Towards an Integrated Europe

Richard E Baldwin

Centre for Economic Policy Research

The Centre for Economic Policy Research is a network of over 200 Research Fellows, based primarily in European universities. The Centre coordinates its Fellows' research activities and communicates their results to the public and private sectors. CEPR is an entrepreneur, developing research initiatives with the producers, consumers and sponsors of research. Established in 1983, CEPR is a European economics research organization with uniquely wide-ranging scope and activities.

CEPR is a registered educational charity. Institutional (core) finance for the Centre is provided through major grants from the Economic and Social Research Council, the Esmée Fairbairn Charitable Trust, the Bank of England, Citibank, the Baring Foundation, 33 other companies and 14 other central banks. None of these organizations gives prior review to the Centre's publications, nor do they necessarily endorse the views expressed therein.

The Centre is pluralist and non-partisan, bringing economic research to bear on the analysis of medium- and long-run policy questions. CEPR research may include views on policy, but the Executive Committee of the Centre does not give prior review to its publications, and the Centre takes no institutional policy positions. The opinions expressed here are those of the author and not those of the Centre for Economic Policy Research.

© Centre for Economic Policy Research, 1994

British Library Cataloguing in Publication Data
A Catalogue record for this book is available from the British Library

ISBN: 1 898128 13 8

Towards an Integrated Europe

To Sarah

Contents

List of Tables

List of Figures

Preface

Trade arrangements in Europe are developing in a piecemeal fashion, driven by urgency, by short-term political considerations, and by economic advantage. Individual agreements have been signed linking the European Union to several Central and East European countries (CEECs), EFTA to several CEECs, a few CEECs to each other, and EU to EFTA. Although the agreements have many similar features, most have been negotiated separately; their coverage differs significantly; and there are no links among them. They involve not only trade relations but also a wide range of economic institutions and political ties. In the background is the intention of most of the European countries not yet in the Union to join it as soon as possible and the endorsement of that goal by the European Councils in Edinburgh (December 1992) and Copenhagen (June 1993).

This maze of bilateral deals is now the framework for European economic and political development. It has no clear, overall structure. Is it the best configuration for promoting pan-European growth and stability? How will these agreements and their interactions influence growth, trade, investment, migration and income disparities in Europe? The European Commission recognized the importance of these questions to all the countries of Europe and their implications for the future prosperity of Central and Eastern Europe. The Commission therefore requested from CEPR a major study by Richard Baldwin (Co-Director of CEPR's International Trade programme) of the external trade environment for Central and Eastern Europe and its broader ramifications. The work has been supported by the Union's PHARE programme, to which we are very grateful.

Richard Baldwin has marshalled the best available empirical evidence and analytic techniques to establish a framework for organizing our thinking on why the structure and pattern of trade arrangements matter. On this basis, he assesses alternative paths towards European economic and political integration.

The economic analysis is objective, but political economy on this scale is likely to lead to strong policy conclusions, as indeed it does here. Baldwin criticizes the 'hub-and-spoke' pattern of existing arrangements and develops a proposal which embodies a specific, dynamic form of 'concentric circles' for the progressive integration with the Union of countries that are not currently member states. Aspects of his proposal will be controversial, but it offers a deeply considered basis for further discussion and ultimately for action. All will benefit from Baldwin's insights and the challenge he puts forward for a more positive and coherent approach to the architecture of Europe.

CEPR research and publications on economic integration, on the economic transformation of the CEECs, on the Union's external trade relations, and on EU enlargement have benefited from a wide range of support, notably from the Community's SPES, ACE and PHARE programmes, the Ford Foundation, and the German Marshall Fund of the United States. This book is published as part of CEPR's programme on Market Integration, Regionalism and the Global Economy (MIRAGE), financed primarily by the Ford Foundation. We are also grateful to the UK Department of Trade and Industry for additional financial support. None of these organizations, however, is in any way responsible for the specific contents of this study. Nor is CEPR, which takes no institutional policy positions, but the Centre is very pleased to commend Richard Baldwin's important work to the urgent attention of both analysts and policy makers.

Richard Portes
28 February 1994

Executive Summary

Communism's demise destroyed the political barriers dividing Europe and shattered East European economic structures including trade arrangements. Integration and reconstruction are under way, but the outcome is still uncertain. If all goes right, economic success in the East could foster prosperity and peace throughout the continent. If all goes wrong, prolonged economic distress in the East could produce catastrophic consequences for Europe. Western Europe can do little to ensure Eastern prosperity; Central and East European Countries (CEECs) must shoulder most of the work and pain. Building a sensible path towards pan-European integration is one way Western Europe can help. This should be a priority.

Reconstruction Without a Plan

Pan-European integration is proceeding, but no one seems to be in charge. Despite this, much progress has been made. The promised liberalizations, especially the EU–CEEC Association Agreements, are important steps. This book identifies three important shortcomings of the current system:

1. Some Eastern nations have not yet been included.
2. The bilateral Association Agreements are 'spokes' separately linking each CEEC to the West European 'hub'. This hub-and-spoke bilateralism tends to marginalize CEECs economically and politically.
3. There is no intermediate step between the Association Agreements (Europe Agreements) and full EU membership.

Not-yet-included Nations

Most industrial trade in Western Europe is duty-free, so duty-free access for CEECs merely levels the playing field. The EU intends to sign Europe Agreements (EAs), or free trade accords with the CEEC-10, so a solution has been promised.

Hub-and-spoke Bilateralism

A railway system, with the capital city as its centre, favours investment in the capital. Similarly, hub-and-spoke bilateralism discourages foreign and domestic investment in CEECs. This may slow Eastern growth. West European firms are harmed by the other side of this investment-deterring effect. Trade barriers between CEECs – and the possibility of future barriers – inhibit normal commercial practices; for example, supplying the region from facilities concentrated in one Eastern country. Intra-CEEC agreements are an imperfect solution. Given the track record of such agreements among developing countries, investors cannot be sure that these piecemeal deals will become effective.

The investment-deterring effect may have enduring repercussions. Suppose a large Central European market emerges. Where will the new industrial concentrations be? Industry is its own best customer, so firms tend to locate near concentrations of other firms. This 'herding instinct' means that once a location gets a head-start, other locations must struggle to catch up. This is a problem since five or ten years of hub-and-spoke bilateralism gives German and Austrian locations a head-start on locations in Slovenia, Poland, Hungary, the Czech Republic and Slovakia. Hub-and-spoke bilateralism may also marginalize CEECs politically.

No Intermediate Stages

EU special-interest politics is likely to prevent an Eastern enlargement for a long time. Without an intermediate stage to allow continued progress, reintegration would stall at the EA stage for decades. Frustrating the aspirations of millions of Central and East Europeans for this long would create political problems for Western Europe. It would also mean missing important economic gains.

At Least Two Decades Before Membership

Simple arguments imply that an Eastern enlargement is improbable for decades:

- *Budget burden* Because CEECs are so poor, so populous and so agricultural, an early Eastern enlargement would be costly. The 64 million people in Visegrad-4, for example, are 2.5 times more agricultural and only 30% as rich as the EU-12 average. This study estimates that admitting Visegraders would increase annual EU spending by 63.6 billion ECU. Financing this would require a drastic cut in EU spending, or an increase (about 60%) in incumbent contributions. Raising taxes or deficits for this would be unpopular with voters. The spending cuts would fall on two extremely powerful interest groups – EU farmers and poor regions, since they receive 80% of EU spending. As a matter of self-defence, coalitions of farmers and poor regions are likely to veto an Eastern enlargement until CEECs become much richer and much less agricultural. This problem is worse for earlier and greater enlargements.
- *Structural funds* A region's income must be below 75% of the EU average to be eligible for the most generous structural spending. If the EU average grows at 2% and Visegrad growth was three times that pace, it would take two decades before the Visegraders passed the 75% cut-off. If they managed to grow 'only' twice as fast as the EU, it would take three decades. The periods are longer for poorer CEECs.
- *CAP spending* The Visegrad countries are blessed with fertile land, well suited to the products most heavily protected by the CAP (e.g. dairy). Consequently, their accession is likely to bankrupt the post-McSharry CAP. One careful study puts the annual cost of extending the CAP to the Visegraders at US $47 billion in 2000. Rising incomes might never change this. Visegrad farmers could be as productive as French or Danish farmers in 20 years, so the most relevant fact is that a Visegrad enlargement would boost the EU landmass by more than a fifth. Further CAP reform is inevitable, but an early Eastern enlargement would significantly alter the nature of the necessary reforms.
- *Voting issues* Under current practices, the Visegrad group would receive more Council of Minister votes than the incumbent poor-four (Spain, Portugal, Ireland and Greece). This would drastically alter EU politics. The problem increases with the size of the enlargement. EU voting reform is foreseen in 1996. One likely reform is to trim the over-representation of small nations. The extent of this could depend on how soon, and how far, the Union enlarges to the East. Small incumbents may have to choose in 1996 between preserving power and enlarging eastwards.

- *The human factor*   Assuming that the obligations of EU membership require capable and experienced people, it is not enough to adopt EU law. Entrants must be trained and experienced personnel must interpret, apply and enforce the laws. Government officials in all CEECs are inexperienced in the design and enforcement of health, safety and environment standards in a market economy. Gaining the necessary experience takes years.

- *Migration*   Chapter 7 suggests that no more than 3–6 million Visegraders would migrate westwards. If they spread themselves thinly about the Union, few problems would arise. If they all settle in Germany and Austria, there would be many problems.

- *Defence and security issues*   If Poland joins, the Union would have a border with Belarus, the Ukraine and Russia (Kaliningrad). This would greatly enrich the foreign policy issues that the EU must resolve. It would also transfer some of the CEECs' security problems to the Union.

- *Deepeners versus wideners*   Maastricht made bold, but vague, commitments to deeper social, economic and political integration. Voting by EU members over the coming decades will decide how the commitments are met. An Eastern enlargement would have important, but unpredictable, effects on the outcome.

- *Early membership on the cheap*   One solution to the budget burden of an early Eastern enlargement would be to exclude entrants from structural spending until they were rich enough not to need it, and from agriculture for however long incumbent EU farmers insist upon. This 'solution' is a recipe for great political complications. Excluding entrants from almost all EU spending programmes is unprecedented. Once the joys of marriage wore off, this second-class status for CEECs could disrupt the EU. To put it colloquially: unpleasantness is unavoidable if second-class ticket holders can vote on what first-class passengers will have for dinner. Specifically, a long transition means that CEECs would vote on reform of structural spending and the CAP. One wonders what stance they would take towards programmes from which they were excluded.

All this suggests that an early Eastern enlargement is likely to be vetoed due to pressure from farmers, poor regions and/or small countries. Of course, the future is full of surprises. Extreme political events could convince West European voters to open their pocket books and admit some CEECs.

The Challenge

The basic long-run design of European integration was decided at the EU's 1993 Copenhagen summit. All CEECs with Europe Agreements can join the EU, eventually. These Agreements and the various CEEC–CEEC trade deals dictate where pan-European integration is now. Europe needs a well-marked path that gets it from here to there.

The required path must correct the system's three shortcomings to avoid political difficulties and seize the economic opportunity presented by Communism's demise. It should be a multispeed path to account for the great diversity among CEECs. Above all, it must be politically viable. Eastern politics poses three large constraints. First, CEECs resist the re-creation of a Council for Mutual Economic Assistance, so one natural route – an Eastern free trade area – is blocked. Second, the path must make the journey to membership easier, not harder; membership is a top CEEC priority. Third, there is no leader among CEECs, so the EU must take the initiative. Western politics imposes more constraints. The path to full EU membership for CEECs must avoid four 'political land mines': agricultural trade, competition for structural spending, migration, and voting in the Council of Ministers. This book argues that an Eastern enlargement is unlikely for at least two decades (absent earthshaking political events). Consequently, a makeshift road will not do. Whatever the path to membership is, it will govern pan-European integration for a very long time.

A Proposal

The proposal envisions two phases. The first would redress the hub-and-spoke bilateralism by embedding the existing Europe Agreements into a proposed 'Association of Association Agreements' (AAA). The second would create an intermediate step – resembling the EEA Agreement without migration – for CEECs that needed it. If the most optimistic timetable for EU enlargement holds, some CEECs – certainly not all – may go straight to membership. The intermediate step would turn the European trade arrangement into three concentric circles. Membership in all three circles should evolve.

Association of Association Agreements

- *Goals* The AAA should rationalize the EU's and CEECs' piecemeal trade liberalizations. It should also redress Europe's hub-and-spoke bilateralism and create a more coherent institutional framework. Finally, it should immediately increase the EU's engagement in the short- and medium-run economic integration of Europe. This stage would concern only CEECs with EU Association Agreements.

- *Content*   The EU and all CEECs with Europe Agreements would be members. The AAA would require CEECs to liberalize equally with all AAA members. This would give CEEC-based firms access to other CEEC markets that was no worse than that accorded to EU-based firms. The Europe Agreement process and the internal political processes of individual CEECs would continue to govern the pace of liberalization. Poland's progress, for example, in lowering tariffs would not be tied to the progress of other CEECs. The AAA would merely require the liberalization to be extended to all AAA members. The proposed AAA would also regionalize the Europe Agreements' provisions on national treatment of establishments, trade in services, government procurement, and financial payments and transfers. The confluence of the Treaty of Rome and the proposed AAA would create a duty-free zone for industrial goods. An industrial firm located in any AAA member state would have (after transition periods) duty-free access to any other AAA market.

- *Does the AAA postpone enlargement?*   High-level politics will decide the date and extent of the first Eastern enlargement. The AAA does not touch on such questions; it addresses more modest problems. CEECs fear that joint treatment is a pretext for postponing enlargement, so the issue must be addressed. There is little joint treatment in the AAA, since it only regionalizes the bilateral liberalization generated by the Europe Agreements. Progress by individual CEECs would continue to be dictated by their internal politics. The proposed AAA might marginally hasten enlargement by boosting CEECs' trade and incomes, and by providing them with a track record on multilateral cooperation in an EU-dominated organization dealing with complicated economic issues. Accession talks are slowed by discovery and discussion of special features of each entrant's economy. By increasing the EU's involvement immediately, the AAA might shorten the eventual accession talks.

- *An institutional framework*   The proposed institution, 'the AAA Authority', should improve Europe's current patchwork of institutional arrangements. It would deal with EU–CEEC and CEEC–CEEC economic relations, namely trade in goods and services, rights of establishment, the liberalization of payments and financial transfers, competition rules, state aids, government procurement and the approximation of laws as covered in the Europe Agreements. In each of these areas the AAA Authority would: (1) play a surveillance and enforcement role to ensure that promised liberalization actually occurred and was not offset by subtle changes in domestic laws or regulations, (2) have a coordinating function for many transition periods and derogations in the Europe Agreements, (3) coordinate EU technical and financial assistance, and (4) assist with the human capital formation necessary to operationalize the approximation of laws foreseen in the EAs.

The EU must dominate the AAA Authority for legal and political reasons, and CEECs wishing to join should be happy with this. The EU would be visibly more engaged in helping CEECs to carry out Europe Agreement measures. The proposed Authority should not be a junior Commission; it should respect the basic Commission mandates.

Benefits of the AAA

Although it would entail no immediate increase in East–West liberalization, the new framework would promote trade and investment on a pan-European basis. The heightened credibility, consistency and predictability of trade policy throughout the AAA region would be good for European business. International commerce abhors uncertainty over future trade and investment policies and lack of transparency. Elimination of hub-and-spoke bilateralism should encourage investment in CEECs and help EU firms to do business there. This would spur CEEC growth. The AAA Authority would help CEECs to form the human capital necessary to run and regulate a market economy. The AAA may also take on additional tasks. It may be a good vehicle for adopting sensible cumulation in rules of origin. It could also provide a forum for rational discussion of safeguard measures. Even without altering the letter or spirit of EA safeguard provisions, such a forum might produce more satisfactory outcomes for all parties.

Stage Two: An Intermediate Step

EU farmers and poor regions are likely to veto an Eastern enlargement for at least two decades. Stage two proposes an intermediate step to allow pan-European integration to proceed. The importance of this step is that it does not require the two-decades-before-membership premise to apply to all CEECs. Optimists hope that Hungary, Poland, the Czech Republic and perhaps Slovenia can join in the year 2000 with a long transition period. Even if this occurs, many CEECs will not make the first wave. For these, the wait may be much longer than two decades.

The EU grants much better access to EFTAn members of the EEA than to CEECs. Some CEECs should be ready for this deeper integration by, say, the end of the decade. Similarly, if CEECs grow rapidly, EU firms will want Single-Market access to CEECs. The proposed intermediate step – an 'Organization for European Integration' (OEI) – would guarantee CEEC and EU firms such access. The OEI should not replace the AAA since not all CEECs would be ready simultaneously.

Duty-free Trade to Single Market Integration

The proposed OEI would help to fulfil the Europe Agreement promise 'to make progress towards realizing between [the EU and each CEEC] the other economic freedoms on which the Community is based'. The Europe Agreements are specific about tariff and quota removal. They are asymmetrically vague about moving beyond this. It is clear what CEECs must do (approximation of laws, etc.). It is not clear what the EU must do. Extending the Single Market to CEECs will not be an easy task, as the EEA negotiations revealed. For example, the EEA forbade contingent protection (anti-dumping etc.), allowed any product approved in one EEA country to be sold freely in all and permitted EEA companies registered in their home country to operate in any EEA country without prior approval of the local authorities. Clearly, this sort of access requires that many rules be enforced credibly and uniformly. This demands a strong institution. The EEA was basically stillborn, so a new more appropriate framework is needed.

No Immediate Action

Unlike the AAA, stage two would require no immediate action. Several years must pass before any CEECs are ready. Nevertheless, good road builders know that it is wise to decide the whole route before laying the first cement.

Shape of the New Agreement

The proposed OEI would avoid all four 'political land mines' mentioned above. As with the EEA, OEI members would participate in the EU's Single Market without agriculture, without transfers and without voting. Unlike the EEA, migration would also be excluded.

New Institution

A strong body (perhaps an extended AAA Authority) would be necessary to deal with competition policy, state aid and mutual recognition of technical standards and regulation. This administration authority should be modelled on the parts of the EU Commission dealing with enforcement and surveillance of the Single Market. Of course, the proposed Administration Authority could not impinge on the mandates of existing EU institutions, so some sort of multi-tier arrangement would be necessary. The awkward two-pillar legal structure of the EEA Agreement is not a good model, but it is indicative. The EFTA Surveillance Authority polices

EFTAns. The EC Commission polices EU nations. The EU has no direct involvement in the EFTA Surveillance Authority. This last item should be changed. As in the AAA Authority, the proposed 'OEI Administration' should be dominated by the EU. The CEECs that want to join the EU should welcome assistance in helping them to adopt Community standards on all Single Market issues. The EU should be interested in extending this assistance to promote trade, investment and growth.

A Pan-European Trade System with Three Concentric Circles

This intermediate step would create a pan-European trade system of three concentric circles. The EU would be the central circle with the smallest membership (at least until the Copenhagen vision is fully realized). The OEI would be the next largest comprising all the EU member states plus the leading CEECs that were not yet Union members. The outer circle, the AAA, would delimit the boundary of a European duty-free zone for industrial products.

Currently, opening this system to Belarus, the Ukraine, Moldova and Russia seems to be politically infeasible. If the political situation changes, there is no economic reason for excluding them from the AAA. On the contrary, there would be important economic benefits in doing so. Deeper-than-AAA integration for the 200 million citizens of these nations is a matter for futurologists.

A Note on Terminology

To avoid infelicitous prose, the terms 'Easterners' or 'Eastern nations' are occasionally used to refer to all former CMEA European countries plus Albania, Slovenia and Croatia (other Balkan states are excluded due to lack of data). Of course, this term is not geographically correct since, for example, Slovenia and the Czech Republic are significantly west of Finland and Greece. The terms are not meant to hide the large differences among these nations.

The acronym CEEC (which stands for Central and East European countries) is used as a noun and an adjective. CEEC-10 refers to the Visegrad-4, Slovenia, the three Baltic states, and Bulgaria and Romania. CEEC-12 adds in Albania and Croatia. Russia, Ukraine, Moldova and Belarus are called the former Soviet Republics-4 (FSR-4).

Acknowledgements

I wish to thank Per Wijkman for numerous discussions over lunch during which much of the content of this book was shaped. Mario Gehring, proof-reader *par excellence*, has made many improvements to the style and accuracy of the text. Sophie Huang worked full-time for two months assisting with this book. In addition to endless data-gathering, she did most of the data manipulation and all the estimation of the gravity model in Chapter 3. Rikard Forslid and Peter Johns provided detailed comments on the theory chapters. Many of the ideas in this book come directly from my work on the CEPR book *Is Bigger Better? The Economics of EC Enlargement*. I wish to thank my co-authors David Begg, Jean-Pierre Danthine, Vittorio Grilli, Jan Haaland, Manfred Neumann, Victor Norman, Tony Venables and Alan Winters. It is quite unfair that the reference to the above book is Baldwin et al. (1992). Richard Portes and Peter Johns have provided important material and intellectual inputs for which I am grateful. Much of the material in this book is drawn from my previous work that has appeared in EFTA and CEPR Occasional Papers.

I benefited greatly from comments I received at an early presentation of this material at the EC Commission. I wish to thank in particular Joly Dixon, Joan Pearce and André Sapir as well as Horst Reichenbach, Dariusz Rosati, Jan Svejnar and Alan Winters. The comments and suggestions of Alan Mayhew, Michael Leigh, Cameron Fraser and Joris Declerck helped greatly. Helen Wallace and László Csaba provided comments on the entire manuscript. Finally, many thanks to James Shepherd, who edited it.

Richard E Baldwin

Introduction

Until recently, millions of men and trillions of dollars of equipment were poised for combat in Europe. The rejection of Communism defused this situation. Above all, the Easterners' desire to share Western affluence and democracy compelled this rejection. Western Europe can do little to help fulfil these desires; most of the pain and work necessarily falls on the shoulders of Central and East Europeans. Building a sensible pan-European trade system is one important task in which Western Europe can help. This would be worth doing.

On the bright side, the right kind of trade system could accelerate the Eastern transformations while reducing the attendant economic pain. This would quicken Eastern growth and lock-in democratic and pro-market reforms. Moreover, the growing spending power of hundreds of millions of Eastern consumers would be a bonanza for West European businesses. Quite simply, an economic success story would foster prosperity and peace throughout the continent.

On the dark side, the wrong kind of trade system could frustrate Eastern aspirations to join Europe, could increase the pain of their transformations and could foster widespread disillusionment with market economics. There is nothing irreversible about the demise of authoritarianism; prolonged economic distress creates political turmoil. Indeed, democracy and capitalism are at risk in parts of Europe. Geography and history dictate that this is a continent-wide problem. Pan-European war is the worse-case scenario. However, any serious unrest or conflict – even if it were limited to the East – could harm Western Europe. Such conflicts often force mass migrations. They always harm investors' confidence. Quite simply, widespread economic failure in the East could have catastrophic consequences for Europe.

Plan of the Book

The book has three parts. Readers in a hurry should read Part 2 first and then Part 3, referring back to Part 1 where necessary.

Part 1

The first part presents material that supports the main arguments in Part 2 (The Problem) and Part 3 (Some Solutions). Many readers may wish to skip this entire Part, referring back to it occasionally for additional detail on points made in Parts 2 and 3. Part 1 is divided into three chapters.

Chapter 1, which is quite short, presents a brief history of the evolution of Western Europe's post-war trade arrangements. It draws some lessons for the new democracies in the central and eastern parts of Europe.

Chapter 2 is the theory chapter. It looks at how trade arrangements can differ and their economic effects. The sections on locational and growth effects cover recent advances in the literature on integration. The final section considers the political economy of trade arrangements.

Chapter 3 projects potential pan-European trade patterns. The results of the chapter guide much of the reasoning in this book. Briefly, the results suggest that East–West trade will be much more important than East–East trade, but the latter will still account for between 20% and 30% of the CEECs' European exports in the long run. The chapter also shows that EU and EFTA exports to the CEECs have the potential to grow at double-digit rates for decades. This suggests that West European exporters have much to gain from pan-European integration.

Part 2

The second part of the book presents and critiques the pan-European trade system of early 1994 and three significant shortcomings are identified:

1.   Some Eastern nations have not yet been included.
2.   Hub-and-spoke bilateralism is an inferior means of organizing trade relations.
3.   The steps to closer integration are extremely uneven. The first two are reasonably gradual: GATT membership followed by free trade agreements with the EU and EFTA covering only trade in manufactures and involving long transition periods. The third step, EU membership, is much larger and more difficult. The shortcoming, therefore, is that there are no intermediate steps between the Europe Agreements and full EU membership.

Chapters 5 and 6 take a more detailed view of shortcomings 2 and 3. The solution to the first shortcoming was promised at the EU's 1993 summit in Copenhagen, so the book devotes little space to it.

The current pan-European trade arrangement is far from the worst possible. The trade liberalization that has already been promised, especially the bilateral deals between the CEECs and the EU, constitutes an important step towards reintegrating the eastern and western parts of the European continent. These Association Agreements (also known as the Europe Agreements) are the foundation of Europe's post-Communist trade system. To put the point more colloquially, this part of the book points out that the pan-European trade system is a half-empty glass. Perceptive readers, however, will understand that this admits that the glass is already half-full.

Part 3

This part of the book discusses several possible solutions to the three shortcomings and the lack of a coherent plan. There is no certain way of knowing which solution is right. Critical parts of the various arguments depend on assumptions concerning events in the distant future. Perhaps the most one can hope for from analysis such as this is that it asks the right questions and stimulates thoughts on how to solve them.

Chapter 7 is a detailed study of the benefits and the difficulties that an Eastern enlargement of the EU would pose. Chapter 8 considers the early-membership-on-the-cheap solution. That is, instead of waiting at least two decades to let in the CEECs, this solution would admit them early but exclude them from most of the financial and some of the economic benefits of membership in order to assuage incumbent special-interest groups. The chapter argues that this is a perilous tactic. There is no clear line between a very long and very broad derogation and second-class EU citizenship. Creating a first- and second-class division for, say, ten years is a recipe for great political difficulties in the EU. Finally, Chapter 9 presents a proposal for improving the current integration process. Its details depend upon many unknowables, so it should be viewed as a thought-piece, not as a blueprint.

PART 1

Preliminaries

1

History

The recent change in Europe's trade arrangements is not the continent's first massive dissolution and subsequent reorganization of trade relations. This chapter looks at Europe's post-Second World War experience and attempts to draw some lessons for its continuing reconstruction.

1.1   Western Europe's Post-war Trade Arrangements

History is one damned thing after another, according to the Henry Ford school of thought. While there is a grain of truth in this, it is often useful to search for clear-cut historical patterns. Such patterns, if they do exist, direct one's attention to critical issues that are likely to arise in the future. As a caution, one should note that there are many fundamental differences between the post-war period and the 1990s.

I am not a historian and this is not a history book. Rather, I selectively draw on facts to build a case that while politics led to the EEC's integration, ·strong commercial forces shaped Western Europe's trade arrangements. These forces operate bilaterally, drawing nations that were outside the 'hub' of Europe (the EEC) ever closer. These forces might have resulted in hub-and-spoke bilateralism in Western Europe. However, each time these forces intensified, the outsiders responded in a way which avoided hub-and-spoke bilateralism, even though trade among them was dwarfed by their trade with the EEC. That is, the non-EEC nations in Western Europe consciously avoided the trap of a hub-and-spoke trade arrangement. Lessons from this should help to guide the continuing reorganization of Europe's trade relations.

1.1.1   *The Early Post-war Period*

The end of the Second World War destroyed trade relations in Europe. The deleterious economic effects of this are manifest, but it did give Europe's leaders a fresh canvas on which to paint Europe's trade arrangements. The first brushstrokes were made by non-European forces. In 1947, the Organization for European Economic Cooperation (OEEC) was set up to administer the US-backed Marshall Plan. Its aim was to promote economic cooperation and to foster trade liberalization (see Molle, 1990; EFTA, 1987). According to EFTA (1987), '[t]he OEEC was very successful in terms of economic results, freeing trade and payments in Western Europe and fashioning effective new methods for the conduct of international economic relations'. Some members, however, very soon found the OEEC too limited to bring about the deeper integration that they felt was necessary to avoid future wars and restore economic strength:

> By the nineteen-fifties strong currents were moving in Western Europe in the direction of a more rapid and more complete integration of its nation States. Some European governments were making plans to go beyond 'co-operation' as exemplified in such inter-governmental organization as the OEEC; they proposed to begin the process of close integration of their national economies and to set up strong central institutions under a common authority to help to bring this about (EFTA, 1987, p. 23).

By 1956 two proposals for further integration were under consideration: the European Economic Community, which proposed a customs union and a commitment to deeper integration, and a looser free-trade area involving all of Western Europe. In 1957, the dominant element of Western Europe's post-war trade arrangement was outlined. Six OEEC members (Belgium, France, West Germany, Italy, Luxembourg and the Netherlands) signed the Treaty of Rome, creating the EEC. Discussions of a wider West European free-trade area agreement soon broke down, leaving the 11 non-EEC members of the OEEC on the sidelines.

Note the parallels with today's Europe. In the late 1950s, many European nations, most of them small, faced the threat of being 'left behind'. Europe's new outsiders have chosen to deal with the Community (and EFTA) on a bilateral basis. In the 1950s, however, the reaction of the outsiders was quite different. Fearing the discrimination and marginalization that might occur if they faced the EEC bilaterally, seven of the non-EEC nations formed their own bloc, the European Free Trade Association (EFTA).[1] The coordinated reaction in the 1950s was greatly facilitated by the leadership of a dominant country, the United Kingdom.

It is instructive to follow the behaviour of the few OEEC members that joined neither the EEC nor EFTA. In 1961 Finland essentially joined

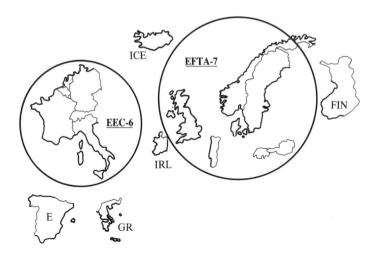

Figure 1.1 West European trade arrangements in the 1960s (non-overlapping circles)

EFTA by signing an Association Agreement.[2] Iceland applied for EFTA membership in 1968, acceding in 1970.[3] Thus by the end of the 1970s, all West European nations had forsaken bilateralism except Spain and Greece (who were under dictatorships), and Ireland (which was neutral and did most of its trade with the United Kingdom). Greece and Turkey both applied for associate EEC membership soon after the Treaty of Rome was signed. Spain signed a preferential trade agreement with the EEC in 1970 and one with EFTA in 1979.

The 1960s saw the trade liberalizations promised by the Treaty of Rome and the Stockholm Convention (EFTA's founding charter) come to fruition. By the late 1960s trade arrangements in Western Europe could be described as two non-overlapping circles. This is depicted schematically in Figure 1.1. What the diagram does not show is the relative economic weight of the two circles. In 1970 the GDP of the EEC nations was more than twice the size of the GDP of EFTA nations.

1.1.2 *Evolution to Two Concentric Circles*

The Political Economy of Discriminatory Market Access

In the early 1960s, EFTA- and EEC-based firms had roughly equal access to each other's markets since the preferential liberalization had only just begun. However, as the barriers began to fall within each group, discriminatory effects began to appear. This discrimination meant lost profit opportunities for exporters in both groups. Accordingly, the progressive reduction of within-group barriers gave rise to increasingly larger political economy pressures for lowering between-group barriers. Consider the example of a British industrial turbine manufacturer whose main rival was a West German manufacturer. In EFTA markets, the British firm had an edge over the West German rival. The edge resulted from EFTA's preferential tariff treatment of British goods. However, in EEC markets the West German firm enjoyed the edge. The commercial importance of these advantages grew as the liberalization of intra-EFTA and intra-EEC trade progressed. Since the EEC-6 market was more than twice the size of the EFTA market in the late 1970s, EFTAns suffered more from the discriminatory tariffs than EEC members.

Domino Effect

This political economy of discriminatory market access led the EFTAns to push for better access to the EEC markets. This initially came in the form of applications for membership in the EEC. As early as 1961, the United Kingdom applied for EC membership unilaterally. Ireland, Denmark and Norway quickly followed. The other EFTAns did not apply for political reasons such as neutrality (Austria, Finland, Sweden and Switzerland) or because they were not heavily dependent on the EEC market (Iceland). After much discussion, France vetoed this first enlargement attempt in 1963, but the same four EFTAns reapplied in 1967. After many delays, membership for the four was granted in 1973. Norway's population (which is profoundly jealous of a sovereignty that they won only in 1905) refused EEC membership in a referendum.

The impending departure of four EFTAns to the EEC was anticipated well in advance. It created a domino effect of the type modelled by Baldwin (1993). The political economy force that tips the dominos might be described as political economy 'jealousy'. Chapter 2 presents the argument in more detail, but the basic idea is elementary. In business, what matters is relative competitiveness. A firm's sales and profits are harmed by anything that lowers its rival's costs. In this light, the 1973 EEC enlargement meant a swelling of the EEC markets and a shrinking of the EFTA ones. Firms based in the remaining EFTA states would suffer a disadvantage (compared with their EEC-based rivals) in more markets and would enjoy an advantage (over their EEC-based rivals) in fewer markets. Accordingly, EFTA industries pressed their governments to redress this situation. The result was bilateral free trade agreements (FTAs) between each remaining EFTAn and the EEC that went into effect when the United Kingdom and others acceded to the EEC.

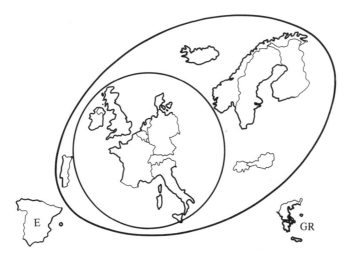

Figure 1.2 West European trade arrangements in the mid-1970s (concentric circles)

The result of all this was that by the mid-1970s trade arrangements in Western Europe had evolved from non-overlapping circles into two concentric ones. This is shown schematically in Figure 1.2. The outer circle, which encompassed both EFTA and EEC nations, represents a unified free trade area for industrial products. Note that the duty-free zone for industrial goods was the result of three types of agreement. The Treaty of Rome guaranteed it within the EEC. The Stockholm Convention guaranteed it within EFTA, and separate bilateral free trade agreements between each EFTAn and the EEC guaranteed it for EFTA–EEC trade. The inner circle was the EEC. These countries were much more thoroughly integrated, even in the mid-1970s. For instance, EEC members had duty-free trade in all products (including agricultural goods), a common external tariff, many common sectoral policies (coal, steel, etc.) and a common labour market.

Again a parallel with the 1990s appears. The EFTAns that chose not to apply for EEC membership – Austria, Finland, Iceland, Sweden, Switzerland and Portugal – were once again faced with the prospect of increased discrimination. Like the CEECs in the 1990s, the EFTAns of the 1970s reacted by signing bilateral FTAs with the EEC. In contrast, however, the EFTAns in the 1970s did so in a coordinated manner (the FTAs were negotiated in parallel and are almost identical). More importantly, the EFTAns continued to maintain strong free trade links among themselves, to avoid marginalization effects. Indeed, the extent of intra-EFTA integration continued to deepen.[4]

Lessons from the behaviour of the EFTAns in the 1970s are critically important for the CEECs in the 1990s. Although each EFTAn did most of its trade with the EEC, they managed to avoid the pitfalls of hub-and-spoke bilateralism. In this light, EFTA of the 1970s and early 1980s should *not* be thought of primarily as a club of countries that trade with each other.[5] EFTA was a group of small countries that had free trade agreements with the EEC and wanted to band together to avoid hub-and-spoke bilateralism.

1.1.3   *The Threat of the Single Market Programme*

The Single European Act, proposed in 1985 and adopted in 1986, is best thought of as a massive liberalization of the EU economies.[6] Its main effect is on the efficiency of each individual member's economy. However, it does have significant trade effects. By removing physical, fiscal and technical barriers to trade, the so-called 1992 programme finally made good on the promise implied by the EEC's commonly used name, the Common Market. Before the Single European Act, firms based in member states enjoyed duty-free access to each other's markets, but they certainly did not enjoy free trade. Intra-EC trade was impeded by a long list of barriers. Some examples are differing technical standards and industrial regulations, capital controls, preferential public procurement, administrative and frontier formalities, VAT and excise tax rate differences and differing transport regulations. Although the great majority of these policies seem negligible individually, the confluence of their effects served to substantially restrict intra-Community trade. Pelkmans and Winters (1988) conservatively estimate that the 1992 programme would reduce real trade costs on intra-EU trade by between 1% and 3%.

For the third time since 1958, non-EU West European nations were threatened by the discriminatory effects of closer integration in the hub of Western Europe. Again EFTA firms prompted their governments to offset the discrimination by seeking closer ties. Again the EFTAns did so in a coordinated way. As we shall see, however, a new element emerged during this exercise.

In the late 1980s, EFTA governments had decided that they must react to the Single Market. Several thought of applying for EU membership (Austria actually did), while others considered bilateral negotiations. Jacques Delors forced the decision in January 1989 by proposing the European Economic Area agreement (initially called the European Economic Space agreement).[7] The agreement is very complex, but for our purposes it can be thought of as bringing the EFTAns into the Single Market, apart from agriculture and the common external tariff. Box 1.1 provides more detail.

Given the political economy forces described above, it is easy to

Box 1.1 The EEA Agreement

It is useful to think of the EEA in terms of Western Europe's two-concentric-circles trade system. The EU's 1992 programme and the EEA combined to deepen the integration among nations encompassed by the outer circle, namely all the EU and EFTA nations except Switzerland. The EEA Agreement extends the EU's 'four freedoms' – the free movement of goods, people, capital and services – to the EFTAns. A large part of the Agreement is identical to the Treaty of Rome; most of its provisions are based on the EU's *Acquis communautaire*. Agricultural products are excluded and various transition periods apply.

- *People, capital and services* Citizens of EEA nations will have the right to seek and hold a job anywhere in the EEA. The freedom to establish businesses in any EEA nation and the mutual recognition of diplomas and professional qualifications (including doctors) are provided for. All capital controls are to be abolished on intra-EEA flows. Nations may not restrict the ownership of land or companies on the basis of nationality. Financial institutions, which are licensed in any EEA nation, can establish branches and provide services without the prior approval of the host country. The Agreement also opens up government procurement to competition from all EEA firms.
- *Goods* The Agreement's aim is to ensure non-discriminatory conditions for the production and marketing of all EEA goods. Most of the formal barriers to intra-West European trade have been removed. The remaining ones are subtle, so the EEA Agreement is vast. About 800 items of EU legislation dealing with free trade have been integrated into the Agreement. More than 12 000 pages of legal text were scrutinized during the talks. There is not room even to describe all the general principles. One worth noting, however, is the Cassis de Dijon, or mutual recognition, principle (established by a 1979 ruling of the European Court of Justice). To avoid cost-raising barriers created by spurious standards, this implies that any product that has been approved in one EEA nation can circulate freely in all. The Agreement contains a general prohibition of 'state aid' (grants, subsidies, soft loans, etc.) that may distort trade. New aid schemes in the EFTA nations are not allowed without the approval of the EFTA Surveillance Authority. The Agreement also requires EEA nations to adjust state monopolies of a commercial nature so that no discrimination

> in the production and marketing of goods or services exists (certain goods, e.g. alcohol, are exempted).
>
> - *Anti-dumping and competition rules* No anti-dumping or countervailing duties will be applied on intra-EEA trade, according to Article 26. The Agreement's competition rules, and the EEA's high level of market integration, make these unnecessary. The main substance of the Agreement's rules on competition are identical to those of the EU. See EFTA (1992) for further detail.

understand why the EFTAns would want to participate in the Single Market. There are, however, two aspects of the EEA that are truly extraordinary. First, the EEA is unbalanced in terms of the rights and obligations of EFTAns in future EU legislation. In essence, it forces the EFTAns to accept future EC legislation (the *Acquis communautaire*) concerning the Single Market, without formal participation in the formation of these new laws.[8] Second, the EEA creates a good deal of supranationality among the EFTAns (see Box 1.2 for details). It forced the EFTAns to speak with one voice on many issues during the negotiations and would oblige them to develop an EFTA position on future EU legislation. This supranationality is extraordinary for two reasons. First, it was the EU that imposed this supranationality on the EFTAns to simplify the task of keeping the Single Market homogeneous. Second, the EFTAns have resisted such supranational authority since the end of the Second World War, so it is astounding that they said they would accept it.

In fact, virtually none of the EFTAns were willing to live with the EEA as it was negotiated. By the end of negotiations on the EEA, Austria, Finland, Sweden, Norway and Switzerland had applied for EU membership. For these countries, the EEA was viewed as a transitional arrangement. Swiss voters rejected the EEA in December 1992, effectively freezing their EU application. Thus, if the accession talks of the four EFTAns are successful (as they are widely expected to be), the EEA will consist of the EU, on the one hand, and Liechtenstein and Iceland, on the other (perhaps with Norway as well).

As far as the current reorganization of Europe's trade arrangement is concerned, the lessons from this episode are twofold. First, it is another example of how the non-EU countries in Western Europe sidestepped the snare of bilateralism. The interesting lesson is that the coordination among outsiders was due largely to direct actions of the EU. The EU found it in its interest to force the outsiders to coordinate with each other. This had nothing to do with the EU's concern about the outsiders' welfare. It was simply a matter of commercial motivation (ensuring consistent application of the 1992 Programme) and practicality (reducing verification costs).

Box 1.2   The EEA institutions

Surveillance and enforcement are essential to achieving non-discrimination in the EEA. Moreover, the Agreement must be continually modified to incorporate new EU laws concerning the Single Market. Accordingly, the Agreement establishes a legal and political system.

- *The legal system*   The legal system has two pillars. EU nations are policed by the EU Commission and the European Court of Justice; EFTA nations by the EFTA Surveillance Authority (ESA) and the EFTA Court. The two legal orders are separate formally, but are intended to create a common European legal system in practice. The Agreement does not alter the rights or obligations of EU institutions. The ESA deals only with matters in EFTA nations. Its main tasks are: to ensure that EFTAn governments fulfil their Agreement obligations; to enforce EEA competition rules (i.e. antitrust and state aid); to make sure that public procurement rules are respected; and to cooperate, exchange information and consult with the EU Commission on general surveillance policy questions and on individual cases. The ESA has wide investigatory powers and can impose fines when competition rules are infringed. It can act on its own initiative. EEA governments, firms and individuals can also lodge complaints. The ESA is led by a College of five Members representing the participating EFTA nations (Liechtenstein is a special case). Decisions are by majority voting and can be appealed to the EFTA Court. The EFTA Court is composed of five judges appointed by EFTA governments. Decisions are taken by majority rule. Its main competencies are: to decide on infringement actions raised by the ESA against an EFTA state; to decide on appeals of ESA decisions; to give advice on interpretations of EEA rules; to settle disputes among EFTA states concerning EEA rules and decisions of the ESA. Cases involving both EFTA and EU parties are decided by the EU Court of Justice.
- *The political system*   The Agreement sets up the EEA Joint Committee and EEA Council; their decisions require unanimity, with EFTAns speaking with one voice. The EEA Council, consisting of members of the Council of the EU, members of the EU Commission and one member of each participating EFTAn state, provides high-level political guidance and impetus for implementing the EEA. A second body, the EEA Joint Committee, is charged with the effective implementation and operation of the EEA. It is responsible for amending the Agreement to

permit simultaneous application of new EU legislation to all EEA trade. Its members consists of representatives of all the contracting parties and it meets at least once a month. If the EEA Joint Commitment decides not to amend the EEA agreement in accordance with new EU legislation, the affected part of the EEA agreement will be 'suspended'. Thus, although the EFTAns do have to approve each new EU measure, they never have the choice between the status quo and accepting the new law. The choice is between accepting the new law and having the whole relevant part of the EEA agreement suspended. The practical implications of such a suspension are unclear. A clause (Article 102, paragraph 6) appears to exempt all rights gained by existing EFTA and EU firms. Thus, the impact of a suspension would appear to fall on future commercial interests.

Notes

1. The UK, Denmark, Sweden, Norway, Portugal, Switzerland and Austria were the original EFTA-7. Tiny Liechtenstein has participated via its customs union with Switzerland.
2. To avoid the appearance of having ties with the Western military alliance, Finland (which is neutral) chose not to become a full EFTA member.
3. Iceland's economy was based largely on natural resource-intensive activities such as fishing. For this reason, the discriminatory treatment of its industrial exports was of much less concern than in other European economies.
4. For example, duty-free treatment was extended to fish, EFTA decided to set up the Industrial Development Fund for Portugal, and Finland became a full EFTA member.
5. Trade among the Nordic economies was important, but Nordic–Alpine trade and intra-Alpine trade was quite modest.
6. It is difficult to know whether to use the current name, the EU, or the one that applied in the 1980s, the EC. Here I substitute EU for EC but not for EEC.
7. The idea was first suggested at a meeting of EFTA and EEC ministers in Luxembourg in 1984. This produced the Luxembourg Declaration. Nothing much happened for five years. The EEA talks began informally in 1989, continuing more formally in 1990 and 1991. It was signed on 2 May 1992 in Oporto, together with an Agreement establishing the EFTA Court of Justice and the EFTA Surveillance Authority.
8. See Baldwin (1992a) for further analysis of the EEA Agreement. The *Acquis communautaire* is the term for EU law. This includes the Treaty of Rome and subsequent treaties and secondary law adopted under the Treaty of Rome. This concerns regulations, directives and decisions as well as the relevant case law of the EU Court of Justice. Each year approximately 2000 new legal acts, decisions and directives are added to the *Acquis*.

2

Theory

This chapter looks at how trade arrangements can affect economic activity. The policy analyses in Chapters 4 and 5 refer to specific parts of the material in this chapter. For this reason, many readers may wish to skip this chapter at first, returning to it when necessary. Much has happened in the field of economic integration in recent years. It is no longer enough to think about 'trade diversion' and 'trade creation'. This chapter attempts to provide a (mostly) non-technical presentation of most of the old and new theory. For readers who have followed the literature on economic integration, it may not be new; for others it may be unnecessarily detailed.

Section 2.1 starts with a listing of the numerous dimensions along which trade arrangements can differ. In the old integration literature, inspired largely by the formation of the EEC, the major distinction was between a free trade area and a customs union, the latter having common external tariffs. In the modern world, trade agreements involve documents that are more than a thousand pages long. Clearly, all this text would not be necessary if the only important issue was the tariffs charged on external imports.

Sections 2.2–2.4 discuss the economic impacts of trade arrangements. These are divided into three large types: allocation effects (Section 2.2), location effects (Section 2.3) and accumulation, or growth, effects (Section 2.4). A cataloguing system that is more standard would divide the effects into two: static and dynamic. The term 'allocation effects' corresponds directly to static effects. These are effects that regard the efficiency with which a static (i.e. fixed) amount of resources is allocated. My third term corresponds direct to growth effects. The commonality of effects considered in Section 2.3 is the accumulation of productive resources, such as physical capital, human capital and knowledge capital (i.e. technology). These two categories provide natural supports for location effects. Section 2.2 considers integration's impact on the location of industrial activity within the region. Thus, from the perspective of the region as a whole, this is simply a spatial allocation of a fixed quantity of resources. However, from the point of view of a particular locality, industrial concentration or deconcentration appears mainly as a change in the quantity of productive factors present. In other words, to the specific locales within the wider region, location effects will appear to be accumulation effects.

In addition to this fairly traditional economic analysis, Section 2.5 considers political economy issues. First, it examines forces that may influence the shape of trade arrangements. Second, it describes channels through which the shape of a trade arrangement, particularly its size and composition, can affect the trade policy adopted by the members.

2.1   How Trade Arrangements Can Differ

The 1960s literature on economic integration considered two basic cases: customs unions and free trade areas, the principal distinction being the treatment of tariffs applied to non-member countries. Trade arrangements that have been signed in the intervening years address a much broader set of issues. Consequently, they can differ along many dimensions. The geographical and commodity coverage of arrangements are the most obvious. However, modern trade arrangements typically consider policies that go far beyond simple tariffs and quotas.

2.1.1   *Barriers to Trade in Goods*

Standard Border Measures

The easiest trade barriers are a tax on imports. Such taxes are called tariffs. Due to a series of successful GATT negotiations, the tariff levels on industrial goods charged by industrialized nations have been greatly reduced.

Quantitative restrictions are another simple type of trade barrier and outright quotas on imports are fairly common. These restrict the quantity of a particular good that may be imported over a certain period (usually a year). The administration of import quotas varies. Some countries issue import licences to various companies and the customs service checks that every consignment of the imported good is accompanied by an import licence.

It is a violation of GATT rules unilaterally to impose quantitative restrictions on goods that have been the subject of tariff negotiation. To avoid this, countries have developed a whole series of 'grey area measures' that are essentially quotas (although their economic effects are different, as described below). These measures have various names, such as Voluntary Export Restrictions (VERs), Voluntary Restraint Agreements (VRAs), Orderly Marketing Arrangements (OMAs), etc. The feature that these barriers share is that the exporting country ends up administering the quota instead of the importing country. These agreements are usually arranged when the importing country threatens to impose another type of protection.

Cost-creating barriers   All the barriers mentioned above create 'rents', i.e. pure profits. By restricting imports into a particular country, these barriers raise the price of imported goods in that country. This creates rents since someone can buy the goods on the international market and sell them at an artificially high price in the protected one. While this type of barrier is important in many countries, they do not affect much trade within the European continent. A large amount of trade in Europe is subject to a host of seemingly minor policies that increase the real cost of importing and exporting goods, especially manufactured ones. When trade barriers entail higher real trade costs, the rents are not gained by anyone. Trade just becomes more difficult, so resources that were previously devoted to making useful goods and services must be diverted to overcoming such barriers. Typical examples of such policies are complicated and slow customs procedures, unnecessary delays in the verification of industrial and health standards as well as the imposition of spurious health, environment or industrial standards. Similarly, some countries make it difficult and expensive for importers to obtain licences or foreign exchange for importing.

Contingent Protection

The GATT is a very pragmatic document. Its framers understood that, on occasion, countries would face the political necessity of imposing trade barriers. The GATT allows three basic ways of doing this.

Safeguards   The first, and least used, is the Safeguard Clause, also known as the Escape Clause. This allows a country to impose import protection when one of its industries suffers due to increased imports. The protection must be temporary and the country is under an obligation to extend compensating concessions to the countries whose exporters are harmed by the temporary protection. (Note that all this reasoning is based on solidly mercantilist principles that ignore all the gains from trade that we discuss below.) The fact that a safeguard measure is temporary and compensation must be made has reduced the use of this means of contingent protection.[1]

Anti-dumping measures   In recent years, anti-dumping and countervailing duties have, to a large extent, replaced safeguard measures. Although the justifications of these so-called unfair trade laws have nothing to do with safeguarding an industry, the rules governing their use are quite flexible. Indeed, anti-dumping duties and countervailing duties (known as AD and CVD in the trade) have become the protectionists' favourite tools, especially in the EU and the United States.

The second means involves what are called anti-dumping duties. Nothing is simple about dumping. From legal and economic perspectives, one quickly runs into great complications. For our purposes, however, we will describe only the main points. Anti-dumping duties are tariffs that are meant to offset a type of pricing behaviour called dumping. This behaviour is defined from the point of view of the importing country (let us call this the home country). A good is said to be dumped if it is imported into the home country at a price below that charged in any other country. Many countries also add a third definition of dumping that involves the cost of production. Under this definition, a good is dumped if it is sold in the home market at a price that is below calculated costs plus some calculated profit margin. The GATT pre-Uruguay Round was extremely vague on how countries could calculate these costs.[2] Given the political will to protect, and sufficiently clever lawyers and accountants to massage the numbers, a country can usually find that a particular good is being dumped in its market. To impose anti-dumping duties, a country must show that the imports are being dumped and that the home-country industry is injured by the dumping. It is important to note that the duties can be imposed without 'compensating' the exporting country.

When anti-dumping duties were first introduced in the 1930s the explicit intention of lawmakers was to prevent an anti-competitive practice known as predatory pricing. If a firm sells below cost for long enough, it may drive its competitors out of the market. This may then leave the 'predator' free to charge high monopoly prices in the future. Such conduct may be harmful irrespective of the predator's nationality. It is, however, especially irksome when the predator is foreign, since the monopoly profits do not accrue to domestic residents.

When phrased this way, anti-dumping laws sound quite reasonable. The problem is that there are many reasons for a firm to charge different prices in different markets. Most of them have nothing to do with predatory pricing. For instance, airlines routinely sell tickets for the same service at different prices in different markets. Indeed, even within a single country, a firm may charge different prices in different cities or regions. Thus, even if 'dumping' occurs, it may stem from normal business practices instead of predatory pricing. A 'grand opening sale' is a form of dumping. When this is true, anti-dumping laws result in having an impact that is exactly opposite to their rationale. They reduce competition and prevent the normal functioning of the markets, instead of promoting 'fair' competition. Very often, the imposition of dumping duties, or the threat of their imposition, force foreign firms to collude with home firms in keeping prices high.

The problem is a serious one. Most economists feel that most cases of 'dumping' (i.e. below-cost sales or price discrimination among countries) are simply firms engaged in normal business practices. Consequently, they think that anti-dumping duties are nothing more than a disguised form of protectionism.

Here is the basic argument for believing that most cases of below-cost sales have nothing to do with predatory pricing, or with any other form of anti-competitive behaviour. Predatory pricing, even when a firm can get away with it, is not always a good idea. Think of the initial losses incurred by the predator as an investment. If this is to be a wise investment, the predatory firm must expect higher than normal profits after it has driven out the competition – high enough to cover the cost of the predation. Now this is not possible in all industries. The key to profitable predation is the existence of barriers that prevent other firms from entering, or re-entering, the market when the predators raise their prices. This is especially difficult in markets that are marked by much international trade. In such markets, many firms would be tempted to redirect their exports to the market where the predators are charging above-normal prices.

Anti-subisidy duties   The third means of raising trade barriers in a GATT-legal manner is called countervailing subsidies. These are duties that are meant to offset subsidies paid to the exporter. The most obvious of these are export subsidies, but also covered are production subsidies that have the effect of distorting trade. The idea behind this legislation is similar to that of dumping.

Non-tariff–non-quota Barriers

The range of protectionist instruments grows constantly. In addition to the barriers mentioned above, various standards are often used to protect domestic industries from import competition. For instance, environmental standards of various types are used. A classic example is that of Mexican tuna. After the US Congress had passed a bill governing fishing practices by US tuna fishermen in the Pacific, the US government imposed trade barriers against all Mexican tuna that did not meet the same standard. Moreover, the barrier was imposed in a way that made it extremely difficult and expensive for Mexican fisherman to comply. Health standards, human rights concerns, concerns of labour laws are all examples of domestic policies that are used to justify import protection. In all these cases there is a mixing of reasonable, intelligent policy making and plain old-fashioned protectionism.

2.1.2 *Barriers to Services Trade*

Most kinds of international trade in services are quite different from trade in goods. For instance, trade in services very often requires the foreign service provider to have a branch or office in the country to which it is exporting (for instance, in banking, insurance and consultants of all kinds). For this reason, barriers to international services trade often take the form of restrictions on the right of foreign firms to establish themselves in the local market. These restrictions are very often a standard part of the regulation of the domestic service industry. In banking, the same authority that oversees domestic banks will be responsible for granting or denying permits to foreign banks that wish to operate in the local market.

Another set of more subtle restrictions on trade in services concerns accreditation of professionals. Medical doctors are a good example of this. Countries generally require doctors to have a licence to practise medicine, and these licences are usually country-specific. Of course, the agency that grants these licences is naturally dominated by local doctors who would rather not face competition from foreign ones. Thus, doctors often find it difficult to export their services by, say, working in a foreign hospital for several months each year. Similar practices restrict trade in many professional services, ranging from car repair to ski instruction. Discriminatory tax treatment sometimes plays a similar role in restricting trade in services.

Many public services, such as telecommunications, were monopolized by national governments in the early post-war period. The justification usually involved the massive fixed investments involved. In telecommunications, however, technology has changed sufficiently to permit several private firms to operate profitably. In many European nations, national laws protect the state monopoly from foreign competition.

2.1.3 *Barriers to Trade in Productive Factors*

Labour Mobility

Most countries place restrictions on foreign workers. The most common is an outright ban on immigration, or strict quotas. For certain types of trade in services, such as construction and harvesting, these immigration laws act as a barrier to trade in services. Similarly, restrictions on travel by sales, marketing and technical staff can hinder trade in goods since much of the world's trade is actually intra-firm. That is, two affiliates of the same country will sell goods to each other. Often, a critical part of this exchange involves services that are provided by foreign employees of the firm.

Capital Mobility

Restrictions on foreign ownership of domestic assets is very widespread. These range from laws that make it difficult for foreigners to buy coastal property to ones that prohibit foreign ownership of domestic firms. These direct prohibitions are only one way to restrict international capital mobility. Another entails taxation of or restrictions on the use of profits earned in the local market. Many developing countries, for instance, limit the amount of profits a foreign company can repatriate. Sometimes these limits are tied to the amount of export earnings the company generates.

Controls on the international flow of financial capital were very common in Western Europe up to the 1992 Single Market programme. These controls take many forms. Some countries make it difficult for foreigners to own stock in domestic companies or to have bank accounts. Other curbs on capital flows entail laws prohibiting domestic residents from having foreign bank accounts. To complement these quantitative restrictions, countries often tax interests and dividends earned by foreigners and domestic residents asymmetrically.

Technology

Technology and information can be thought of as a factor of production (see Section 2.1.4). Moreover, all countries have policies that affect international flows of intellectual property (this is the general term for patents, copyrights, trademarks, etc.). Since intellectual property is often expensive to create and cheap to copy, countries often face the temptation to allow domestic firms to steal foreign firms' intellectual property. To prevent this, several international agreements that guarantee certain standard property rights have been signed by many nations. The Uruguay Round agreement incorporated many of these into the GATT itself.

An issue that is likely to become more prominent in coming years is that of foreign participation in government-sponsored or assisted research and development (R&D) projects. This is in some ways a restriction on international trade in property rights. It is similar to restrictions on foreign firms' ability to bid on government procurement contracts.

2.1.4 *Corporate Behaviour*

In some markets, such as Japan, private firms are alleged to act in concert to prevent foreign firms from selling. These practices, known as restrictive business practices, restrict import competition and trade. Very often the allegations assert that large companies band together with bureaucrats in order to erect many intangible barriers to foreign goods. This sort of collusion is harmful for the domestic economy and almost all nations have laws – called competition laws in Europe and antitrust laws in the United States – that forbid it. Nonetheless, since local industry is often very influential with local politicians and bureaucrats, restrictive business practices that impede imports are often ignored. As a result, there are increasing calls to include competition policy on the agenda for the next round of GATT talks.

Competition policy is closely related to anti-dumping and countervailing duties. For instance, members of the EU are not allowed to impose either of these duties on each others' exports even if dumping is occurring and even if the domestic industry is harmed. In the place of these duties, the EU Commission has an agency that polices anti-competitive practices and excessive government subsidies.

2.1.5 *Government Behaviour*

In Western Europe, government spending accounts for about one-quarter of all purchases of goods and services. Consequently, a government's policies concerning foreigners' rights to compete for these sales may constitute an important restraint of trade. The set of issues surrounding this comes under the heading of 'government procurement'. One important element of the 1992 Single Market programme was to increase the extent to which all EU firms could compete on a fair basis for government contracts in all EU nations.

Another way in which government behaviour indirectly affects trade is called state aid. For example, several EU governments support their steel and car industries with massive subsidies paid for with tax receipts. A common form of these is for a state-owned firm to run a deficit. This sort of subsidization can impede international trade, since it may prevent the domestic firm from going out of business.

2.2 Allocation Efficiency Effects

Every economy must decide how to allocate its resources to the production of various goods and decide how to allocate the output among its citizens.

In a market economy, these allocations are the outcome of countless decisions made primarily by private citizens acting in their own best interests. An allocation based on greed cannot possibly be good for a society, unless it is restrained and coordinated by some mechanism. Competition among firms facing market-determined prices is the dominant restraining and coordinating force in a market economy. Such competition in factor markets forces the factor prices to reflect their true scarcity and productivity. Competition in the goods market forces firms to charge prices that broadly reflect the cost of the resources used to make them. On the demand side, when consumers must pay the true cost of goods, their purchasing pattern implicitly allocates resources to the production of goods in a way that accurately reflects consumers' preferences. In other words, they are implicitly voting on the allocation of productive resources by buying certain goods instead of others.

In this sense, market-determined prices in a competitive economy constitute a very clever information system. Competitive prices are how firms tell consumers about the true costs of making various goods. Purchase patterns are how consumers tell firms about their preferences.

Barriers that hinder competition among firms and/or constrict consumers' ability to choose among goods disrupt this information flow. Consequently, such barriers tend to worsen the allocation efficiency of an economy. More specifically, when competition is restrained – by government policies or collusion – self-interested firms naturally take advantage of this by raising prices above costs. This reduces the efficiency of the economy since prices that do not reflect the true costs of production typically lead to an inefficient allocation of resources. Government policy that interferes with market pricing similarly reduces efficiency, since such interference distorts the price-based communication among producers and between producers and consumers. Thus even if competition checks the behaviour of self-interested firms, distorted prices are translated into a false and inefficient allocation of the nation's resources.

Government-imposed barriers to the international transactions are extremely common. These barriers hinder international competition among firms and distort the market determination of prices. As such, they typically reduce the efficiency with which the market allocates resources. This section explores in more detail several channels through which barriers reduce the efficiency with which a market economy allocates resources.

The majority of all trade involves goods, industrial products in particular. Moreover, the state of the data and the state of economists' understanding of this sort of trade is by far the most advanced. Consequently, this section is by far the longest. We look first at trade in industrial goods, turning in the first case to the analysis of competitive industries and then to that of imperfectly competitive industries.

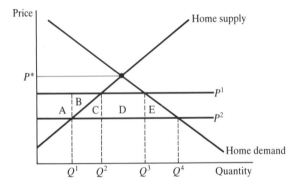

Figure 2.1 The well-known tariff analysis diagram

2.2.1 *Allocation Effects in Competitive Industries*

We start with the most basic analysis. Although this analysis is well known, we review it to fix ideas and introduce notation. In particular, we wish to introduce a distinction between trade barriers that create rents (tariffs, quotas, etc.) and those that simply raise the real cost of trade (excessive bureaucratic delays, etc.).

Standard Analysis of MFN Barriers

Barriers that raise the cost of importing foreign goods artificially distort the relative prices of domestic and foreign goods. This harms economic efficiency. The classic analysis of these effects is shown in Figure 2.1. For example, consider a country's market for electric stoves. To keep things simple, suppose that the domestic economy is small enough so that its demand for stoves will not affect the world price (i.e. the import supply curve is flat at the world price of P^2) and domestic and imported stoves are perfect substitutes. Import barriers of all types raise the local consumer price of imported goods above the international one. The figure shows the case where a trade barrier increases the local price of imports from the world price P^2 to P^1. There are four effects of this price rise:

1. The price of domestically produced stoves also rises to P^1 since domestic stoves could not compete with imports at a higher price and there is no reason to sell them for less.
2. The domestic price increase raises domestic production from Q^1 to Q^2.
3. The higher price of imports and domestic stoves reduces consumption from Q^4 to Q^3.

4. The combination of higher domestic output and lower domestic consumption reduces imports from Q^4–Q^1 to Q^3–Q^2 since imports identically equal consumption minus production.

Welfare Analysis   The well-known analysis in the figure is valid for any trade barrier that introduces a wedge between international and local prices. However, when we turn to the welfare analysis, a sharp distinction must be made between:

- Barriers that create the wedge by 'artificial' measures such as tariffs, quotas, foreign export restraints, import licensing fees, etc. The identifying characteristic of such barriers is that the price gap P^1–P^2 does not represent a real cost – it is simply pocketed by someone. We call these rent-creating barriers (RCBs).
- Barriers that create the wedge by raising the real cost of importing goods. For example, barriers such as excessive bureaucratic restrictions and spurious industrial standards introduce a gap between world and local prices, but this gap is not pocketed by anyone. Rather it represents the cost of real resources that must be devoted to overcoming the barriers. We call these cost-creating barriers (CCBs).

Rent-creating Barriers   The classic example of a rent-creating barrier is a tariff. In this case, there are three welfare effects in addition to the four positive effects mentioned above:

1. The government collects revenue equal to imports times the tariff, i.e. area D.
2. Consumers lose since they pay more for stoves. The loss consists of two parts: (i) The price increase, P^1–P^2, times all the stoves they buy at the increased price, i.e. the areas $A + B + C + D$ and (ii) the area E, which equals what consumers would pay to have the right to buy the extra stoves Q^4–Q^3 at the world price. At the higher price people consume and pay for fewer stoves. However, even though they no longer pay for the extra stoves, they are unhappy about the lower consumption. Area E is a measure of this unhappiness.
3. Home producers gain from the higher price. The gain consists of two parts: (i) the price rise times the number of stoves they sold at the old price (area A) and (ii) area B, which is the profit they make selling the extra stoves Q^2–Q^1 at the new price.

The gains to the government and firms are less than the loss to consumers. Adding up the gains and losses to all domestic residents, the country as a whole loses by the area C plus E. This is the pure loss due to allocation inefficiencies induced by the tariff. Area C represents the loss due to the inefficient allocation of domestic resources. The country is using resources that are worth P^1 to make stoves when it could have bought the stoves at a cost of P^2 on the world market. Area E represents the allocation inefficiency on the consumers' part. The tariff distorts prices so that consumers do not face the true cost of stoves. Consequently, they allocate their expenditures inefficiently, buying too few stoves as opposed to other goods. Obviously the impact of a tariff removal is just the reverse of the above reasoning.

Quantitative restrictions, such as import quotas and voluntary export restraints, constitute another major type of rent-creating barrier. A quota that reduces imports to Q^3 minus Q^2 would have the effect of raising the price of imports to P^1 and would therefore have the same positive effects as the tariff studied above. Indeed, if the quota is enforced by an import-licensing scheme, and the government sold the licences at a price which just equalled the gap between local and international prices, the welfare effects would be identical. In fact, if the government gave away the licences to domestic citizens or firms, the net welfare would still be the same. The difference would be that the rent (area D) would be pocketed by a private citizen or firm instead of the Treasury.

In some cases, however, it is the foreign firm or the foreign government that holds the rights to the rent. Indeed throughout the industrialized world, it is extremely common for trade barriers to be arranged so that the wedge is earned by foreigners. One reason for this is that the rent is used as a carrot to soothe the anger of foreigner companies and governments at having a trade barrier imposed. Examples of this are voluntary export restraints (VERs), price-raising arrangements made to avoid dumping duties and international cartelization of markets such as textiles and clothing (the Multi-Fibre Agreement) and steel. In all these cases the net loss to the protecting country is even greater, since less of the loss to domestic consumers is offset by gains to other domestic interests. Specifically, the total static cost of the barrier is C plus D plus E.

It is important to note that the primary effect of the tariff is to redistribute money from consumers to domestic firms and the Treasury. Indeed, it is easy to show that a 10% tariff is exactly like a 10% sales tax together with a 10% subsidy to domestic producers. In this sense, tariffs are an inefficient means of taxing citizens and subsidizing domestic production.

Cost-creating Barriers   West European countries often restrict imports by subjecting them to a whole range of policies that increase the real cost of importing. The net cost to the nation of imposing this sort of barrier is again C plus D plus E.

One of the most important types of such barriers involves industrial and health standards that are chosen at least in part to restrict imports. For example, some countries refuse to accept safety tests that are performed in foreign countries, even in highly industrialized nations. This forces importers to retest their products in the local country. In addition to raising the real cost of imported goods, this sort of barrier delays the introduction of new products. While this clearly harms consumers, domestic producers may benefit since it may give them time to introduce competing varieties.

A related set of cost-raising barriers consists of unusual industrial, health and environmental standards. These involve countries imposing standards that differ from internationally recognized norms. The net effect is to protect domestic producers or service providers. Domestic firms design their products with these standards in mind while foreign firms, for whom the domestic market may be relatively unimportant, are unlikely to do so. Bringing imported products into conformity raises the real cost of imports.

One reason this sort of barrier is so common is that the government agencies charged with formulating and enforcing standards are often 'captured' by special-interest groups representing the industries they are supposed to regulate. That is, domestic firms and service providers that gain from having standards that reduce import competition often play an important role in setting the standards. For example, even if the government formally decides on standards, a domestic industry association often suggests or approves the standards.

Of course, nations do need health, environmental and industrial standards. One solution to the problem of setting standards without unduly restricting international trade and competition is to participate in international groups that adopt standard regulations. Another, which the EU Single Market programme adopted for many issues, is that of mutual recognition. Under this principle, products that have been approved under the rules of any EU country will be accepted as approved in all EU markets.

Standard Effects of Import Barriers on Exporters

So far, we have focused on the domestic impact of domestic trade barriers. The opposite side of the equation – the impact of trade barriers on the exporter's country – is our next subject. As before, we make simplifying assumptions to highlight the economic logic. Specifically, we assume that there are only two countries labelled country 1 and country 2. Figure 2.2, which shows the markets in countries 1 and 2 for electric stoves, is drawn assuming that 1-made and 2-made stoves are indistinguishable to consumers. The right diagram shows 2's supply and demand curves. For prices above the intersection of 2's supply and demand, 2 has an excess of supply of stoves that it will export. In the left diagram the MD curve shows 1's import demand (this is simply 1's total demand curve minus 1's supply curve), and MS shows the import supply curve. Assuming that initially

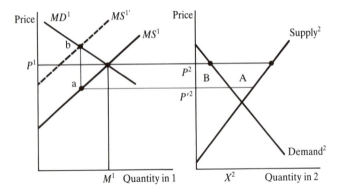

Figure 2.2 The impact of protection on an exporting country

there is free trade in stoves between the two countries, MS is also 2's export supply curve. The free trade equilibrium prices and quantities are shown as P^1, M^1, P^2 and X^2. Note that P^1 equals P^2 due to free trade.

Next, consider the impact on 2 of a rent-creating import barrier imposed by 1. To be specific, suppose 1's government imposes an import tariff equal to the distance between points a and b in the diagram. The import tax can be represented as a shift back in the MS curve, since each level of local price in 1 corresponds to a lower level of imports. The net effect is a wedge between the price of stoves in 1 and 2. This drives down the price received by 2's exporters. As a consequence, producers and consumer in 2 face a lower price for stoves. The positive effects of these price changes are straightforward. Consumption and imports in 1 fall and domestic production rises. Production and exports in 2 fall, while consumption rises. Using the analysis above, it is easy to see that 2-based producers lose more than 2's consumers and the government gains. That is, the lower prices harm 2's producers by the area $A + B$. Country 2's consumers gain from lower prices by the area B. Country 2's net loss is therefore equal to A.

It is easy to use this diagram to analyse the impact of a wide variety of import-restricting policies on the welfare of exporting countries.

Standard Analysis of Geographically Discriminatory Barriers

When a country maintains geographically discriminatory trade barriers – for instance, when Poland maintains higher barriers against imports from Lithuania than it does against imports from Germany – the analysis becomes slightly more complicated.

Let us take the case of a discriminatory tariff. Domestic importers wishing to buy products from abroad usually search for the lowest-priced

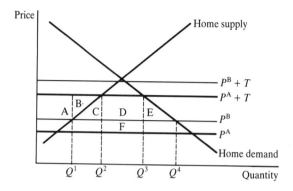

Figure 2.3 Trade creation and trade diversion

products that meets their needs. Broadly, this search is in the national interest since it reduces the cost to the nation of acquiring the good. If the home government imposes different tariff rates on the imports from different countries, the prices that guide the importers' search will be warped. Consequently, the importers will not necessarily buy from the lowest-cost producer; they buy from the country whose price plus the relevant tariff is lowest. The tariff distorts the price signals, so the private importers' choice may be misguided from the social point of view. In other words, importers face a price that equals the true cost to the nation plus the tariff. Since the tariff is paid to the home government, it is not a true cost to the nation. Thus lower tariffs against only certain countries' goods may actually lead importers to switch from low- to high-cost foreign suppliers. From the national standpoint, this 'trade diversion' constitutes a loss. This loss mitigates and may reverse the usual gains from liberalization.

Figure 2.3 shows the analysis for any barrier that raises the price of imports in a geographically discriminatory manner. The figure considers the case of two potential sources of imports, countries A and B. To set the stage, suppose that initially the home country imposes a trade barrier that raises the local price of all imports above the international price by T as shown in the figure. As before, we assume that the country is small enough to face a flat import supply curve from all countries. Clearly, it would cost home consumers P^A plus T to import from country A and P^B plus T to import from B, so all imports would come from A. Competition from imports fixes the price of local goods at $P^A + T$, and imports at Q^3 minus Q^2.

Next, suppose that the home country signs a free trade agreement with B but not with A. This discriminatory liberalization artificially changes the relative competitiveness of goods from A and B. Indeed, now goods from B cost P^B while those from A cost $P^A + T$. Naturally, home consumers will divert all of their import demand from A towards B. There are four positive effects:

1. The preferential liberalization increases competition from imports and thereby forces down the price of locally made goods to P^B.
2. Some high-cost home production is replaced by lower-cost imports. This amount is equal to $Q^2 - Q^1$.
3. Imports from A are entirely replaced by imports from B.
4. Consumption rises to Q^4.

Welfare Analysis   Again welfare analysis requires us to distinguish between rent- and cost-creating barriers. The simplest rent-creating policy is that of a government tariff. In this case, the government loses all tariff revenue due to the diversion of trade from A to B. This loss equals D + F. The lower price benefits home consumers by an amount equal to A + B + C + D + E, and domestic producers are harmed by A plus B. The net impact on the home country's welfare equals the two triangles (C plus E) minus the rectangle F. This amount may be positive or negative.

Traditional analysis classifies the welfare effects of a discriminatory tariff cut into 'trade creation' and 'trade diversion'. The cost of trade diversion, area F, stems from the fact that after the discriminatory liberalization, the country buys from a higher-cost international supplier. The trade creation gains, areas C plus E, are exactly equal to the gains we saw from an non-discriminatory tariff cut above. The source of the gain is also the same, consisting of a reduced producer distortion (area C) and a reduced consumer distortion (area E).

The fact that a country can lose when it liberalizes on a discriminatory basis has created a very large literature on theory (see Lipsey, 1960). This has identified many rules of thumb about when a discriminatory liberalization is likely to increase national welfare. Perhaps the most enduring and most intuitive one concerns the fraction of total imports that come from other members of the preferential trading area. It is easy to understand this using Figure 2.3. In the case presented above, the home country initially imports none of the goods from the country with which it signs the free trade agreement. Consequently, the discriminatory tariff cut could, and in this case did, lead home consumers to switch from a low-cost supplier to a high-cost one. This opened the door to a possible welfare loss from the bilateral free trade agreement. For comparison, suppose instead that the free trade deal was signed with country A. Since A was already the low-cost supplier, there is no possibility that tariff discrimination would force home consumers to switch to higher-cost suppliers. Consequently, the liberalization would unambiguously make the home country better off.

Actual trade between countries is made up of thousands of products, so to be complete one should go through thousands of diagrams like Figure 2.3 to check whether the home country would gain or lose from a preferential trade arrangement. An obvious shortcut, however, is simply to look at how much trade the home country does with its intended partners. If it already imports a great deal from its partners, then it is likely that its partners were the low-cost suppliers even before liberalization. Consequently, the discriminatory tariff cuts on imports from these countries are likely to lead to little switching. Clearly, this rule of thumb is not infallible.

We assumed above that the gap was caused by a home government tariff. However, as discussed above, many import barriers raise the local price above foreign prices, but do not generate revenue for the home government. For instance, many governments strike deals with foreign firms limiting the amount of goods that they will sell in the home market, or forcing foreign firms to raise their prices to avoid anti-dumping duties. In such cases, it is the foreigners who earn the profit equal to the area $D + F$ prior to liberalization. Thus when a discriminatory tariff reduction destroys these profits, there is no loss to the home country to offset the gains of lower prices. The gain from liberalization is $C + D + E$.

Removing Cost-raising Barriers   The welfare analysis is also quite different from the tariff case when considering trade barriers that impose real costs on imports. If the price wedge T was due to, say, excessive bureaucratic delays, then eliminating the barrier in a discriminatory manner (i.e. only against imports from country B) would have all the positive and normative effects mentioned above except the one dealing with government revenue. Consequently, the liberalizing nation gains as a whole, even though trade is diverted. The size of the gain is $C + D + E$.

The last two results are quite important, since many trade barriers are either the cost-raising or the rent-creating type in which foreigners get the rents. It would seem that trade within Europe has been impeded by a very long list of cost-raising barriers. For instance, the financial system underpinning intra-CEEC trade is less developed than the one for East–West trade. The same is true of telecommunications and postal services. The implication of the above analysis is that removing cost-raising barriers alone on a regional – as opposed to multilateral – basis cannot lead to a worsening of welfare due to trade diversion.

The Cost of Rules of Origin

Any preferential trade agreement requires 'rules of origin' that specify how customs officials determine the origins of particular products in order to know which trade barriers to apply. The absence of such rules would create an incentive to reroute trade artificially in order to avoid trade barriers. For instance, consider a free trade area between a country that imposes a high tariff on Taiwanese radios and one that imposes a low tariff on them. An importer based in the high-tariff country may attempt to avoid the high duty by importing the radio into the low-tariff one and then re-export it into the importer's own country duty-free. Rules of origin are needed to prevent this 'trade deflection'. Rules of origin can be very complicated. For instance, the main body of the Interim Agreement between Poland and the EU agreement fills 13 pages; Protocol 4, which describes how to determine whether a product originates in Poland or the EU, is over 60 pages long with all its Annexes. The rules of origin become more complicated as countries' trade arrangements become more complicated. A brief explanation of common rules of origin and an example (the EFTA–EU rules of origin) are presented in Box 2.1.

Rules of origin can significantly affect the allocation efficiency effects of a preferential trade agreement, although the economic impact varies greatly depending upon the exact wording of the rules. Nonetheless, these rules, together with the preferential access embodied in a preferential trade agreement, tend to protect producers of intermediate materials and components by forcing final producers to buy more local inputs. They may also unintentionally harm the interests of third countries. For instance, consider a manufacturer of products that fall under the Harmonized System heading number 8208 (knives and cutting blades for mechanical appliances). Suppose that prior to Poland's free trade agreement with the EU, the manufacturer imported some components from, say, Lithuania. Under the free trade agreement, the Polish manufacturer's product is granted preferential access to the EU only if at least 40% of its value is added in either Poland or the EU. This restriction may induce the Polish firm to switch from the Lithuanian supplier to a higher-cost EU-based supplier in order to meet the 40% value-added rule.

A common provision that is aimed at reducing this artificial switching of suppliers induced by rules of origin provision is called 'cumulation'. Continuing to use our Polish example, a cumulative system would require at least 40% of the value of the final product to be added in Poland, or any other country (such as the Czech Republic and Hungary) with which the EU had a similar preferential trade agreement.

Rules of origin can impose heavy administrative costs on exporters and importers which force an artificial distortion of trade. Herin (1986) documents the cost of the rules of origin for intra-EFTA and EFTA–EU trade. He found that these rules were so complex that many EFTA- and EU-based exporters preferred to pay the higher, non-preferential tariff rather than incur the administrative costs necessary to qualify for zero-tariff treatment under the EU–EFTA free trade agreements. Specifically, in 1984 a fifth of the EU's exports to EFTA and a quarter of EFTA exports to

Box 2.1 An example of rules of origin

One of the most common forms of rules of origin is based on the concept of 'change in tariff heading'. According to this concept, an article completed in one country from materials originating in another is said to originate in the second country if the processing was sufficient to change the tariff classification of the article. Another popular concept, which is often combined with change of tariff heading, involves minimum value added. That is, for a product to be considered as originating from country A, a certain percentage of its final value (often at least 40%) must have been added in country A.

EFTA–EU Rules of Origin
Before the European Economic Area agreement, trade between EFTA and EU states was governed by individual bilateral free trade agreements; one between each EFTAn and the EU. Additionally EFTA was a free trade area itself, so trade in manufactured products was duty-free among EFTAns. Since each EFTAn maintained different tariffs against third countries, a complicated set of origin rules was imposed to prevent tariff circumvention. Consider, for example, an Austrian-based firm that wished to obtain duty-free treatment for its exports to the EU. To do so, the firm would have to prove that its product originates in Austria. According to the rules, its product originates in Austria only if it fulfils one of the following criteria:

1. It is wholly produced in Austria.
2. It is produced with materials from third countries provided that:
    - *All* materials, parts and components imported from countries not members of EFTA or the EU are classified under a four-digit Customs Cooperation Council Nomenclature (CCCN) heading which is different from that for the final product.
    - For certain finished products, additional limitations were imposed restricting the value of inputs from non-EFTA, non-EU sources.

To fulfil these conditions, the exporter must maintain up-to-date records of:

- The tariff classification of all materials imported from non-EFTA, non-EU countries and the tariff classification of all its finished products.

- The tariff classification and origin of all products imported from subcontractors in other EFTA or EU countries.
- The value of materials imported from non-EFTA, non-EU nations which are of the same tariff classification as the finished product.

See Herin (1986) for more details.

the EU were subject to the non-preferential tariff. Of course, the one-fifth figure also reflects the fact the tariffs on trade among industrialized countries are quite low as a result of tariff-cutting in successive GATT rounds.

Inside a customs union like the EU, none of these rules are necessary for intra-EU trade, at least in principle. However, even though the EU-12 have had common external tariffs, they have until very recently maintained national quotas on some non-EU imports. (The cases of Italian quotas on Japanese cars and French quotas on bananas from Latin America have been much reported in the press.) To enforce these quotas, time-consuming customs procedures were necessary. The example of bananas shows how complicated trade arrangements can lead to hidden costs. France, which maintains preferential trade arrangements with its former colonies, discriminated against bananas imported from Latin America. Germany, however, bought most of its bananas from Latin America since they are the low-cost producers. France had to maintain customs surveillance to prevent cheap bananas from slipping across the German border.

2.2.2 *Allocation Effects in Imperfectly Competitive Industries*

International trade in goods typically increases competition in local markets. Import protection, in contrast, typically decreases it. Since competition is the central pillar of market economies, the pro-competitive effect of trade liberalization is an important channel through which liberalization increases allocation efficiency. This effect occurs when trade liberalization intensifies competition between foreign and domestic firms and thereby restrains anti-competitive behaviour both domestically and abroad.

Traditional Analysis

The domestic market of a small country may not support a large number of firms, especially in industries in which scale economies are important. This can cause problems, since small numbers of firms tend to collude and exploit consumers by raising prices. Competition from imports is an important means of restraining the monopoly power of domestic firms. This subsection presents the traditional analysis of import competition on the competitive behaviour of domestic firms.

Domestic Monopolist and Import Competition with Homogeneous Products
Consider the case of a domestic monopolist in a country where imports are initially forbidden. It is well known that a monopolist will restrict sales to raise prices and profits. In particular, a monopolist chooses sales at the level where the extra revenue from selling one more unit just equals the extra cost of producing it. It is useful to break down the extra revenue (i.e. marginal revenue) into direct and indirect components. The direct part is the price that the firm receives for the extra unit it sells. The indirect effect is the extent to which the extra sale marginally depresses the market price, thereby reducing the revenue the firm receives on all its sales. The fact that firms with market power take account of this indirect effect is what leads to economically inefficient pricing. Were it not for the indirect effect, the firm would set price equal to marginal cost, and consumers would then face the true cost of the good. As we shall see, the crucial impact of import competition on the monopoly pricing of domestic firms concerns the indirect effect.

To study the impact of import competition on the monopolist's position, suppose that imports are allowed. In this simple example, competition from imports completely eliminates the indirect effect. If consumers have unlimited access to imports at the world price, all the monopolist's price-setting power is destroyed. The monopolist cannot charge a higher price since it would lose all its customers to imports. Moreover, there is no reason to charge less, so the international price becomes the domestic price. These two facts combine to remove the indirect effect mentioned above. Since the international price is the true cost to the country of making or consuming the good, pricing efficiency is restored. Imposing a tariff will raise the domestic price to the international one plus the tariff. The tariff means that consumers no longer face the true cost of the good, so an inefficient allocation of resources results. Nonetheless, the unrestricted ability of consumers to import destroys the power of the domestic monopoly.

As before, the positive analyses of a tariff and of other rent-creating barriers are fairly similar. However, the welfare impact depends, in an important way, on who gets the rents (if any) created by a trade barrier. Since there is nothing essentially different between the perfect and imperfect competition cases on this point, we do not repeat the welfare analysis.

Imperfect Substitutes The above example clearly illustrates the pro-competitive effect of imports. It is, however, quite unrealistic. Import

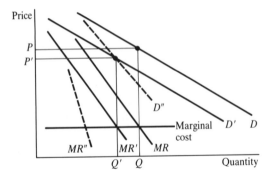

Figure 2.4 Quotas versus tariffs with imperfect competition

competition rarely destroys a domestic firm's ability to set prices. Figure 2.4 shows the more general case where imports are an imperfect substitute for domestic goods, so consumers' ability to buy imports still leaves the domestic firm some price-setting freedom.[3]

In Figure 2.4 the demand curve and corresponding marginal revenue curve for home goods are shown as D and MR for a given tariff on imports. As usual, the home firm would sell Q units at a price of P. If the tariff on imports is lowered, foreign goods will be sold at a reduced price, inducing some of the domestic firm's customers to switch to imports. Consequently, the demand for home goods at any price is reduced. This is shown as a shift of D to D'. Normally this will also shift in the marginal revenue curve to MR'. The net result will be lower prices of imports and domestic goods. More to the point, the market power of the domestic firm is reduced. By market power, we mean the extent to which the home firm charges a price that exceeds marginal cost. Clearly, in this example the domestic firm's mark-up is reduced (the price is lower but marginal cost is constant). This leads to lower prices and output of the home goods, with the usual impact on profits and consumer welfare. That is, the price reduction creates greater benefits for domestic consumers than losses to domestic producers. Furthermore, since prices more closely reflect true costs, the efficiency with which resources are allocated is improved.

Non-equivalence of Tariffs and Quantitative Restrictions   Next, consider the effects of reducing imports through the use of a quantitative restriction such as a quota instead of a tariff. In Figure 2.4 the demand curve with a quota intersects the demand curve for tariff at Q'. The reason for this is simple. If the home firm charged P' with the quota, the local price of imports would be just the same as the local price with the tariff. Consequently, the amount of home good demanded at P' would be the same as under the tariff, namely Q'.

Note, however, that the demand curve facing the home firm when the restriction is a quantitative restriction, i.e. D'', is steeper than it is for a tariff. To understand the reason for this, think about what a quota is. If the domestic firm raises its price, some consumers may wish to switch to the imported goods. With a tariff, their switching will not bid up the price of imported goods too much because of the unlimited supply of imports, so many will switch. However, with a quota the increased demand stemming from switching consumers will bid up the price of the limited quantity of imports permitted under the quota. Of course, this higher price of imported goods will discourage some domestic consumers from switching. The bottom line is that if the domestic firm raises its price by a given amount, it will lose fewer sales with a quota than it will with a tariff. Graphically, this means that the demand curve is steeper. The implication of the steeper demand curve is that the corresponding marginal revenue curve MR'' is to the left of the marginal revenue curve with a tariff. Clearly, this will lead to a higher domestic price than under the tariff.

The key result here is a comparison of the impact of tariffs and quotas on market power of local firms. Here we saw that a tariff and a quota that limited imports equally led to different prices of the domestic substitute. In particular, the quota leads to higher prices than the tariff. The intuition for this result is the same as before. With a tariff, consumers always have the alternative of importing. With a quantitative restriction, they have the alternative only for the fixed number of imported goods permitted. Thus, with a quantitative restriction, the domestic firm does not face import competition on the margin.

More Recent Analysis

Most of the traditional analysis presented above was developed in the 1960s and 1970s in large part due to academic interest in the impact of the formation of the EEC. Over this period, however, economists largely ignored scale economies and imperfect competition in their formal work. Advancement in the profession's understanding of economies of scale in production and imperfect competition in product markets has been reflected in a set of new analyses of the economic impact of trade arrangements.

The Venables–Smith Pro-competitive Effect   Most trade in industrial products is intra-industry due to scale economies and imperfect competition. The pro-competitive forces of liberalization of such trade has been shown to have particularly large allocation efficiency effects by Venables and Smith (1988) and Gasorek, Smith and Venables (1992). To see why this is so, note that firms that sell to various markets in Europe tend to treat these markets as segmented in the sense that they think that their sales in one market does not affect the price for their goods in other markets. It is possible for them to charge different prices due to a whole host of seemingly minor policy differences. Two types of policy are relevant: those that raise the cost of entering a particular market (licensing and bureaucratic requirements that make it expensive for foreign firms to establish local branches to help with marketing and after-sales service, spurious product standards that require foreign firms to modify their product, etc.) and policies that raise the real cost of trade (customs inspections and delays, VAT refund procedures, etc.).

Although each of these barriers seems minor in isolation, the net effect is to fragment the EU market into many small markets. Evidence of this fragmentation can be found in the fact that different European firms, offering quite similar products, typically have very different market shares in various EU markets. The cost-raising policies imply that foreign suppliers typically have a smaller share of the local market. Indeed, if these trade costs are high enough, foreign firms may decide not to incur the market-entry costs, so eventually they have a zero market share. The net effect is that local firms often have the lion's share of the market, with foreign producers playing a marginal role. Often this reflects the fact that the political power of the local firms lead to the 'minor' policy differences being chosen in such a way as to give an artificial edge to the local industry.

This sort of fragmentation of markets leads to too little competition and too many firms, each operating at inefficient scales of production. Even if firms are not earning large pure profits, fragmentation is harmful since inefficient scales of production result in high prices. Trade arrangements can change this situation by lowering the real costs of trade and market-entry costs. Lowering trade costs tends to even out the shares of local and foreign firms. If costs fall far enough, foreign firms that previously did not bother selling to the home market may start to do so. Similarly, lowering market-entry costs tends to increase the presence of foreign firms, putting additional competitive pressure on home ones. The overall effect is to reduce the profit that firms earn in their home market but increases their profits in foreign markets. If the home market is very important then liberalization will squeeze total profits. This will drive out some firms, so the remaining ones can operate at a more efficient scale. The lower average costs can have a large impact on welfare in addition to the real trade cost savings.

A liberalization that is as sweeping as the EU's Single Market programme may have the additional effect of removing the segmentation of the various national markets. That is, it may force firms to adopt a single pricing strategy for the entire European market. This would lead to further rationalization, and thereby a further lowering of average costs and prices.

Collusion and Trade Liberalization   Domestic firms often engage in implicit or explicit anti-competition arrangements that raise market prices above costs. In addition to exploiting consumers, such arrangements usually worsen the allocation efficiency by distorting prices and supporting inefficient scales of production. Virtually every market economy has laws that prohibit or circumscribe this sort of anti-competitive behaviour. The problem, however, is that it is extremely difficult to implement such laws in a manner that is not disruptive to normal business practices. For instance, regulations that prohibit mergers of large firms based solely on market-share criteria may have the unintentional effect of preventing perfectly sensible and economically efficient rationalization. Competition from imported goods is an effective way of disciplining such arrangements without running the risk of excessive government intervention.

The point is that domestic firms often find it much harder to sustain collusive arrangements with foreign ones, especially when there are many potential foreign suppliers of the good. To explain the economics of this point, it is necessary to describe modern economic thinking on collusion. Collusion is a cooperation among firms that might otherwise be competitors. This cooperation allows them to raise prices and thereby increase profits. According to the new thinking, the pillar holding up such cooperation is the threat posed by the lower prices and profits that would occur if the cooperation broke down and a price war ensued.

For the sake of argument, let us consider the difficulty of supporting collusion among a handful of firms in a market that was shut off from the rest of the world. In this case the threat of a breakdown of cooperation would be great. With only a few producers, the production capacity of each is fairly large relative to the market. Thus if any of them significantly increased production (by running their factories for two or three shifts a day), prices would fall by a considerable amount. Moreover, since all the firms depend entirely on the home market, such a reduction in prices would pose a serious threat to their profitability. Collusion would be relatively easy to support since the consequences of not cooperating would be dire.

Let us contrast this with the case of a fairly small, open economy where there are many foreign firms participating. Clearly, it would be difficult for the home firms alone to collude and drive up prices since foreign suppliers would step in. Moreover, since the production capacities of domestic firms are relatively small, foreign firms would be relatively less worried about retaliation by home firms if they did not cooperate. Since many of the foreign firms may view the home market as relatively small and unimportant, they are unlikely to be very concerned by a price war in the home market. The result of all this is organizing cooperation with foreign producers in the home market alone would be difficult, since foreign firms would not greatly fear a price war in the home market. Of course, one possible outcome is that domestic and foreign firms attempt to collude in all markets. While this is possible, the difficulties of orchestrating a cartel rise rapidly with the number of participants.

2.3   Location Effects

Trade, investment and migration barriers influence location of productive activity. Consequently one very important – but much neglected – aspect of integration is the effect of a trade arrangement on the region's economic geography. Data in Europe, for instance, show a very strong link between peripherality and per capita income levels. Of course, peripherality is a relative concept, so one needs to be careful. (Is Iceland on the outskirts of Europe or conveniently placed between the European and North American markets?) Indisputably, it is far too facile to think that geographical location is the only or even the main determinant of relative incomes. Nevertheless, location matters. Switzerland is more centrally located than Portugal and it is pretty easy to believe that being right in the middle of Europe's industrial heartland gives Swiss industry an edge not enjoyed by Portuguese industry.

2.3.1   *Krugman–Venables Theory*

Paul Krugman, Tony Venables and others have recently developed a set of tools that help us think systematically about how policy can affect the agglomeration of economic activity on a very large scale. The tools address two fundamental questions. Why and where do industries concentrate geographically? This 'new location theory' is quite distinct from the classic approach. Alfred Marshall listed three main reasons why industries concentrate in geographically small areas: labour market pooling, supply of non-traded intermediate goods, and technological spillovers. Krugman, in his excellent book, *Geography and Trade* (1991), argues that these three effects best explain fairly small economic concentrations such as a single city or small cluster of cities. The location of economic activity in Europe, however, displays a much grander pattern. For instance, the concentration of industrial activity currently seen in northern Italy covers hundreds of kilometres. This very large-scale agglomeration suggests that there are much broader forces governing Europe's economic geography.

Basic Analytic Framework

The basic approach to understanding this grand scale of agglomeration relies on two economic forces: (1) increasing returns to scale in production that are internal to the firm, and (2) trade costs. Note that technology-based externalities – e.g. knowledge spillovers, non-traded intermediates, etc. – are not part of this approach. In fact they are assumed away in order to sharpen the focus of the analysis. Since trade costs and scale economies are at the very heart of the theory, it is worth discussing them in more detail.

Increasing returns simply mean that average costs fall as the scale of production rises. There are many reasons for this, but the most common and intuitive are fixed costs. If selling requires a firm to build a factory, undertake R&D, invest in advertisement, or establish a marketing and after-sales service network, then the firm faces falling average costs. The costs of any or all of the previously mentioned items are substantially fixed. That is, even if the firm fails to sell a single unit of output, it must still pay for the set-up costs.

The notion of trade cost is less well established. The classic trade cost is the expense of shipping a product from the point of production to the point of sale. However, we should not limit ourselves to this. Transport cost is only the tip of the iceberg. Modern business involves much more than making goods and loading them onto a truck. To take a very practical example, let us consider what it would require to sell fresh pasta in Western Europe, assuming that the product is made in Italy. Most food in Europe is sold through local supermarkets and small shops, so the pasta maker must somehow get the goods onto the shelves of these stores. How does this occur? The pasta maker must have a sales force that goes out and tells the local stores about the pasta and tries to convince them that they should order some because they will make money selling it. This must be done in the local language. In order to prevent chaos in this selling effort, the pasta maker must have a marketing staff that directs the effort throughout Europe. Moreover, the necessary information flow is not one-way. The pasta maker has to find out about consumers' ever-changing likes and dislikes concerning every aspect of the product: package size, spiciness, ingredients, how long the product must stay fresh, etc.

The point of this discussion is to bring out the importance of distance. All the activities mentioned above typically get harder – and therefore more expensive – the further away consumers are from the headquarters in Italy. There is the financial cost and time demand of travelling, the difficulty and cost of communicating between increasingly different cultures and languages. Think about the problems facing an Italian trying to manage local-language marketing and sales effort in Italy, in France, in the United Kingdom and in Iceland. The further away a market is from Italy, the more difficult it becomes. Of course, this is not always the case; the New Zealand culture is much closer to England's than is that of France. Moreover, with fresh pasta, shipments must be frequent and the manufacturer must take back the product that goes bad before it sells. Obviously this is a special case, but the point is general. Trade costs involve much, much more than shipping the product.

Why Location Matters to Firms   Scale economies force firms to decide where to locate. Trade costs mean that the decision has important implications for profits. If average production costs fall with the scale of production at a particular location, then firms face serious trade-offs in their location decisions. Concentrating productive capacity lowers average costs but raises the costs of selling output to dispersed customers. The point can be made clear by considering the converse case of constant returns to scale with small trade costs. In this case the optimal location decision of a firm is trivial, but ridiculous. To avoid even very small transport costs each firm would have to place a small amount of manufacturing capacity right next to each of its customers. Every consumer would have a scaled-down model of all manufacturing plants located in his or her own garden! The absence of scale economies implies that this other-worldly distribution of economic activity would be just as efficient as the massive concentration that we observe in the modern world.

Before considering how all this affects location, an aside is in order. Once we open the door to increasing returns to scale, we must deal with imperfect competition. If average cost falls with output, there is a strong tendency for a small number of firms to dominate. In such cases it is quite unlikely that they would act in a perfectly competitive manner. Thus, imperfect competition will necessarily be involved in the Krugman–Venables framework. Imperfect competition *per se* plays only a minor role in the framework, but it is an unavoidable aspect of the models.

Equilibrium Location of Industry

Circular Causality   We now turn to the core mechanism of the Krugman–Venables framework. Firms facing scale economies would prefer to concentrate production. Other things being equal (e.g. production cost), firms would want to locate near the largest market in order to reduce trade costs. This line of reasoning starts to turn circles on itself. For many sectors, industry is its own best customer. Thus firms want to be where other firms are located. Firms that sell goods directly to consumers face a similar circularity. Their customers are located where the jobs are, and the jobs tend to be concentrated where firms are located. Accordingly, there is a mutually amplifying interaction between transport-costs-avoidance and market-size determination. Firms' desires to be near customers tend to concentrate demand for intermediate and final products, and this agglomeration of firms' and workers' purchasing power tends to attract more firms.

Thus there is a circular mechanism involving transportation-costs-avoidance (firms' wishes to be near large markets) and market size (firms' location decisions influence market size). We refer to this as circular causality.

An Illustration   To elucidate this reasoning, let us imagine a country in which there are only two locations (the coast and the interior), only two economic activities (farming and manufacturing) and two types of labourers (farmers and workers). Farmers are assumed to be tied to their land and are divided evenly between the two locations. Manufactured goods can be made on the coast or in the interior, but setting up a factory involves a large fixed cost. In an established factory, the labour required to produce manufactured goods rises linearly with the output. Furthermore, a firm located in one locale must incur some costs to sell to consumers located in the other. Finally, let us suppose that demand for manufactured goods in each locale is proportional to its population of farmers and industrial workers.

If the fixed cost is large enough, then each firm will want to have only one factory, so its choice is to locate on the coast or in the interior. Given the transport costs, it wants to locate in the region with the higher population. But in our simple model, the population in the two regions differs only by the number of industrial workers (farmers are assumed to stay on their land). The question of how many workers are in each region, though, depends upon the location decision of all firms. There are two stable outcomes: all industry either located on the coast or in the interior.

The outcome has implications for real wages. By assumption, the labour of farmers and workers cannot be substituted, so the location of industry will not impact on farmers' physical marginal productivity; this depends only on the ratio of farmers to land. However, the location of industry affects farmers' real wages through the price of industrial goods. Due to trade costs, industrial goods are more expensive in the region without industry. Higher prices means lower real wages, so farmers should be concerned about industry location. Workers' wages are, of course, equal, no matter in which region the industry is located since they will be living near the industry.

So far, we have biased the model towards spectacular outcomes. All the industry is located in one region or the other. Let us suppose that only half of the industrial workers in each region are mobile. In this case, the industrial wages in the two regions would adjust to prevent complete concentration. To work through this assertion, let us assume instead that all industry moved to the coast, taking with it half of the interior's workers. The remaining interior workers would have nothing to do. As a result, it is very likely that they would be willing to work for a lower wage than that earned by coastal workers. If trade costs were not too high, the low wages in the interior would attract some firms back to the interior. In fact, that difference in wages would have to be large enough to offset the trade cost disadvantage incurred by firms that chose to locate in the small interior market.

Of course, the simple model has left out many realistic effects – but it serves the purpose of illustration. The future research agenda for economic geography is vast, on both a theoretical and an empirical level. The question of what regional integration does to industrial concentration is important, but as yet it is not well understood. Even more detailed questions such as what are the best policies in order to help disadvantaged regions are even more pressing (at least in Europe) but are even less well understood. There is much informal reasoning and 'common wisdom' (e.g. the central government should build more physical infrastructure such as roads and telecommunications systems, and promote more investment in human capital by building and improving schools). In fact these policies have failed dismally in some cases (southern Italy) but have enjoyed some success in others (Ireland and Portugal).

Implications

Multiple Equilibria   This simple example shows us two very important and very general results. First, note that we have not assumed any of Marshall's externalities. There are no technological spillovers or advantages from labour pooling. Thus it is understandable why concentration of industrial activity occurs in industries with such different technologies as financial services and cars. The second is that, in general, we have multiple stable equilibria. In the above example, total concentration on the coast and total concentration in the interior are both stable outcomes. Thus, history can matter.[4] Another implication of this is that temporary policies can, by shifting the economy between stable equilibria, have effects that last even after the policy has been discontinued (it is fashionable to call this effect 'hysteresis').

Expectations Matter   The simple story above avoided the issue of time and therefore questions of firms' expectations. But this should not prevent us from realizing that location decisions are often very expensive to reverse. Building a factory or locating a headquarters in a particular place generally entails a commitment of 10 to 30 years. Consequently, location decisions will typically be made with an eye to future policies and conditions, not just current ones. A key point is that future policy, and therefore uncertainty about future policy, can have important effects on location. Indeed, expectations may be at least as important as current policy.

This has worthwhile implications for the economies in transition. Firms deciding upon where to locate their investments must form judgements about the future policies that the governments of various competing nations will pursue. Consequently, the governments of the CEECs should consider engaging in strategies that send positive signals to investors about future policies. One obvious example is joining an international organiza-tion, such as the GATT, which credibly enforces a set of rules. Another is the signing of free trade agreements with the EU. We shall return to this issue of credible policies when considering proposals for the reorganization of trade relations in post-Communist Europe.

Location is one area in which self-fulfilling expectations may play an important role. We saw that multiple stable equilibria are endemic to location models. The question of which equilibrium the economy arrives at has not been answered. It would be natural to assume that industry would go to the region with a head-start in industrialization. Some reflection on the decision process of firms, however, reveals that this need not be the case. If all the firms believe, for one reason or another, that a particular region will become the centre and they act on these beliefs, then that is where the centre will be. The beliefs may become a self-fulfilling prophecy.

Small Policy Changes May Have Large Effects   Another implication of multiple equilibria and the importance of expectations is that seemingly small policy changes may have large effects on industrial concentrations. Think about the original simple story of two identical regions. Initially this is a knife-edge model. Any slight advantage accruing to one locale will tend to divert all industry to that locale. Thus policy changes that seem small may have large location effects. Moreover, the same policy may have entirely different effects before and after the concentration question has already been resolved. In equilibrium, firms are not just indifferent to locating in the two places. They definitely prefer to be where all the others are. The circular causality of location provides the 'winner' with some breathing space. For instance, Germany already has a massive concentration of industry, making it a very attractive place to locate. Accordingly, the German government can impose taxes and regulations (up to some limit) on firms located in Germany without causing considerable relocation. A new region wishing to attract industry does not have this luxury.

The implications for the CEECs should be clear. The rapid discarding of policies that disfavour industrial activity (e.g. foreign exchange rationing, restrictions on the repatriation of profits, excessive regulation of commercial activity) may pay handsome rewards for many years. Failure to do so may harm very long-term consequences.

The Political Economy of Location   A slight extension of this model helps us to apply this reasoning to real-world concerns and develop some political economy arguments. 'Farmers' was a shorthand for productive factors that do not move. Land is another obvious one. More generally, certain types of workers are more likely to move than others. This is true for international migration. It also holds for migration between regions within a country. For instance, highly skilled workers tend to move around more, even within a single country. Indeed, one could imagine a whole range of factors marked by varying degrees of mobility as measured by the wage gaps they would tolerate without moving. The logic of the simple example suggests that these highly mobile factors – capital, technology and highly skilled workers – will not care very much where the concentration takes place. The less mobile factors will. If these less mobile factors – e.g. land, farmers and medium-skilled workers – tend to be the low-paid factors, then industry relocation will take on the tone of a rich-versus-poor debate. This is what has happened in Western Europe.

2.3.2   *Trade Arrangements and Location Effects*

The U-shaped Relationship of Trade Costs and Concentration

Krugman and Venables (1989) show that the link between trade barriers (or trade costs more generally) and industry location is not simple and monotonic. The easiest way to see this is to consider two identical countries under two extreme cases: prohibitive trade costs and no trade costs. With no trade costs, the circular causation discussed above does not operate. Firms would tend to spread out in search of low-cost immobile factors, such as land. Starting from this pole a slight rise in trade barriers would lead to increased concentration. The opposite occurs at the other extreme. If trade costs are initially prohibitive, location will be decentralized since firms would be forced to produce locally. If trade barriers fall to just below the prohibitive level, the circular causation activates and some firms would relocate in search of larger markets. The point is illustrated in Figure 2.5.

More generally, let us consider one small and one large region that are separated by prohibitive barriers. In order for producers in the small country to cover their fixed costs with lower sales, prices must be higher in the small country than in the large one. As the barriers come down, trade tends to narrow this price gap thereby driving some firms in the smaller market to relocate to the large one. Not all firms leave, however, since the reduced competition in the small countries means increased market share

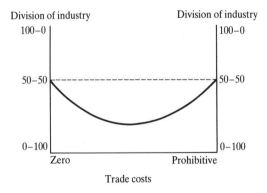

Figure 2.5 The U-shaped relation of concentration and openness

for the remaining firms. Moreover, the centralizing force is also mitigated by wage differences, presuming that some labour is immobile. Thus, a growing unevenness in dispersion is accompanied by increasing wage differentials. This latter fact means that there is a tension between a firm's desire to be in the low-wage region and its desire to avoid trade costs. That is, locating in the large market minimizes trade costs, but it maximizes wage costs.

This negative relationship between even industrial dispersion and trade costs (lower costs–more uneven dispersion) continues only so far. At some point the negative relationship turns around. If trade costs continue to fall, location in the small market looks increasingly better. The trade-cost disadvantage fades and the wage-cost advantage rises. At some point firms move from the large market back to the small one. In doing this, they drive small country wages back up towards the large country wages. Once we get to zero trade costs, we are back to the even distribution, but now wages are as high in the small country as they are in the large one.

Political Economy of Shock Treatment Liberalization

It is interesting to apply this analysis to the political economy of liberalization. Let us suppose initially that countries in a region of the world impose quite high tariff and non-tariff barriers on intra-regional trade. This line of reasoning suggests that a gradualist approach to market opening may be self-defeating. As the barriers begin to come down, the industrial profits and wages in the smaller countries fall and those in the larger ones rise. Moreover, relocation of industrial activity would show up as investment-led growth in the large market and investment-led recession in the smaller ones.

Of course, consumers in the small country gain from lower prices and the increased choices provided by imports. In politics, however, consumer voices are often ignored. It is evident that anti-liberalization forces in the small markets would gain strength. They would oppose further liberalization and, depending upon the balance of political power, industrial firm owners and workers in the small country might well reverse the liberalization.

At least in theory, none of this would happen if the countries went straight to zero trade costs. Even if this is not possible, going close to free trade would mean that small-region industrial workers would support slightly more liberation and would oppose slightly more protection, as long as the decision was restricted to marginal changes in policy.

2.4   Accumulation (Growth) Effects

Policy makers and economists generally believe that economic integration is an engine of growth. The basic link between integration and growth is simple to describe. It is dictated by the logic of growth. Growth in per capita output requires the accumulation of some factor of production (using the term broadly, to include knowledge capital, i.e. the stock of knowledge, as a factor of production). Consequently, international trade arrangements influence growth by affecting the accumulation of factors. Most accumulation of productive factors is intentional and it is called investment. Accordingly, we can say that trade affects growth mainly via its effect on investment in human capital, physical capital or knowledge capital. The qualification 'mainly' is necessary, since trade may also affect unintentional accumulation. For instance, by speeding the international dissemination of technological progress, trade may hasten growth without directly affecting investment.

Growth effects fall naturally into two categories: medium term and long term. An instance of medium-term effects is that of induced physical capital formation. For all the reasons documented above, closer integration improves the efficiency with which productive factors are combined to produce output. As a side-effect, this efficiency gain makes the region a better place to invest, so more investment occurs. The result is that the initial efficiency gains are boosted by induced capital formation. While the above-normal capital formation is occurring, the economies experience a medium-term growth effect. This effect is only medium term, since it will eventually peter out. As the amount of capital per worker rises, the marginal incentive to invest in more capital diminishes and eventually the above-normal capital formation stops. A good example of this is the investment boom that Spain experienced around the time of its accession to the EU.

Long-term growth effects involve a permanent change in the rate of accumulation, and thereby a permanent change in the rate of growth. It is much harder to find examples of this. Besides, the economics of it are necessarily more complicated, as we shall see below.

2.4.1   Medium-run Accumulation: Induce Capital Formation

Neoclassical growth literature, started by Solow (1956), provides a simple way for thinking about the medium-term growth effects of trade liberalization. The Solow model provides the simplest way of determining the capital stock at any point in time. In particular, it assumes that the fraction of output invested is constant and that all investment comes from domestic sources. The next assumption concerns the relationship between capital and output. A nation's aggregate output is related to its supplies of productive factors and the level of technology according to:

$$Y_t = A_t K_t^a L_t^{1-a} \tag{2.1}$$

where the factors of production are physical capital (K) and labour (L); The variable A is total factor productivity, i.e. knowledge capital. Finally, it is assumed that a constant fraction of the capital stock depreciates each year.

To understand growth in this model, it is first necessary to understand how the level of the capital stock is determined, and Figure 2.6 assists in this task. Both L and A are assumed constant to simplify matters. The Y/L^* curve is concave due to the assumed diminishing returns to capital holding L constant. The depreciation/L schedule is straight since the amount of depreciation per worker increases linearly with the level of the capital stock. The savings/L curve has a shape similar to that of the Y/L curve since savings is a constant fraction of output.

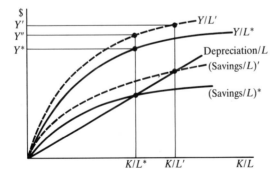

Figure 2.6   Induced capital formation in the Solow model

Notable things occur at intersections or tangencies in economics diagrams. Since there are no tangencies in this one, the equilibrium capital–labour ratio must be where the savings/L and the depreciation/L curves cross, i.e. K/L^*. The reason is simple. If the capital–labour ratio were lower, the savings per worker would exceed the depreciation per worker. This would cause the level of the capital stock to rise compared with the labour force. If the capital–labour ratio were higher, the reverse would be true. This sort of equilibrium in a dynamic model is called a 'steady state' since it is the state of the model where motion stops. In this case, the 'state' is K/L and the 'motion' is a rise or fall in K/L.

Trade and Growth Effects

The simple medium-term growth effects can be illustrated with Figure 2.6. Let us consider a liberalization programme for which the allocation efficiency effects have been estimated. For example, suppose it has been estimated that a particular programme would increase GDP by, say, 1%. The way this is usually calculated is by adding up all the static allocation effects. In other words, the impact is calculated assuming that there will be no change in the capital stock. However, the only way Y can rise by 1% without an increase in K or L is for A to rise by 1%. In the figure, this corresponds to a shift upwards in the Y/L curve to Y/L'. With a constant investment rate, this would directly increase per capita savings to savings/L'.

The estimated allocation effect is the output increase that would occur without any change in the capital–labour ratio, i.e. Y'' minus Y^*. But clearly this is an incomplete analysis, since the old steady-state capital–labour ratio is no longer valid. As the K/L ratio rose towards the new steady-state level, there would be a knock-on increase in GDP per capita. This knock-on effect is the medium-run growth effect, i.e. the induced capital-formation effect. Its eventual impact on GDP is the difference between Y'' and Y'.

The induced capital-formation effect argues that market integration should coincide with investment-led growth. After all, an increase in integration that is large enough to have a noticeable economy-wide impact is also likely to increase the productivity of the capital stock. The resulting faster accumulation of capital, i.e. induced-capital formation, will provide the economy with more resources, thus augmenting the output gains due to increased static efficiency. The same sort of pro-investment effect could also induce a higher rate of investment in human capital and knowledge capital.

Measuring Dynamic Effects with the Aggregate GDP Approach

The aggregate GDP approach does much violence to the details of the composition of output. After all, it is somewhat blunt to speak of output as if the economy produced only one good. Counterbalancing this, however, is the fact that equation (2.1) is widely used and, more to the point, its simple structure allows us to use estimates of the static efficiency gains from market integration to measure the dynamic effects. That is, if the economy is to produce, say, 1.5% more output with the same amount of inputs, then it must be that the path of *A* in equation (2.1) shifts up by 1.5%. As it turns out, this is sufficient to force out the implied dynamic effects. Specifically, differentiating equation (2.1) with respect to *A* and gathering terms, we see that:

$$\% \Delta GDP = (\% \Delta A)\left(1 + \frac{a}{1-a}\right) \tag{2.2}$$

where %*Δ* means 'percentage change in'. This is the sum of the static efficiency effect and the induced capital (human and physical) formation effect.

Adjustment Period   It will take decades to reach the new higher steady-state GDP, since even if the static efficiency gains are rapidly phased in, factor accumulation takes time. A simple approximation (assuming a constant savings rate) allows us to gauge how much time. Using equation (2.1) and the conditions that relate the capital stock to investment and depreciation, the dynamics around the steady state can be approximated by:

$$\frac{\mathrm{d}Y/Y}{\mathrm{d}t} = (n + \eta + \delta)(1 - a - \beta)(\ln Y^* - \ln Y_t) \tag{2.3}$$

where Y^* is the new steady-state level of per capita output. That is, per capita GDP rises towards its new steady state in a way that closes a certain percentage of the gap between the current level and the steady-state level each year. This certain percentage equals $(n + \eta + \delta)(1 - a)$, where *n* is the population growth rate, η is the rate of productivity advance and δ is the depreciation rate. Thus during the transition, Y/L, H/L and K/L should grow faster than their long-run rates, with both H/L and K/L further above their trends than Y/L. This comes from the fact that Y/L is driven by faster than the 'normal' accumulation of factors, but the transmission is muted since *a* is less than unity.

Note that this approximation implies that the adjustment process is not linear. Rather, the extra growth is heavily front-loaded. To illustrate this point, take *a* to be two-thirds, δ to be 13% per annum and a total factor productivity growth (i.e. η) to be 2% per annum. This generates a $(n + \eta + \delta)(1 - a)$ equal to 5%, implying a half-life of about 14 years. Consider what this means for the impact on Europe of the 1992 programme. Gasiorek, Smith and Venables (1992) estimate that the Single Market programme would lead to static efficiency gains that would add

1.5% to the EC output without altering the level of input. From equation (2.2) we see that the factor accumulation effects on capital would eventually add another 3%. The static efficiency gains would probably all be realized within 5–10 years. The first extra 1% (from factor accumulation) would be spread over the first 8 years, the second 1% spread over the subsequent 14 years and so on. To the average observer, this effect would show up as 'investment-led growth'.

The transition time that we obtain assuming a constant investment rate is shorter than that obtained when we allow intertemporal optimization. When we allow re-optimization on the saving rate, citizens understand that they will be wealthier in the future. This makes them feel wealthier today, and so increases consumption somewhat today. This reduces the saving rate and thereby postpones attainment of the new steady state.

Output is Not Welfare   In studying the induced capital accumulation effect, it is critical to bear in mind the fact that extra output is not a measure of extra welfare. Citizens must forgo consumption to accumulate the extra capital. Thus the increase in future consumption is largely and perhaps entirely offset by the necessary forgone consumption during the transition path. Baldwin (1992b) shows that the welfare effects depend on the wedge between the social and private return to capital, and provides some numerical estimates of the welfare effects of the 1992 programme. The general finding is that welfare effects stemming from induced capital formation are more than an order of magnitude smaller than those resulting from the static effects.

Problems with the Aggregate GDP Approach

The estimates of dynamic effects that come from the aggregate GDP approach are very rough and do not reach the high standards of empirical rigour attained in many other branches of economics. These calculations are really nothing more than an illustration of the common-wisdom propositions that growth effects may easily be more important than static ones. Indeed, it is probably best to think of them as merely indicative. Samuel Johnson's quip about a dog walking on its hind legs is an apt way to summarize the point of these rough calculations: the interest lies not in that it is done well, but rather that it is done at all.

Assuming the existence of an aggregate output function, such as equation (2.1), allowed an easy and transparent estimate of medium-run dynamic effects. The aggregate GDP approach has many limitations, however, which must be kept in mind. The limitations stem from two sources. First, GDP functions generally do not have well-specified microfoundations, unless very restrictive assumptions are made. The second, and more practical, limitation is that integration does not affect all sectors equally. Consequently the static efficiency gains may be biased towards sectors that are intensive in the use of human or physical capital. Such biases, however, invalidate the procedure we used to force out the initial change in marginal products from existing estimates of total static gains. To see this, recall that the rough calculation above required us to assume that the liberalization raised the marginal productivity of all factors proportionally. That is, we viewed the static efficiency effect as a Hicks-neutral technological change.

To give an illustration of the importance of this shortcoming, let us consider the medium-run growth effects of the EC's 1992 programme. Although the current integration of the EC is extremely broad, it does not affect all sectors and it does not affect all sectors equally. For example:

- The pro-competitive effect should impact much more on industries with increasing returns to scale than on the constant-returns-to-scale sector.
- The reduction in trade cost should affect traded goods more than untraded ones.
- The mobility of labour existed for many years in the EC, but harmonization of standards and mutual recognition of professional qualifications will boost mobility of certain types of labour more than others.
- The EU and the removal of capital controls should encourage capital mobility more than labour mobility.
- The fact that certain EC economies were always more open and integrated than others before the 1992 programme also implies that monetary and economic union will have different impacts on different countries.

Of course many more such examples exist. The fact that European integration does not affect all sectors and all countries equally is likely to have important implications for quantitative estimates. This is especially true for the induced capital-formation effects since the reforms may increase the productivity of certain factors more than others. Given that the static efficiency impact of the 1992 programme will almost certainly fall more heavily on traded goods and scale-economy goods, the Stolper–Samuelson theorem suggests that the rewards to physical and human capital might rise *more* than the average amount.

2.4.2   *Ceaseless Accumulation: The 'New' Growth Theory*

Continual output growth per person requires the continual accumulation of factors of production. In the Solow model, and the neoclassical model more generally, this ceaseless accumulation takes the form of productivity-boosting knowledge. However, in the Solow model the rate of productivity growth is taken as given. The model does not attempt to address its determinants. Consequently, it would be entirely futile to use this framework to organize our thinking about the long-term growth effects of trade arrangements. The major contribution of the 'new' growth theory, which many view as having started with Romer (1983, 1986), is to endogenize the ceaseless accumulation of factors. Since accumulation is the key focus, the best of these models concentrate on specifying the microfoundations of accumulation. In particular, they carefully lay out the private costs and benefits to investing in more capital, more skills or more technical progress. Precisely because endogenous growth models delve into the private costs and benefits of accumulation, they permit consideration of a much wider range of economic channels by which trade affects growth.

Basic Logic of Endogenous Growth Models

Before turning to the ways in which trade arrangements can affect long-term growth, we address the logic of endogenous growth theory and briefly review several important models.

The key to endogenizing output growth is to endogenize investment. To do this convincingly, one must lay out the microfoundations of individuals' investment decisions. Whatever the details of these microfoundations, the bottom line will be that the rate of investment depends on the costs and benefits of investing. Now clearly, if the rate of investment is to remain constant in the long run, then the private net return on new investments should also remain constant in the long run. This brings us to the first crucial aspect of an endogenous growth model. The necessity for the real return to investment is to be non-diminishing in the capital stock.

To see this point more clearly, let us consider the relationship between the private return on investment and the economy's capital–labour ratio. In the Solow model the return on investment declined as the capital–labour ratio rose due to diminishing social returns on capital (holding the labour forces constant). Clearly, this situation will not be marked by continuous growth, absent exogenous shocks. Growth would slow as the rising capital–labour ratio forced down the return on investment. In contrast, if there are increasing returns on capital, we should see the return on investment increase as the capital–labour ratio rose. Since investors would want to do increasingly more investing as the private return rose, this situation would correspond to an ever-rising rate of growth. Since continually rising growth rates is not one of the world's problems, we ignore this case.

At the dénouement of several Sherlock Holmes novels, the great detective remarks that if one has eliminated all possible answers to a problem except one, the remaining answer, however unlikely, must be the solution. Applying this reasoning leads us to conclude that continuous growth requires that the returns on capital are exactly constant. The point is quite general. Ceaseless growth requires ceaseless accumulation and ceaseless accumulation requires that the return on accumulation does not fall as the capital stock rises.

As it turns out, this requirement places a large stumbling-block in the path of builders of endogenous growth models. A constant marginal return on investment implies a private return on investing that is unrelated to amount of investment that has been done. That means that private investors think that the gap between the cost of and the benefit of investing is constant no matter how much investing they do. This is a problem, since it implies that private investors' demand for capital is not well behaved. 'Not well behaved' means that, depending upon the relationship between the cost and benefit of investing, private investors will want to do no investing, an infinite amount of investing, or will be entirely indifferent to how much they do. If the cost exceeds the return, no one will invest. If the return exceeds the cost, everyone would wish to invest an infinite amount. If the cost equals the return, then no one cares how much they invest. The rate of investment and therefore the rate of growth is zero, infinite or undetermined by the actions of investors. It should be clear that this type of set-up is not going to be much good for studying the determinants of growth or the growth effects of various government policies.

Three important lessons should be learned from this:

- The growth rate of output depends upon the rate of accumulation of factors, i.e. the rate of investment.
- To make the rate of GDP growth endogenous, it is necessary to endogenize the rate of investment. In a market economy, this means detailing the cost and benefits of investment faced by private, self-interested investors.
- Continual growth requires that the return on investment is not diminishing in the capital stock.

To go beyond shallow models of growth, we are going to want the decision of private investors to be well behaved. This requires that private investors perceive their personal returns on investing to be diminishing in their own levels of investment. This requirement leads us to the following important conclusion. If the private investment decision is to be well behaved, there must be a 'wedge' between the public and private return on investment that implies that the private return is perceived as diminishing as the capital stock rises, but social- or economy-wide return does not. We now turn to several sophisticated endogenous growth models. Note that each model displays two critical features: (1) a wedge between the private and public (i.e. aggregate) rate of return on investment, and (2) a public rate of return that is not diminishing in the aggregate capital stock.

Three Main Varieties of the 'New' Growth Models

There are many ways of classifying the numerous models of endogenous growth that now exist. It is most useful to sort them into categories according to which type of factor they assume to be accumulating: physical capital, human capital or knowledge capital. This brings to the fore a pivotal distinction between primary factors, which do not accumulate (or accumulate for reasons that are not addressed in the model), and factors that do accumulate. Most models take labour and land as primary factors ('non-reproducible factors' is an equivalent term for primary factors). Several models allow more than one type to accumulate, but even in these, one factor usually plays the dominant role, at least in the motivation of the model.

Knowledge Capital   Robert Solow taught us long ago that technical progress is the driving force behind long-term per capita income growth. The first category of new growth theories picks up on Solow's insight by endogenizing technical progress. Technical progress is nothing other than knowledge creation, and ceaseless technical knowledge leads to a continually rising stock of knowledge. To stress the similarities with the other models, technical progress can be thought of as the accumulation of productivity-boosting 'knowledge capital'.

In the earliest of these models (Romer, 1983, 1986), the microfoundations of knowledge creation and knowledge spillovers were somewhat vague. Private firms, who are assumed to be small compared with the whole economy, individually face diminishing returns on their investments in knowledge creation. Yet from an economy-wide perspective the rate of return on investment does not fall due to technological spillovers in production. That is, the productivity of an investment that a firm installs today depends positively upon how much investment has been done in the past. The reason this is so was not fully explained in Romer's early models. The cumulative action of many small firms raises the economy-wide capital stock, and thereby continually prevents the private return on investment from falling. Here the wedge between private and social return on investment relies on technological spillovers in the output sector. These models have the attractive feature that firms' investment decisions are well behaved since the technology spillover introduces a public–private wedge. As a result, the amount of investment that private firms wish to do responds sensibly to changes such as tax incentives, trade liberalization, etc.

A set of more recent models focuses more explicitly on the microfoundations of innovation, that is, the decisions by firms to invest in productivity-boosting innovations. In these models, private firms invest in knowledge creation because it provides them with an edge over other firms. The profit earned in exploiting this advantage provides a return on the knowledge-creation investment. From the economy-wide point of view the net result of this profit-motivated activity is output growth. That is, the economy's primary factors produce more and more output each year due to this endless stream of innovations. In these models private knowledge creation has an unintentional side-effect – a contribution to the public stock of knowledge. The models assume that this unintentional spillover feeds back into the economy by raising the productivity of resources employed in innovating. This unintentional side-effect creates the private-versus-social wedge in these models. Thus, unlike the early models, knowledge spillovers affect the productivity of resources located in the innovation sector instead of the output sector.

Another common feature of these models is their assumption (explicitly or implicitly) that there is a 'production function' for knowledge that specifies the relationship among primary resources devoted to innovation, the existing stock of innovations and the discovery of innovations. It is useful to think of the production function for innovations as a great book in the sky with an infinite number of pages. Each page contains the blueprints for a new product or an innovation. Everyone in the economy knows about the book and all know the quantity of primary resources needed to read the pages. Whoever reads a page first gets an infinite patent on the innovation on that particular page. While it costs real resources to 'read a page', doing so provides a continual stream of profits from exploitation of the resulting patent.

There are two sub-varieties of these innovation models: product innovation and process innovation. In the production innovation models, output growth is driven by a constant flow of product innovations that raises primary factor productivity. The new products are interpreted as intermediate goods, so the productivity-raising effect is interpreted as reflecting the manner in which a finer division of labour permits greater specialization and efficiency. Development of a new variety yields the developer an infinite life patent; it also contributes to the public stock of knowledge due to the non-appropriability of some of the newly created knowledge. The patent affords the developer a return on R&D investment; the knowledge spillover feeds back into innovation by lowering the development cost of additional new products. Thus although new products garner increasingly smaller market shares (and profits) due to the progressively larger number of competitors, they can be developed at a progressively lower cost. Given proper assumptions on the magnitude of the knowledge feedback, the result is a time-invariant rate of return on labour invested in R&D activity. This leads profit-motivated firms to invest a constant fraction of the economy's primary resources in production development, thereby resulting in a constant flow of new products and constant income growth.

Technological spillovers in innovation create a wedge between the private and public returns on innovation investment. To use the great-book-in-the-sky parallel, the usefulness of the blueprint on each page is the same, however the information on each page is encoded. While it takes time to decipher the blueprint on each new page, the amount of time diminishes with each new page turned since innovators learn from past decoding experiences. In this analogy, the spillover is that everyone learns all the past decoding lessons free.

A separate line of thought has been pursued by the process-innovation models.[5] Unlike the product-innovation models, these innovations may drive some existing firms out of business. The reason is simple. Instead of creating a new product that can be sold side by side with existing products, process innovations allow the innovator to make existing products more cheaply. This means that the owner of the innovation may find it worth while to charge a price that drives competitors out of business. The profits earned by innovators from exploiting this edge compensate them for the R&D costs. However, even as the most recent innovator is luxuriating in profits, other firms are developing processes that have even lower manufacturing costs. When one of them succeeds, the previous king-of-the-hill is deposed. This ceaseless search for cost-lowering innovations leads to a ceaseless accumulation of knowledge and drives manufacturing productivity ever higher. 'Creative destruction' is the term that Schumpeter (1942) used to describe the process.

As with product-innovation models, the private-versus-social wedge in these models appears in the innovation sector. However, the technology spillover takes a different form. The 'production function' for innovations does not change in the sense that the amount of resources necessary to obtain an innovation does not change. What does change is the nature of the resulting innovation. Each innovation is clearly better than the last. There is a spillover in that each innovator begins to start working directly on the frontier of knowledge. Using the great-book comparison, the page-reading cost (in terms of primary resources) does not change, but the usefulness of the blueprint is increasing with every page. The technological spillover is like assuming that each innovator is able to read all the previously turned pages free, so that they do not have to reinvent the wheel.

One model in the process-innovation vein, which is especially important for understanding real-world process innovation, is the 'quality ladders' of Helpman and Grossman (1991). This is a model where each subsequent page of the great book reveals a process that allows the page-turners to raise the quality of their products without increasing the manufacturing cost. This is important to understanding modern technical progress since for many innovative industries, such as personal computers and consumer electronics, it is difficult to classify advances as product innovations or process innovations. Let us take the example of portable radios. Electronics firms make more or less the same products using more or less the same process, but each year the radios are clearly superior – lighter, more durable, more powerful, with better sound, etc.

Political Economy of Creative Destruction The concept of creative destruction is extremely important in understanding how an economy directed by selfish motives can, year after year, produce more and more from the same primary factors. Each time a new product or process is developed, part (or all) of the value of previous inventions is destroyed. Schumpeter wrote:[6]

> The fundamental impulse that sets and keeps the capitalist engine in motion comes from the new consumer goods, the new methods of production or transportation, the new markets, ... [This process] incessantly revolutionizes the economic structure from within, incessantly destroying the old one, incessantly creating a new one. This process of Creative Destruction is the essential fact about capitalism. (Cited in Aghion and Howitt, 1990.)

Since most economists would agree with Schumpeter's assessment, it is worth considering the political economy of creative destruction. Many existing firms and industries wield political influence that far exceeds their numbers or even their weight in the economy. This fact is often cited as an explanation of why nations so frequently adopt import barriers that help the few at the expense of the many. The same fact, however, would suggest that existing firms may attempt to stifle technical progress. After all, technical progress will threaten their current position in the market. The current leaders have knowledge that gives them an edge over other firms. Like any good owner of capital, these firms will resist a move to increase competition. Unfortunately, resisting competition in this context means resisting the introduction of new technology. Thus selfish firms, left to their own devices, will attempt to stifle the economy's growth by suppressing the introduction of new technology. That is, the existing firms may be quite capable of matching the technical progress and thereby maintaining their positions, but clearly they would rather not have to do so. Thus just as competition was essential to an efficient static allocation of resources, competition, or at least the threat of it, is a necessary condition for technical progress.

Another of Schumpeter's ideas – the trade-off between dynamic and static efficiency – is closely related to this, yet it is widely misunderstood. Schumpeter pointed out that innovation is costly and so a firm must expect to earn what may appear to be above-normal profits to compensate it for its knowledge-creation investment. While above-normal profits may be considered inefficient from a static point of view, they are necessary for dynamic efficiency (i.e. optimal investing in knowledge creation). This trade-off, however, is widely misunderstood to justify market power on the behalf of existing firms and government policies that protect such market power. A closer look, however, reveals no such trade-off. What is needed is that innovators earn a fair return on their knowledge capital. If we properly account for all inputs, including knowledge capital, a dynamically efficient economy does not require 'above-normal profits'.

This point is especially important in the context of Central and Eastern Europe. In an attempt to promote domestic industry, governments may strive to protect existing firms from competition. The idea is that protection would raise the return on introducing productivity-enhancing technology and thereby promote technical progress and growth. The weak link in this chain of reasoning is the last. Unless existing firms are threatened by new technologies, they have very little incentive continually to invest in new productivity-boosting knowledge.

Human Capital Lucas (1988) opened a new line of thinking in the endogenous growth literature by focusing on the contribution of human capital to GDP growth. Human capital is the skill of workers. It is considered capital since skill embodied in workers can produce a flow of service for an extended period, just as a capital good can. Models that focus on human capital accumulation do not differ in their fundamental economic structure from those already discussed. The basic logic of ceaseless accumulation must be respected. In particular, the economy-wide rate of return on investing in human capital cannot be forever falling or rising. Moreover, to ensure the well-behaved nature of the self-interested investment decisions of private citizens and firms, the models must have some way of introducing a wedge between the private and social (i.e. economy-wide) rates of return

We start with a trivial relabelling. First, it is obvious that by calling it 'capital' instead of 'human capital' we could interpret the first endogenous growth models presented above as showing that human capital can be a source of growth. What is interesting about models that focus on human capital is that they provide a particularly convincing story behind the existence of the private–social wedge. People invest in raising their skill level because they anticipate that there will be a lot of capital that will allow them to turn high skill levels into high salaries. Similarly, firms invest in new plant and equipment because they expect there to be a lot of skilled workers to make the factories produce a profit. The wedge exists since undertaking the investments in human capital do not take account of the output-boosting effect of the capital formation that their actions will induce.

One interesting application of this approach is to understand the spectacular growth experienced by Japan and West Germany after the Second World War. In both cases, the economies suffered a large loss of physical and human capital, and the loss in physical capital was by far the larger of the two. Given the implications of diminishing returns to K (physical capital) and H (human capital) taken separately, this means that the post-war economies of Japan and West Germany were extremely good places to invest physical capital. They had a large amount of human capital compared with physical capital, so the return on the latter was extraordinarily high. Following the usual logic that a high rate of return attracts a high rate of investment, the theory predicts that Japan and West Germany should have experienced above-normal growth during this period. Moreover, the growth should have been investment-led.

Physical Capital The least popular variety of the new growth models focuses on physical capital accumulation as the engine of growth, although, as we saw above, physical capital appears in many models. One of the few articles to take this approach seriously is Romer (1987), which is appropriately entitled 'Crazy explanations for the productivity slowdown'. Moreover, the verbal arguments in the model make it clear that what is really being assumed is that physical capital faces non-diminishing returns because of the technology that is embodied in capital. The unpopularity of the models stems from empirical evidence rather than from theoretical objections. Many economists have attempted to measure the aggregate output elasticity of the aggregate capital stock, both the social and the private rates of return. All these studies find diminishing returns on investment. The main conclusion of this line of thinking is a negative result. The accumulation of physical capital is not to be considered a driving force of growth. Rather, its continual accumulation either is a side-effect of the accumulation of productivity-boosting knowledge or its importance is intertwined with some other factor such as human capital.

Long-run Growth Effects of Trade Arrangements

After all these preliminaries, we are finally ready to discuss the permanent growth effects of trade arrangements. One of the certain lessons of growth theory is that sustained GDP growth requires sustained productivity growth, and sustained productivity growth requires continual accumulation of knowledge. This line of reasoning directs us to investigate the impact on the private return on innovation of an international market. An international version of the Romer model proves to be a useful workhorse for this task. Let us consider a world with two countries (call them home and foreign) which are both identical to the model described above.

Market Size, Competition and Knowledge Spillover Effects In our first thought-experiment, each country is initially closed. The experiment is what would happen when free trade in intermediary goods was permitted. To keep effects separate, we assume for the moment that there are no international spillovers of knowledge. To use the great-book-in-the-sky analogy, home and foreign innovators do not learn from each others' past decoding experiences, only from domestic ones.

Having done most of the spadework, we go straight to the heart of the matter: the benefit and cost of innovating in the integrated world equilibrium as opposed to the benefit and cost in autarky. Since the developer of a new intermediate good will receive a share of world consumption expenditure in every period (recall that each innovation has an infinite-lived patent), the value of having a patent – and therefore the value of innovating – will be affected in two conflicting ways. On the one hand, the access to a larger market boosts the profitability of innovation, while, on the other, the increased competition from existing foreign innovations reduces the R&D profitability. In general, we cannot say what the net effect would be.

Now let us consider the impact on the value of innovating. Suppose that we could open international flows of knowledge without opening trade. While this is highly unlikely to happen in the real world (except via espionage), it is a convenient thought-experiment. The effect would be a decrease in the cost of innovation in both countries. Clearly, this would increase the private return on innovation, draw more resources into innovation and thereby stimulate long-run growth. In terms of the great-book metaphor, this would be like foreign and domestic innovators exchanging tips on how to decode the blueprints more quickly. Since it is entirely possible that this exchange would make both groups into faster decoders, it would lower the cost of investing in innovation.

Putting the three effects together eliminates all the ambiguity. Opening trade between two previously closed, identical economies definitely raises growth rates in both countries.

As a note, we should mention the redundancy effect. In a model with more structure on the innovation technology, the exact ordering of intermediate goods development may lead to a substantial overlap in home and foreign varieties without international trade. Thus, an additional effect of trade on growth is to prevent redundant R&D efforts. The next subsection, however, argues that rivalry in R&D is not all bad for the rate of innovation.

Pro-competitive Effects on Innovators In the above discussion, import competition by itself was an anti-growth effect since it reduces the profitability of innovation. This does not match informal analyses that argue that import competition increases growth by disciplining domestic firms – forcing them to quicken their pace of innovation in order to match international competition. The critical distinction is between competition among innovations and competition among innovators.

To build understanding of the pro-growth effect of import competition, consider a static set-up. Suppose a firm has a monopoly on innovation in its industry. Say that its profits would be a positive number Π^N if it does not innovate and $\Pi^1 - F$ if it does (F is the cost of the innovation). The profit-motivated firm innovates only if $\Pi^1 - F$ is greater than Π^N. Note that $\Pi^1 - F > \Pi^N > 0$. It may happen that even though innovation is profitable ($\Pi^1 - F > 0$), the monopolist prefers to stay with the old technology and thus avoid the R&D costs. Contrast this with the other extreme assumption of free entry into innovation. In this instance, the firm does not have the luxury of comparing the innovation and no-innovation profits. If the incumbent does not innovate, someone else will. Thus innovation occurs whenever it is profitable.

It should be obvious that the threat of innovation by foreign firms would move the situation for the monopoly-innovator case towards the perfect-competition one. In this manner, import competition can spur innovation and growth. Note that the competition here is not among innovations; it is among innovators.

Several policy conclusions stem from this thinking.[7] In the modern world, innovation is done by established firms. Since there are many barriers to entry, innovation activity itself is marked by imperfect competition. The fact that competition (or even the threat of it) from foreign firms changes the rate of innovation of existing firms is important. For instance, evidence that a particular liberalization has driven some innovative firms out of business cannot be used to argue that innovation in the country has slowed. It is entirely possible that import competition raises the rate of innovation of remaining firms enough to result in a higher economy-wide progress.

Trade in intellectual property rights, even without trade in goods, can have a similar pro-growth effect. That is, even if a domestic firm has a monopoly on domestic innovation, the ability of potential rivals to purchase foreign technology will put pressure to innovate faster. Since foreign technology often comes bundled with direct investment, foreign direct investment may stimulate productivity growth of domestic firms.

Innovation and International Capital Market Integration The often-repeated phrase 'investment is the key to growth' suggests that whereas trade arrangements impact on financial markets, they may also affect the rate of investment and therefore long-run output growth. In the simple Romer model described above, we introduce a wedge intended to be a reduced-form measure of capital market imperfection. If international integration ameliorates the capital market imperfections and thus the wedge, the result would be faster growth.

Let us take the example of an inefficient financial sector; inefficient in the sense that it creates a wide spread between the return earned by savers and the cost of funds available to investors. This spread may be the result of backwards-banking technology, or it may simply be due to monopoly power in the banking sector. Whatever the cause, competition from foreign financial firms has the potential of narrowing the gap between interest rates facing savers and investors. Inspection of the equilibrium condition shows that a lower phi (that was our symbol for the capital market imperfection wedge) would result in a higher J (the value of introducing an innovation) for any level of H_1 (the total amount of labour devoted to innovation). Consequently, reducing the intermediation wedge will raise the equilibrium quantity of resources devoted to innovation and the GDP growth rate.

Another example involves risk. Individual savers who cannot diversify their wealth act more risk-aversely towards new investments than when they are well diversified. The point is that when one's wealth is spread over many assets, the poor performance of some tends to be offset by the good performance of others. Thus diversification allows people, and banks, to be less concerned about the variability of any single investment: instead they focus more on average returns. The net effect is to lower the risk premium demanded on investments. This translates into a lower cost of capital to innovators and a faster rate of innovation. The opening of international markets, as is now happening in Eastern Europe, may lower the cost of capital by lowering risk premiums. Moreover, allowing foreign financial firms to participate in the creation of capital markets could also spur investment in knowledge creation.

Growth Effects of Comparative Advantage in R&D   A fundamental gain from trade stems from the fact that it allows countries to specialize in what they do well and trade for the rest. The same applies to innovation. If knowledge spills over internationally then, by allowing some countries to focus on innovation and others on production, trade may raise all growth rates. Consider small countries such as Iceland, Norway or Slovenia. Clearly, none of them could maintain a high standard of living if it had to be self-sufficient in innovation. Think of the fraction of national resources that would have to be diverted into research and development if every improved process and every new product had to be developed at home.

Poverty Traps, Take-offs and the Big Push   The growth rates of countries display striking and persistent differences.[8] Some countries seem to be on a high growth path for decades at a time, others limp along at 1–2% per year and yet others seem to be stuck with zero or even negative growth rates. This real-world fact has created several new growth models that can account for this and the basic feature of all such models is multiple-equilibrium growth paths. That is, there will be a stable equilibrium in which very few of the economy's primary resources are devoted to accumulation and one (or more) in which a good deal of resources are devoted to it. The former is the poverty trap and the latter is the medium-growth path. A take-off happens when something occurs to shift the economy from the low-growth stable equilibrium to medium-growth equilibrium. The 'big push' made famous by Rosenstein-Rodan (1943) is one example of something that will shift the economy between growth paths.

The formalization of such ideas is generally problematic. One convincing model of this phenomenon is that of Azariadis and Drazen (1990). The basic idea can be seen with a slight modification of the human capital model described above. Let us assume that the relationship between the growth of human capital and the amount of time spent in training or education depends on the initial level of human capital. In particular, the higher the starting level of human capital, the more efficient is the accumulation process. However, efficiency increases only up to a limit. The economics of this assumption is very appealing. The effectiveness of education and training in a country depends in part on the general level of education and skill that already exists. If everyone in a child's family already knows how to read, the child can easily get help at home. This makes the child's time at school more efficient. The same applies to on-the-job training. If a worker's colleagues are all very highly skilled, the firm may find it much easier to train new workers and raise the skill level of the existing workforce. Of course, there are limits to this sort of spillover and they may be most important at very low levels of skill.

This small modification can create a poverty trap. With a very low level of human capital, the cost of acquiring skills will be very high, so the return on investing in skills may be quite low. As a result, it may exceed people's willingness to forgo consumption today to invest in skill formation. In this case, there is no accumulation of human capital and therefore no growth. This is a stable equilibrium since if no one finds it worth while to invest, the situation will never change. Clearly, a 'big push' would be needed to increase the initial level of human skill to lift the economy out of the zero-growth equilibrium, or poverty trap. Once this rises above a certain cut-off level, a 'take-off' would occur. Privately motivated investment in skills would continue. The result would be a rising rate of growth that converged to a steady level.

This process could be exactly reversed by the opposite of a 'big push', which we could call a 'big drag'. For instance, suppose a shock of some sort causes a large reduction in the level of human capital. The result could be a halt in the private accumulation of growth. In our simple model, skills never depreciate, so output does not actually fall. In the real world, however, a workforce may experience a declining skill level that would lead to negative output growth.

2.5 Political Economy Effects

For the most part, analysts examine the political economy forces that lead to the formations of preferential trading blocs. A very different question is addressed in this section, namely how trade arrangements themselves affect policy choices. There are two major applications of this. The first is how changing the membership of a trade bloc influences the desire of non-members to join. The second deals with the question of how the composition of a trading bloc's membership affects its policies.

2.5.1 *Political Economy Theory*

Economics is labelled the dismal science because of its gloomy view of human nature. Economists take it as axiomatic that greed governs human behaviour and that the consumption of goods and services is the object of this greed. That is, people work, save and vote to maximize their own wellbeing. Economists also apply this dismal approach to politics, assuming that greed governs politicians' behaviour. However, it is assumed that power, rather than consumption, is the aim of policy makers' greed. Power in this context is the probability of getting or staying elected. This is an oversimplification, but it is didactic. By ignoring many confounding considerations, one can arrive quickly at the core logic of political economy. With this in hand, complications can be introduced without swamping the analytic framework. The alternative approach of admitting from the start that everything affects everything can result in muddled thinking.

One might think that a government, which is concerned only with power and is elected by voters that care only about consumption, would choose policies that maximized the material welfare of the electorate. While this may be true in a utopian society, it is never so in the real world. The trouble is that any political system distorts politicians' views of the welfare of the electorate. The three most important of these political distortions involve the costs that voters face in obtaining information about the nature and effect of policies, the cost of voting and the cost of organizing an effective political force. Because of these distortions, a politician's quest for political support conflicts very frequently with the maximization of national welfare. The political system is a prism through which the government looks when trying to judge how their actions will impact on the economy.

This application of the dismal science to politics is called the endogenous policy approach, since it presumes that policy is endogenous to (i.e. determined by) the economic system. Many prevalent traits of trade policy throughout the world can be understood with this approach. For instance, in virtually every country cheap imports are condemned. From the point of view of national welfare, this is ludicrous. Quite simply, consumers benefit and producers lose from cheaper imports, but the consumers' monetary gains outweigh the losses of the firms. All becomes clear when one realizes that elected governments do not care about national welfare. They care about political support. Because consumers are rarely organized into an effective political force, and because domestic firms and labour unions usually are, the losses of consumers are heavily discounted by the body-politic. This is the prism of politics.

Another very common feature of protection is accounted for by an extension of this reasoning. In nearly all industrialized countries, tariff rates follow a pattern that is called 'tariff escalation'. That is, tariffs on primary and intermediate products are generally lower than those on consumers goods. The reason is that the 'consumers' of primary and intermediate goods are firms. For such goods, both domestic producers and consumers are organized, so the government tends to grant less protection.

To apply this approach to trade arrangements, the pure-greed motivation of policy makers needs to be amplified. We must assume that certain policy choices are made for reasons that are determined outside the political–economic system.[9] It is these events that are the ultimate cause of the changes in trade arrangements and changes in more detailed policies that follow from these.

The Domino Theory of Regionalism

It is very curious how regional liberalization swept the world trading system like wildfire while the multilateral GATT talks proceeded like a glacier. The domino theory posits that the current wave of regionalism stems from idiosyncratic events that are multiplied many times over by a domino effect (see Baldwin, 1992d). The recent wave of regionalism in Western Europe provides an excellent example.

In 1985 the EU-12 decided to create a Single Market to renew their drive towards unity. The primary motives were geopolitical and philosophical, rather than commercial. For the sake of argument, these motives are taken as given. Whatever its *raison d'être*, the EU 1992 project produced what might be called the political economy jealousy effect. Box 2.2 presents a

Box 2.2 The political economy 'jealousy' effect

The jealousy effect depends on two steps: closer integration in the EEC harms the profits of exporters in EFTA, and this profit loss leads EFTA-based industry to press their governments for better market access. The second reflects simple principles of political economy and needs no further explanation. To understand the first step more formally, consider a simple duopoly between an EEC firm and an EFTA firm where the two sell in both the EEC and the EFTA markets. The figure below shows the impact on the EFTA firm's sales and profits in the EEC market. The EFTA firm's cost curves (*MC* is marginal costs; *AC* is average costs) and its residual demand (EEC market demand minus the EEC firm's sales) and residual marginal revenue curves are drawn in the figure. The initial operating profit (profit gross of fixed costs) equals the area ABCD. Now suppose the EEC firm's cost of doing business in the EEC market falls (due, say, to closer EEC integration, or a widening of the EEC) but the EFTA firm's are unchanged. For the moment, assume that the cost reduction is limited to the EEC market so nothing changes in the EFTA market. A lowering of the EEC firm's marginal costs relative to the EFTA firm's will surely lead to higher sales by the EEC firm. This will shift inwards the residual demand facing the EFTA firm. This is depicted as a shift of the residual demand curve to *RD'* and a corresponding shift of residual marginal revenue curve to *RMR'*. The EFTA firm's sales and profits drop: sales fall to *Q* and profit is reduced to EFGH. If the loss is great enough, the EFTA firm may consider relocating to the EEC.

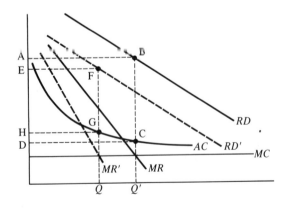

detailed economic analysis. The basic point can be illustrated with an anecdote.

Two campers, who have just settled down in their tent, hear the roar of a hungry bear very close by. One camper sits up and starts putting on his running shoes. The other camper says: 'What are you doing? You can't outrun a bear!' The first camper, who continues tying his laces, replies: 'Oh, I don't have to outrun the bear. I just have to outrun you'. Similarly, in business relative competitiveness is the key to success. That is, a firm is harmed by anything that helps its rivals. In this case, closer EU integration posed a threat to non-EU exporters who depended heavily on the EU market. Cheaper and easier intra-EU trade would reduce the relative competitiveness of non-EU firms, thereby harming their sales and profits.

Non-EU exporters throughout the region, especially those based in EFTA nations, recognized the threat and called for their governments to counter the losses. Moreover, since non-EU firms could be expected to react by shifting manufacturing to the EU, many non-EU industrial labour unions echoed the call for action. The EFTA governments' original solution, the European Economic Area arrangement, was quickly eclipsed by a drive for full membership. In 1989 and 1991, respectively, Austria and Sweden decided to join.

Now the domino effect began to operate. The pending EU enlargement made the potential loss of competitiveness even more threatening. That is, each EFTA nation individually faced the prospect of losing out in the EU-12 markets *and* in the markets of those EFTAns acceding to the EU. Since the combined EU and EFTA markets, on average, account for three-quarters of EFTA exports, the pressure on the hold-outs mounted. Finland, Norway and Switzerland requested EU membership in 1992. The Icelandic government, which is giving much thought to joining, has so far been deterred by the EU's common fishery policy.

Asymmetric Lobbying Effects

The political economy forces driving this domino effect are strengthened by a peculiar tendency of special-interest groups; they usually fight harder to avoid losses than they do to secure gains. In this light it is important that joining the regional integration in Europe would allow firms based in non-member countries to avoid damage as well as to win new commercial opportunities. While there may be many explanations for this asymmetric phenomenon, a simple economic interpretation based on unrecoverable investments (sunk costs, in economists' jargon) seems to fit the facts. Entry into most industries and markets involves large unrecoverable investments in product development, training, brand-name advertisement and production capacity. In such situations, established firms can earn positive profits without attracting new firms, but only in so far as these profits constitute a fair return on the entry investments. A more technical way of saying this is that sunk costs create quasi-rents.

Let us take it as given that a particular export industry has already incurred the sunk costs and consider the industry's incentive to lobby. If a country's exporters obtain additional access to foreign markets, their sales and profits will typically rise. The increase in pure profit, however, will attract new competition, so the size of the gains must be limited. In the extreme, entry continues until all pure profit disappears. Correspondingly, the incentive to lobby for new export opportunities will be limited, and, in the extreme, will disappear altogether. That is, lobbying in a successful industry attracts entry that offsets the benefits of the lobbying.

Next, consider the reaction of an established firm to an unanticipated policy change (such as the 1992 programme) that would reduce its relative competitiveness and profitability. For example, suppose that the change would wipe out half its quasi-rents, so it is earning a below-market return on its sunk capital. Since it would not actually be losing money, the firm would not shut down. More to the point, the firm should be willing to spend up to half its quasi-rents on lobbying for membership, if doing so would reverse the loss of relative competitiveness. Finally, as long as the lobbying merely restores profitability to a normal market rate, no new entrants would be attracted. Consequently, the benefit to lobbying is greater in industries that are in trouble, than it is in industries that are doing well (see Baldwin, 1992f). A more colloquial way of expressing this is that losers lobby harder than winners.

Implications for the Reconstruction of European Trade Arrangements The ramifications of the domino effect and asymmetric lobbying have implications for regional trading arrangements in Europe. For instance, if a new European free trade zone was created that encompassed CEECs and the EU, then it is likely that many CEECs would be interested in joining. At the same time, however, it may be true that before the free trade zone was a *fait accompli*, these same CEECs might all say that they would not want to join.

2.5.2 *Political Economy of Trade Negotiations*

Exports are good and imports are bad, according to mercantilistic thinking.[10] This reasoning has been thoroughly debunked and most policy makers denounce it in public. Nevertheless, mercantilism is still the paramount force behind trade liberalization. Politically powerful export industries in search of new export markets compel their governments to negotiate trade deals. For the export industries, access to foreign markets is the prize. For the government, the political support of exporters is the reward. The cost, as far as politicians are concerned, consists of having to allow foreigners access to the domestic market. Reciprocal liberalization angers domestic import-competing industries. This is a cost to governing politicians since the import-competing industries may reduce political support for the government, or they may increase their support for the political opposition. Domestic consumers, who benefit directly from liberalization, carry little political weight since they are almost never organized.[11] In short, from the politicians' point of view exports are good and imports are bad.

This notion is commonly expressed in more sophisticated language. Political leaders often say that trade is good because trade creates jobs. This is utter nonsense from the medium- or long-run economic perspective. An increase in exports may temporarily create more jobs when the economy is in a recession; in the long run, however, unemployment is determined by the structure of the labour market. By altering the allocation of a nation's resources, trade may change the types of jobs that are available. Trade does not, however, alter the number of jobs available in the long run. Political leaders are right in saying trade is good, but they point to the wrong reason. Trade is good because it improves the allocation of domestic resources and stimulates growth.

Political Economy Juggernaut

Given the pre-eminence of this trade-creates-jobs thinking among policy makers, international negotiation based on an exchange of market access is a stroke of genius. In chasing the mirage of job creation, governments end up choosing policies that benefit their nations. More precisely, insisting that market access be exchanged reciprocally arrays the political power of exporters against the political power of protectionists. The result is a political economy juggernaut. Growth throughout the world makes access to foreign markets increasingly attractive. This leads exporters continually to press their governments to negotiate further market-opening deals. As growth continues, fostered by international market opening, the juggernaut rolls forward, slowly but surely grinding down trade barriers.

Mercantilistic Law of the Jungle

The problem with this mechanism is that it may create a sort of law of the jungle. Since market access is the currency of exchange, countries with large markets can afford to buy a large amount of preferential access. Countries with small markets cannot or, worse, may be coerced into lopsided agreements. The genius of the GATT was to civilize this law of the jungle without subverting the political economy forces underpinning it. The trick was to strap the principle of unconditional most-favoured-nation (MFN) onto the juggernaut.[12] The result is that pro-liberalization exporters in the large markets end up opening markets worldwide for all nations, large and small.

2.5.3   *Political Economy Effects of Trade Arrangements*

Just as a nation's trade policy reflects the composition of its economy, membership of the EU will almost certainly influence European trade policy. For instance, it is quite easy to understand why the United States has highly protectionist laws concerning marine shipping, while Switzerland does not. The point is simply that there is no Swiss marine shipping industry. Swiss politicians face no political pressure for protection. In its absence, the general welfare of Swiss consumers and businesses prevails. To take a counter-example, this is not true for Danish dairy farmers. Here a very powerful group managed to push up milk prices, thereby harming Danish consumers more than it helped Danish producers. In a perfect world, where it was costless for all Danish voters to know about such policies as well as for them to organize and vote against them, this sort of protection would not exist.[13] Alas, this is like the camper who sits down to breakfast and says: 'If we had some bacon, we could have bacon and eggs – if we had some eggs.'

Gerrymandering Effect

Gerrymandering is the rearrangement of electoral districts in a way that permits one party to increase the number of its representatives that are likely to win. Although gerrymandering in the formal sense of the word is an action that is undertaken consciously, one can think of any redistriction as having a gerrymandering effect. That is, changing the political boundary of a district tends to change the objectives of the policy makers representing that district. This is the gerrymandering effect.

Changing the membership of a trade arrangement will have a gerrymandering effect. Examples of this are close at hand. For instance, the entry of Spain into the EU forced a rethinking of the latter's free trade agreement with Israel. The bone of contention in this case was citrus fruits, which is an important industry in both Spain and Israel but a rather minor one in other EU countries.

As far as an Eastern enlargement of the EU is concerned, a couple of facts are worth noting. Many advanced CEECs have agricultural sectors that are fairly similar to those of the northern EU incumbents – such as

France and Germany – that are major recipients of CAP money. Thus, other things being equal, one might expect that an eastern enlargement would lead the EU to be less likely to liberalize temperate farm products. Additionally, since low-wage Eastern labour might tend to specialize in labour-intensive products, such as apparel and footwear, the gerrymander-ing effect suggests that CEEC membership would make the EU less forward-looking on the liberalization of trade in such goods.

The Too-small-to-matter Syndrome

The too-small-to-matter syndrome currently observed in Europe is a direct result of this law of the jungle. The GATT's MFN principle does not apply to regional trade liberalizations. Consequently, the EU is perfectly free to negotiate preferential trade agreements with countries such as Sweden and the Czech Republic while ignoring Slovenia and Malta. The political economy forces at work here are straightforward. EU exporters have an interest in gaining access to all foreign markets, but their interest is more or less proportional to the size of the market in question. This means that they push harder for market-opening initiatives with large markets. If there is some fixed cost to pressing for a trade agreement, EU exporters may not find it worth asking for an Association Agreement with a very small nation such as Slovenia. Without this sort of pressure from exporters, the EU is unlikely to move. Politicians know that some import-competing firms will be harmed by such market opening. Consequently, the political costs of market opening with very small countries often outweigh the political benefits. The result is that small countries are ignored. This is the too-small-to-matter syndrome.

The implications of this for individual CEECs, especially the small ones, should be unmistakable. To gain and maintain the EU's attention, they must become more commercially interesting to EU exporters. One way to do this would be to band together into a regional trade area.

2.5.4   *Formal Measures of Voting Power and Biases*

An important implication of an EU enlargement concerns the impact of EU decision making. In order to understand the magnitude of this effect, one would like to measure how important would be the votes of new members. Gauging the power that the CEECs would have as members is a daunting task. To do this correctly, one would have to forecast the major issues that will arise in the Council of Ministers and how every one of the members would vote. As well as being difficult, the results would be quite arbitrary, since reasonable people could differ over the forecasted issues and positions. An alternative approach, which goes to the other extreme of treating voting positions on issues as totally random, has created a large literature on the impact of EU enlargement on power. One of the principal tools is the Shapley index, also known as the Shapley–Shubik index (SSI).

The Shapley–Shubik Index measures how likely it is for a particular country's vote to switch a losing coalition into a winning one. More specifically, we define a country's vote as 'pivotal' when the addition of its vote to a particular coalition switches that coalition from losing to winning. The SSI is the number of times a particular country could be pivotal divided by the total number of times that any country could be pivotal. It is helpful to think of the SSI in the following way. Suppose that each time a country is pivotal, it asks for and may be granted a special gift. In this light, a country's SSI equals its expected fraction of all special gifts awarded.

To clarify this, consider a model of the Council of Ministers. Using this model, we first measure power of the incumbents and then ask how power changes under two examples of enlargement. Before enlargement, there are only three countries, called A, B and C. Their representatives in the Council of Ministers have numbers of votes equal to 40, 35, and 25, respectively. Finally, suppose that a simple majority (51%) is required to pass any particular proposal.

Box 2.3 presents the analysis of power in this example. The way to proceed is to first list all the losing coalitions (i.e. the countries that vote 'yes' on a particular proposal but do not have sufficient votes to pass the proposal). Second, we count how many losing coalitions a particular country could switch into winning ones. Finally, we divide the number of pivots a particular country could perform by the total number of pivots all countries could perform. Turning to the base case in our example, a simple majority requires 51 votes, so the only losing coalitions are made up of single countries. These are listed on the left-hand side of Box 2.3. Note that either of the other countries could play the pivotal position in every one of the losing coalitions. For instance, country A could, by switching its 'no' vote to a 'yes', give B a victory (in the second listed losing coalition). It could do the same thing for C in the third losing coalition. Inspection of the example shows that there are six pivots. Country A accounts for a third of all the pivots. Countries B and C also account for a third. Thus in this very specific sense, A, B and C are all equally powerful and their SSIs are all equal. More formally, what we are really assuming is that each of the six situations where a pivot exists are equally likely to occur. If this is the case, then we could use the law of large numbers to assert that the average outcome of a large number of votes would be that each country was pivotal in a third of the votes.

Let us pause for a moment to consider the lessons of this simple example. First and most importantly, the number of votes a country has does not

Box 2.3 Numerical examples of power index calculations

The impact of various enlargements on the power of incumbents

Base case voting:
Weights: A = 40, B = 35, C = 25; total votes = 100, majority = 51 votes

Losing coalitions:	No. of pivots	Pivots per country		SSI
A versus B,C	2	A	2	0.333
B versus A,C	2	B	2	0.333
C versus A,B	2	C	2	0.333
Total pivots = 6				

Enlargement example 1
Weights: A = 40, B = 35, C = 25, D = 25; total votes = 125, majority = 63 votes

Losing coalitions:	No. of pivots	Pivots per country		SSI
A versus B,C,D	3	A	6	0.5
B versus A,C,D	1	B	2	0.166
C versus A,B,D	1	C	2	0.166
D versus A,B,C	1	D	2	0.166
B,C versus A,D	2			
B,D versus A,C	2			
C,D versus A,B	2			
Total pivots = 12				

Enlargement example 2
Weights: A = 40, B = 35, C = 25, D = 25; total votes = 135, majority = 69 votes

Losing coalitions:	No. of pivots	Pivots per country		SSI
A versus B,C,D	2	A	4	0.333
B versus A,C,D	2	B	4	0.333
C versus A,B,D	0	C	0	0
D versus A,B,C	2	D	4	0.333

A,C versus B,D	2
B,C versus A,D	2
C,D versus A,B	2
Total pivots = 12	

measure its power. Power depends upon a complex interaction of the majority rule and the number of votes that other countries have. As a general conclusion, it is definitely not sufficient to examine the number of votes each member has in order to gauge its power. Second, in this example the small countries (in terms of number of votes) have disproportionate power. This is not a general conclusion, but it is often the case.

By way of criticism, note that the set-up we are using provides only a shallow depiction of a real-world voting process. For instance, the questions of who sets the voting agenda, how coalitions are formed and how intensively each country holds its various positions are not considered. In a sense, the equal probability of each coalition occurring and each country switching its vote is meant to deal with this shallowness. The idea is that all these things would average out over a large number of votes on a broad range of issues. Thus, this measure of power is really a very long-term concept. Another way of looking at this is as a measure of power in the abstract. It tells us how powerful a country is likely to be on a randomly chosen issue. Of course, on particular issues, various countries may be much more or much less powerful. There are many other drawbacks to this concept. For references to the relevant literature, see Widgren (1993).

We turn now to the question of how an enlargement of our model Council of Ministers affects the voting power of the incumbents. The first enlargement, example 1, involves a new 'small' member country. Country D has the same number of votes as the smallest incumbent. The impact of this enlargement is to raise the voting power of the high-weight country (from 0.333 to 0.5) and to lower the power of other incumbents (from 0.333 to 0.166). Heuristically, the new member's votes are a close substitute for those of the incumbent low-weight countries, so the enlargement weakens their power. However, the presence of many low-weight countries increases the power of the large country since now it will be sought after as a tiebreaker in even more instances.

Enlargement example 2 consists of the entry of a medium-sized country. The impact on voting behaviour here is more significant in some sense. Since country D has 35 votes, it turns out that the smallest incumbent (country C) loses all of its power. The point is that any coalition that has enough votes to win has no need of country C. This exact result is rather an oddity, and changing around the number of votes slightly, or small changes to the majority rule will alter the outcome. Nevertheless, it serves to illustrate the point that enlarging a voting institution may change power in very unexpected ways. Moreover, the number of votes accorded to the entrants is not by any means all we need to know.

Notes

1. It is called contingent protection, since the import barrier is imposed contingent on certain criteria.
2. The Uruguay Round settlement makes dumping proceedings somewhat less arbitrary and, more importantly, the duties temporary rather than permanent.
3. Helpman and Krugman (1989) provide a very readable presentation of these and other related issues. The presentation in this section draws heavily on their work.
4. More technically, the steady state depends upon initial conditions.
5. A little-known article (Krugman, 1988, later published in Krugman, 1990) first outlined this approach. The basic modelling framework in Krugman (1988) comes from Shleifer (1986).
6. Note that literary styles do not seem to be governed by a quality ladder. Modern economists rarely approach the eloquence of the great neoclassical ones.
7. See Baldwin (1992c) for a more thorough working through of this pro-growth effect of import competition.
8. This subsection draws heavily on Azariadis and Drazen (1990).
9. Sufficiently tortuous reasoning can often be used to explain even these 'exogenous' choices. Since understanding, not intellectual purity, is the goal, certain choices are just taken as given.
10. Mercantilism is an economic doctrine from the seventeenth and eighteen centuries.
11. An important exception is when the consumer is industry. That is, in the case of imported intermediate goods, the domestic consumers and domestic producers are both industries.
12. The principle of unconditional most-favoured-nation (MFN) treatment in the context of negotiation means that countries must open up their markets to all countries with MFN status when they offer to open it up to any country. Perhaps a better term would be non-discrimination.
13. Even if voters wished to subsidize dairy farmers, say in order to preserve the countryside, the analysis in Section 2.2 can be used to show that a direct subsidy would be more cost-effective than import protection.

3

Potential Trade Patterns

The fall of the Iron Curtain led to a radical change in the economic map of Europe. More than 100 million people live in Central and Eastern Europe, and more than 200 million are in Russia, the Ukraine, Moldova and Belarus. Although these 300 million consumers/workers/savers are currently poorer than the 370 million in Western Europe, some – and perhaps many – of them will catch up. This process may take decades, even in the most successful CEECs. During the catch-up phase, markets in the successful CEECs are likely to grow two or three times faster than those in Western Europe. This rapid growth, together with the sheer numbers of Easterners, will fundamentally alter the economic map of Europe.

The gains that this opening provides for the Easterners are quite easy to understand. What has been under-appreciated is the promise that this holds out for Western Europe. The sudden opening of a vast new market to the East constitutes a great opportunity for Western Europe. Its businesses should benefit from access to a large and growing market. Its consumers should benefit from lower prices and a wider selection of goods. Its universities and enterprises should gain from the expertise and knowledge of Eastern scientists. West European businesses are in an ideal position to capitalize on this unprecedented opportunity. Recent events, historical evidence and geographical proximity suggest that the nations of Western Europe and those of Central and Eastern Europe are natural trading partners. For example, trade between EU member states and the CEECs has already increased at double-digit rates since the changes in the 1989 regimes. This is even more striking when one realizes that many CEECs have experienced drops in income that rival those of the Great Depression of the 1930s.

Trade between the eastern and western parts of the continent was suppressed by two distinct restraints before 1989. The first consisted of explicit government policies of suppressing East–West trade. The manner in which this suppression was imposed varied from country to country, but usually involved import licensing, state monopolies on foreign trade, foreign exchange restrictions and direct central planning. The second restraint on East–West trade was less direct. Due to the growth-inhibiting aspects of central planning, the income levels in Central and Eastern Europe were below what they should have been. Since trade tends to expand with output and income, East–West trade was lower than it should have been since incomes in the East were lower. As the CEECs complete their transitions to market economies and begin to catch up to West European levels of per capita income, their trading patterns will change. A critical question in the evaluation of potential trading arrangements is: What will the CEECs' trade look like? The importance of this question is matched only by its difficulty.

To get an idea of a pan-European common market the potential trade pattern for Europe is estimated in this chapter. As in previous studies of this type, a model of bilateral trade is estimated on historical West European data. The trade potential is obtained by applying the resulting model to East–West and East–East trade flows. In essence, this asks: What would pan-European trade look like, if the East was as integrated (with the West and itself) as Western Europe is today?

The main tool employed in this chapter is an analytic framework that explains bilateral trade relationships based on per capita GDP, total GDP and geographical distance between partners. This parsimonious framework, introduced in 1966 and known as the gravity model, has been used by many analysts to explain trade patterns in many parts of the world. Despite its simplicity, the model explains the actual pattern of trade remarkably well.

The plan of this chapter is as follows. Section 3.1 presents the theoretical foundations, empirical methodologies and estimation of the model. Section 3.2 gives the results, namely, projections of potential trade flows in Europe under two scenarios, which correspond to the removal of the two types of barriers that have impeded East–West trade. Section 3.3 compares these results with those of other authors.

3.1 The Gravity Model

Economists are not good at predicting the impact of drastic policy changes even in the short run. Predicting trade flows two or three decades after a radical transformation of the CEEC economies takes us well into the 'twilight zone' of economic understanding. The best way to proceed in such circumstances is to admit that any answers will be little more than a rough guess, and then to base that guess on simple and transparent assumptions.

3.1.1   *Theoretical Foundations and Empirical Methodologies*

The gravity model used to have a poor reputation among reputable economists. Starting with Wang and Winters (1991), it has come back into fashion. One problem that lowered its respectability was its oft-asserted lack of theoretical foundations. In contrast to popular belief, it does have such foundations and these are reviewed below. General issues surrounding the empirical implementation of the model are also discussed.

Theoretical Foundations of the Gravity Model

The gravity model consists of a single equation. This asserts that the bilateral trade flow from country x to country i depends upon five factors: the GDPs of the two countries, their populations, and the distance between them.[1] More formally, the gravity equation is written as follows:

$$X_{xi} = \beta_0 + \beta_1\left(\frac{GDP_i}{POP_i}\right) + \beta_2 GDP_i + \beta_3\left(\frac{GDP_x}{POP_x}\right) + \beta_4 GDP_x + \beta_5 Dist_{xi}$$
$$+ \text{dummies} \tag{3.1}$$

All variables are in logs, X_{xi} represents exports for the exporter (country x) to the importer (country i), GDP and POP are total GDP and populations of the relevant countries, $Dist_{xi}$ is the distance between the two countries. A variety of dummies are often added to these five main variables. A common, and exactly equivalent, specification takes population and GDP as entering separately instead of as GDP and per capita GDP.

Intuition   While the gravity model has long played a role in policy research, the gravity model as defined by equation (3.1) may appear strange to many trade theorists. Specifically, it may not be immediately obvious why one includes the GDP and population variable of both the importer and the exporter. To understand the equation in a simple and intuitive way, let us consider the analogy of an individual family's pattern of purchases.

A family lives near two shopping areas. Factors influencing how much the family buys at each shopping area may be divided into those that concern the family's characteristics and those that relate to the particular shopping area's traits. For instance, the richer the family becomes per capita, the more they will tend to spend on goods from both shopping areas. Similarly, holding constant the per capita income of the family but increasing the family's total income – and thereby the size of the family –

would increase the amount bought at both sites. The division of purchases between the two shopping areas would depend primarily on the various characteristics of the shopping areas themselves. It is likely that the family would buy relatively more from the area that offered the wider selection of goods. Also, other things being equal, the family will tend to do more of their shopping at the nearby shopping area.

In the gravity model, as with the family, a country's total purchases from foreign countries increases with per capita and total income. In other words, the importer's GDP and GDP per capita should be taken as measures of income. The gravity model also assumes that the selection of goods a particular country has to offer is positively correlated with the exporting country's per capita and total GDP. Thus, other things being equal, a particular country tends to import more from a large, rich partner. Using the family analogy, the exporter's GDP and per capita GDP in the gravity model are a measure of output and the variety of output. Finally, distance dampens trade since it is generally more convenient and cheaper to buy from nearby countries.

A Gravity Relationship in the Frictionless Krugman Model In the simplest Krugman model of intra-industry trade, a gravity-like equation is easily derived. In that model, tastes in all countries are symmetric and are given by a constant elasticity of substitution utility function. The monopolistic competition equilibrium involves each firm producing an identical amount of output and charging an identical price, with free entry determining how many products a country must produce to ensure full employment of its resources. In this special arrangement, consumers in each country buy an equal amount of each variety no matter where it is produced; also, the number of varieties produced by a country is proportional to its resources and therefore also proportional to its GDP. Clearly, then, the exports of any country increase with its own GDP as do the imports of any country. Putting these together, it is clear that the sizes (income levels) of both the importing and the exporting countries will affect the level of bilateral trade. If we went beyond the model and assumed that distance increases the consumer prices of products, we would observe that consumers would buy more of the goods produced close to them. This addition would yield the standard gravity equation. This line of thought is worked out in Chapter 8 of Helpman and Krugman (1985).

Bergstrand Bergstrand (1989) works out a formal model that is akin to the Krugman–Helpman model but allows greater flexibility. Demand for goods in the Bergstrand model is generated by a nested Cobb–Douglas–CES–Stone–Geary utility function. This permits him to find that demand depends upon relative prices and domestic income. On the supply side,

Bergstrand allows for monopolistic competition where products differ in factor intensity. This implies that a nation's output, and therefore its trade pattern, depends upon its level of income. In particular, income per capita rises as the capital–labour ratio increases. Thus, the elasticity on income per capita need not be unity.

Huang (1993) pieces together the following interpretations of the coefficients on the five main right-hand-side variables in the gravity model. The coefficient on the importer's per capita income is the importer's income demand elasticity. Thus, if traded goods are so-called luxury goods, the point estimate should be greater than unity and less than unity if they are so-called necessities. The coefficient on the importer's total GDP simply reflects size-effects, so the point estimate should be positive. The exporter's per capita GDP should be thought of as a measure of output per person and thus as an indirect measure of the exporter's capital–labour ratio. Thus if traded goods are, on average, relatively capital intensive, the estimated coefficient on per capita GDP should be positive. This inference comes from the Rybczynski theorem. A higher capital–labour ratio shifts an economy towards an output mix with heavier weight on capital-intensive goods. If traded goods are capital-intensive then this shift in output mix will show up as an increase in trade.[2] As stressed by the Helpman–Krugman interpretation, the exporter's total GDP simply reflects how large a range of differentiated products the country has to offer. The point estimate should therefore be positive.

Finally, distance is taken as an important determinant of relative prices. Specifically, relative prices of goods in different countries can be modelled as depending upon distance and other factors. These other factors are modelled as a stochastic error term, assumed to be orthogonal to the other right-hand-side variables. Clearly, then, the estimated coefficient for distance should be negative. If the model is estimated on disaggregated trade data, we expect the distance point estimates to be more negative for goods that are difficult to transport and sell at long distances.

Empirical Implementation

Several generic issues arise when trying to implement the gravity model on actual data. The first is the level of aggregation and country-coverage of the model, the second concerns whether to run the model on real or nominal data and the third relates to the measurement of distance.

Aggregation and Country Coverage   It should be clear from the intuitive explanation that the model should work best on industrial goods. These are often differentiated products subject to internal-scale economies in production. Krugman and others have shown that this can lead to massive two-way trade in similar products between similar countries. Thus, GDP and per capita GDP are good measures of the demand for imports and the supply of exports. Similarly, the model should fit very poorly for trade flows involving natural resources such as oil. The reason is that the source of the trade has very little to do with the exporter's GDP. It is related to the exporter's resource endowment.

Fortunately for this exercise, most trade in Western Europe involves industrial products. Moreover, the resource endowments in all Europe (with a few exceptions such as Norway and Russia) are fairly similar by world standards. This means that considering only aggregate trade in all goods should not create many difficulties.

The country-coverage chosen is mostly a matter of the projections one wishes to undertake. As Huang (1993) argued, the estimated coefficients on the gravity equation will reflect the income elasticities, the capital–labour ratios and the general level of integration among the countries in the data sample. Thus in this chapter we choose to estimate the model on data for West European nations, since we want to project how trade flows in Europe when the East becomes as integrated as the current West European nations are today.

Zeros in the Trade Data   If we select a large sample of countries and years, we find almost inevitably a few bilateral trade relations for which there is no reported trade. This is a problem, since the model is usually estimated in logs, and the log of zero is undefined. The literature has adopted three approaches to the problem. The first is simply to discard all such bilateral flows from the sample. The second is to substitute small values for the zeros. The third is to use estimating techniques, such as Tobit, which explicitly take account of truncated data for the independent variable. Without question, the third method is the right approach. It is, however, somewhat more difficult and most studies show that the resulting estimates are not substantially affected by the choice of approach. See Wang and Winters (1991) for a more thorough discussion of this issue.

Imports versus Exports   The usual source of trade data is the UN's *COMTRADE* database, or a publication that uses it, such as the IMF's *Direction of Trade Yearbook*. Each country reports its imports and exports by partner country. This provides two observations on every bilateral trade flow. For example, France reports its exports to Germany and Germany reports the same flow as German imports from France. This double observation might inspire econometricians, but most trade economists simply choose one source or the other. The most common choice is to rely on import data on the assumption that most countries monitor their imports more carefully than their exports.

Nominal versus Real   Trade is not a nominal phenomenon, so the gravity model should be regressed on real values of the data. Obtaining real values is often difficult, so many authors run their regressions on a single year of nominal data. To see that this is a valid procedure, note that real GDP is just nominal GDP divided by a price index. This is also true for the left-hand-side variable. When we take logs of a gravity model specified in real terms, the price indices enter linearly. Consequently, estimation on nominal data is identical to estimations on real data apart from the value of the constant term.[3] In the nominal data regression, the logs of all the price indices, multiplied by their relevant coefficients, are all estimated with the constant. Once we wish to use panel data, however, it is necessary explicitly to use real data. Moreover, given the long and sizeable swings in exchange rates, a single year of data may substantially under- or overestimate a country's GDP. Clearly, using a panel of several years of real data is preferable to a single year of nominal data.

Distance   Any reasonable microfoundations of the gravity model would indicate that relative prices of trade goods should enter the estimating equation. (Recall the family shopping pattern analogy.) One surprising aspect of the gravity equation is that it fits the data quite well even without relative prices. This is possible to explain by using a simple example.

Consider trade in clothing and, furthermore, assume that trade barriers do not matter. Specifically, consider Germany's imports of men's shirts from the United Kingdom and the United States. Wages are much higher in the United States than in the United Kingdom, but the wage difference exists because UK labour is less productive. Consequently, the total production cost of a similar-quality shirt is likely to be roughly the same in the United States and the United Kingdom. More precisely, the United Kingdom and the United States will both make a similar-quality shirt only if the total production costs in the two locations are roughly the same. Here is where distance counts. If US and UK manufacturers can manufacture shirts at roughly the same cost, the relative price of US and UK shirts in Germany should reflect trade costs.[4]

Given all this, it is certainly true that various factors (such as the exchange rate) may depend on the relative productivity and wages of US and UK workers. Accordingly, the relative prices of US and UK shirts in Germany may vary from year to year. However, these prices cannot do so for too long. We can model relative prices as white noise and in estimations this shows up as the error term.

The measurement of distance is a difficult issue in the gravity model. Some authors try to measure transport distance. For example, they would try to discover the route Swiss exports take on their way to the United States. One route may send the goods through Rotterdam to New York.

Another may take them via Genoa or Marseilles. Each time one must decide whether rail or road distance is most relevant as well as which ports. Clearly, there is no correct answer to any of these questions. An alternative approach, adopted in this section, is to rely on straight-line (in fact great-circle) distances between capitals. This strategy has its own set of problems but it is at least extremely transparent.

3.1.2   *Data and Estimation*[5]

The model was estimated on trade flows among the EC and EFTA nations and between these nations and the United States, Japan, Canada and Turkey. Belgium and Luxembourg are treated together, as are Switzerland and Liechtenstein, so there were 17 exporting countries and 20 partners (a country's trade with itself is not reported). Trade between Iceland and Turkey was zero, so the sample consists of 339 bilateral flows. Annual observations on each of these bilateral flows were obtained for the period 1979 to 1988, inclusive. The bilateral trade flow data were taken from the UN's *COMTRADE* database. These figures reflect aggregate merchandise trade and are expressed in nominal dollars. They were converted to real dollars using prices indices published by Eurostat in *Commerce Extérieur*, 1992 Yearbook. Use of these price indices required us to employ the export data of each reporter.

GDP and population data for all countries and all years were taken from the Summers and Heston (1988) database. The GDP numbers in this database are corrected for price differences and are expressed in 1985 international dollars. We used straight-line distances between capitals as our measure of distance. The 17 exporters and 20 partners (minus the Iceland–Turkey flow) over ten years yielded 3390 observations.

Estimation

The gravity equation was expanded to include dummies for adjacency and an EEA dummy (that is, a dummy for mutual membership in the outer concentric circle described in the discussion on Europe's historical trade arrangements in Chapter 1). Additionally, the GDP and per capita GDP variables were separated into GDP and population for convenience.

We first estimated the equation with ordinary least squares. The results are shown in the first row of Table 3.1. All the parameters are highly significant (the lowest *t*-statistic is 5) and the R^2 high, but the Durbin–Watson statistic indicates serial correlation. Employing a random-effects estimator with a maximum likelihood correction for first-order autocorrelation, we obtain the estimates in the third row of the table.[6] The actual

Table 3.1 Gravity model regression results

			Exporter		Importer					
	C	DIS	Pop.	GDP/Pop.	Pop.	GDP/Pop.	ADJ	EEA	R^2	DW
OLS	− 19.7	− 0.83	0.79	1.40	0.78	1.17	0.26	0.58	0.85	0.24
	(33)	(31)	(76)	(38)	(73)	(39)	(5)	(10)		
AR1	− 17.5	− 0.88	0.77	1.16	0.79	1.22	0.28	0.53	0.99	2.39
	(12)	(11)	(26)	(13)	(25)	(16)	(2)	(3)		

Notes: OLS = ordinary least squares; AR1 = random effects with maximum likelihood correction for first-order autoregressive error. DIS = distance, Pop = population, ADJ = adjacency dummy, EEA = EU + EFTA dummy. *t*-statistics (absolute values) are listed below point estimates.

point estimates do not change greatly, but the summary statistics do. Again, all variables are significant. The AR1 coefficients are the ones we employ here.

3.2 The Results: Projecting Europe's Trade Potential

This section reports potential trade flows and patterns for two distinctive scenarios which correspond to the elimination of the two distinct restraints on trade between Eastern and Western Europe under the old Communist regimes. The first is a medium-run scenario where it is assumed that the CEECs become as integrated into European trade as was the average West European country (EU plus EFTA) in the 1980s. In this scenario, incomes are held constant at their 1989 levels. The second scenario should be thought of as long run. It is assumed that the per capita incomes of the CEECs and FSR-4 catch up to the levels of the poorer West European nations.

The simplicity of the gravity model permits us to project trade flows for countries that have only the most basic data available. In fact, we need only population, GDP and the geographical distances between countries to project potential trade flows. Trade potentials were estimated for Albania, Croatia, the Czech Republic, Bulgaria, Estonia, Hungary, Latvia, Lithuania, Poland, Romania, Slovakia and Slovenia, Russia, Ukraine, Belarus and Moldova.

3.2.1 *Medium-term Trade Potentials*

It is a simple mechanical exercise to insert data (GDP, population and distance) into the estimated equation for any pair of countries. The implicit economic assumption is that the Eastern nations become as closely integrated with each other as Western Europe and the Westerners were during the 1980s. We use GDP data from 1989 for the medium-run projection. This has two merits. First, it isolates the impact of the first of the two constraints on East–West trade mentioned above. The other reflects the fact that it will take many CEECs many years to return to their 1989 per capita income levels. Thus, this may be thought of as the medium-run potential.

The Eastern GDP data are for 1989 and were taken from *Planecon*. Although there are many sources of GDP estimates, *Planecon* was the most complete we could find that was corrected for price differences. The 1989 data in dollars were rebased to 1985 to match the data used in estimations. Population figures are for 1989 and were taken from the World Bank's population database. Straight-line distances were calculated using a commercial software package. Appendix 3.1 at the end of this chapter lists all the Eastern GDP and population data used.

The result is a large trade matrix that lists all the bilateral trade flows among the EFTA-6, the EU-12, the CEEC-12 and the FSR-4. This and the matrix for the income catch-up scenario are presented in their entirety in the Appendix. The figures give potential trade flows measured in 1985 dollars.

Volume Results for Western Europe's Exports

The potential trade matrix contains over 450 numbers. To obtain an idea of what the results mean, we aggregate along several dimensions. The first is total potential exports by country. We first consider the numbers for West European nations.

These numbers are shown in Table 3.2. For comparison, the actual 1989 trade flows, the ratio of potential to actual and the differences between potential and actual are shown. The first set of columns show Western exports to the CEECs (that were not part of the former USSR); the next shows the figures for the former USSR; and the last set shows the figures for the sum of the first two sets. The table indicates that the potential exports of West European countries to the East far outstrip the actual exports in 1989. For instance, potential exports of the EU-12 to the CEECs and FSRs should have been roughly twice as large, exceeding their actual exports by US $34.7 billion. The second-from-last column in the table shows the ratio of potential to actual for the various countries. All these figures (except Finland's) are greater than unity and most of them are well above two. Finland, which had special commercial ties with the former USSR, is the only country projected to reduce its exports to the East. Clearly, the figures in Table 3.2 show that there is a very large medium-term potential for export growth from Western Europe to the East.

CEEC versus former USSR Breakdown   It is interesting to break down these total figures into extra exports to the CEECs and extra exports to the former

Table 3.2 Potential and actual exports to the East in 1989 (billions of US dollars, except ratios)

	CEEC-12 less Baltic States				Former USSR				Total			
	Actual	Potential	Ratio	Difference	Actual	Potential	Ratio	Difference	Actual	Potential	Ratio	Difference
Austria	2.0	5.6	2.8	3.6	0.8	1.6	2.0	0.8	2.8	7.1	2.6	4.4
Finland	0.2	0.8	3.2	0.5	3.1	2.3	0.7	-0.9	3.4	3.0	0.9	-0.3
Iceland	0	0	1.5	0	0	0.1	1.2	0	0.1	0.1	1.3	0
Norway	0.1	0.6	4.5	0.5	0.2	0.9	5.6	0.7	0.3	1.5	5.1	1.2
Sweden	0.8	1.3	1.8	0.6	0.3	2.2	6.4	1.9	1.1	3.5	3.2	2.4
Switzerland	1.0	2.0	2.0	1.0	0.6	1.5	2.7	0.9	1.6	3.5	2.2	1.9
EFTA-6	4.2	10.4	2.5	6.2	5.0	8.4	1.7	3.4	9.2	18.8	2.1	9.6
FANS	3.1	8.3	2.7	5.2	4.4	6.9	1.6	2.5	7.5	15.2	2.0	7.7
Belgium/Lux.	0.7	1.6	2.5	1.0	0.5	1.4	2.9	0.9	1.1	3.1	2.7	1.9
Germany	9.0	10.3	1.2	1.3	5.7	7.1	1.3	1.4	14.6	17.4	1.2	2.7
Denmark	0.3	1.1	3.5	0.8	0.2	1.2	5.3	1.0	0.5	2.3	4.3	1.7
Spain	0.8	1.8	2.3	1.0	0.4	1.8	5.0	1.4	1.1	3.5	3.1	2.4
France	1.9	5.8	3.0	3.8	1.6	5.2	3.3	3.6	3.5	10.9	3.1	7.4
Greece	0.3	0.7	2.3	0.4	0.1	0.6	4.3	0.5	0.4	1.2	2.9	0.8
Ireland	0.1	0.2	2.1	0.1	0.1	0.2	4.2	0.2	0.2	0.5	2.8	0.3
Italy	3.0	7.5	2.5	4.5	2.4	5.1	2.1	2.7	5.4	12.6	2.4	7.3
Netherlands	1.0	2.1	2.1	1.1	0.6	1.9	3.0	1.3	1.6	3.9	2.5	2.4
Portugal	0	0.3	11.2	0.3	0.1	0.4	3.3	0.3	0.1	0.7	5.0	0.6
UK	1.1	4.7	4.1	3.6	1.0	4.6	4.5	3.6	2.2	9.3	4.3	7.2
EU-12	18.2	36.0	2.0	17.9	12.6	29.4	2.3	16.8	30.8	65.5	2.1	34.7

USSR. One good reason for doing so is that many expect the economic performance of most of the CEECs to be greatly superior to that of the former Soviet Republics (excluding the Baltic States).[7] As a consequence, it is likely that it will take much longer for the FSR-4 to fulfil the assumptions of this medium-term scenario, i.e. to become as integrated with Western Europe as Western Europe was with itself in the 1980s. The first and second sets of columns in Table 3.2 permit this breakdown. Roughly, half the total potential export increase is projected to go to the former USSR market. This simply reflects the size and wealth of the former USSR in 1989.

The patterns of the potential–actual ratios are also worth noting. These reveal the extent of the trade diversion that was caused by the various East–West barriers. Apart from the cases of Austria, Germany, France and Italy, the ratios are higher for the former USSR than they are for the CEEC-9. This indicates that Western exports to the former USSR were generally suppressed to a greater extent than those to the CEECs. For the four exceptions, however, it appears that exports to the CEECs have the potential to expand much more than those to the former USSR. Note that Finland's exports to the former USSR are projected to fall but Finland's exports to the CEECs should grow.

Differences Among the EU-12   To emphasize the effects that are most likely to appear in the medium term, consider the exports to the CEECs only. The largest actual and potential exporter is clearly Germany, followed closely by Italy. Indeed, in 1989, Germany accounted for almost half of all EU-12 exports to the CEECs.

Note that there is a substantial bias in terms of which countries are projected to do the most extra exporting to the CEECs. The EU-12 together should export an extra US $16.8 billion to the CEECs, but the poor-four (Spain, Portugal, Greece and Ireland) are projected to account for only US $1.6 billion of this. In absolute dollar amounts, the 'winners' will be the United Kingdom, France and Italy. These dollar figures, however, hide the pattern of implied growth. For instance, in terms of percentage growth of existing exports, the poor-four all are projected to expand more than the EU-12 average, with Portugal having the highest ratio of all.

The current enlargement of the EU-12 to include Finland, Austria, Norway and Sweden ('the FANS'), will alter the picture somewhat. In particular, Austria with its population of only 7.8 million is projected to export as much to the CEECs as France. Taking the FANS together, export potential is US $8.3 billion. Recalling that trade policy is usually based on mercantilistic reasoning, this begins to suggest that the accession of the FANS will shift the EU's attitude towards opening trade with the CEECs. We expand upon this below when we consider export patterns.

Table 3.3   Potential and actual exports for CEECs in 1989 for which data were available (billions of 1985 US dollars except for ratios)

	CSFR	Hungary	Poland	Romania	Albania	Bulgaria	Former USSR
EU-12							
Actual	2.6	2.6	4.0	2.5	0.1	0.5	15.1
Potential	12.5	4.5	8.5	3.0	0.3	2.9	31.2
Ratio	4.8	1.7	2.1	1.2	2.6	5.2	2.1
Difference	9.9	1.8	4.5	0.6	0.2	2.3	16.1
EFTA							
Actual	0.8	0.9	1.0	0.2	0.0	0.1	4.4
Potential	4.6	1.5	1.9	0.6	0.0	0.5	8.7
Ratio	5.5	1.7	2.0	3.2	1.9	7.3	2.0
Difference	3.7	0.6	1.0	0.4	0.0	0.4	4.4
CEECs + USSR							
Actual	6.6	4.1	5.2	4.2			
Potential	4.1	2.2	3.8	1.6			
Ratio	0.6	0.5	0.7	0.4			
Difference	−2.4	−1.9	−1.5	−2.5			
CEECs			•				
Actual	2.7	1.8	2.2	1.8			
Potential	2.8	1.4	1.8	0.8			
Ratio	1.0	0.8	0.8	0.4			
Difference	0.1	−0.4	−0.5	−1.0			

Volume Results for Eastern Europe's Exports

Discussing actual trade flows for the CEECs is problematic due to data problems. During the CMEA period, intra-CEEC trade was conducted in 'transferable rubles' that was not a standardized unit of measure *vis-à-vis* hard currencies. Thus, we can compare actual and estimated potential trade only for a few countries. Table 3.3 shows the figures for all CEECs for which the necessary data were listed in the IMF's *1992 Direction of Trade Statistics Yearbook*.

The first two sets of rows in the table show actual and potential exports (medium-run scenario) to the EU-12 and the EFTA-6. The row showing the ratio of potential to actual exports to the EU-12 clearly indicates the possibility of great trade growth. The ratios vary from 1.2 for Romania to 5.2 for Bulgaria. The variance reflects the fact that the CEECs, even in 1989, were at quite different stages of openness. For instance, Hungary had already embarked on a programme of liberalization before 1989. The dollar amount of extra trade projected is quite large. For the Czech Republic taken together with Slovakia, the total is almost US $10 billion.

The third and fourth sets of rows show the CEECs' trade with other CEECs and the former USSR.[8] Here a very different picture emerges. The third set of rows shows the trade-diverting effect of the CMEA trading

Table 3.4 Potential exports of CEEC-12 and FSR-4, 1989 (millions of 1985 US dollars)

Exporter	Market				
	CEEC-12	EFTA-6	FSR-4	EC-12	Total
Albania	54	41	33	259	387
Bulgaria	711	521	500	2 869	4 602
Romania	824	599	813	3 025	5 261
Croatia	941	876	361	3 360	5 538
Hungary	1 418	1 505	761	4 485	8 170
Czech Republic	1 525	2 156	863	9 034	13 579
Slovakia	1 244	2 415	500	3 457	7 617
Slovenia	835	886	339	3 857	5 917
Estonia	159	488	270	714	1 631
Latvia	326	458	511	1 280	2 575
Lithuania	443	401	626	1 411	2 882
Poland	1 759	1 914	2 030	8 479	14 182
CEEC-12	10 242	12 260	7 607	42 230	72 340
Russia	3 831	4 731	3 408	16 795	28 766
Ukraine	2 275	1 679	3 045	7 178	14 176
Moldova	269	186	340	871	1 665
Belarus	1 066	791	1 513	2 944	6 313
FSR-4	7 440	7 387	8 306	27 788	50 921

system. The ratios of potential to actual trade are all less than unity, suggesting that there was too much East–East trade in 1989. The extent of this diversion varies from about 160% too much for Romania, to about 40% too much for Poland. A great deal of this trade diversion concerned the former USSR itself. The fourth set of rows illustrates this point. Considering only CEEC–CEEC trade, the ratios of potential to actual are closer to unity. This indicates that the trade-diverting impact of the CMEA on CEEC–CEEC trade was less severe than on CEEC–USSR trade. This finding is supported by other studies discussed below. The absolute dollar differences also show that most of the diversion was to the USSR. Indeed, for the CSFR, the model predicts that for the medium-run scenario exports to other CEECs should rise by US $100 million.

The medium-run potentials for all the CEEC-12 and the FSR-4 are listed in Table 3.4. The total European exports are broken down into four main markets: the EU-12, the EFTA-6, the CEEC-12 and the FSR-4. Taken together, the potential exports of this region are quite significant. Adding up total European exports of the CEECs and the FSRs produces a figure of over US $120 billion. To get an idea as to the magnitude of this number, note that intra-EU trade in 1989 was about US $680 billion.

Trade Pattern Results for West Europe

Figure 3.1 shows the potential export pattern for West European nations. The total European market is divided into four large areas: the EU-12, the

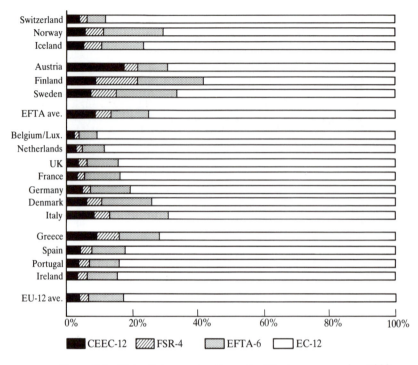

Figure 3.1 Potential export patterns for Western economies, 1989

EFTA-6, the FSR-4 and the CEEC-12. It is immediately obvious that the West European market dominates the exports of all nations. Austria and Finland are both projected to have a little more than 20% of their European export sales going to the East; the EU-12 average (weighted according to trade volumes) is below 10%. Looking at the EU-12 alone as a market for exports we see that it accounts for more than 80% of the European markets for all the EU-12 except Denmark, Greece and Italy. Interestingly, the EU-12 is projected to be systematically more important for the EFTAns that are not likely to join the EU (Iceland, Norway and Switzerland), than it is for those that are.

On average, the CEEC-12 are projected to account for only 4% of the EU-12's sales; the same figure for the FSR-4 market is only 3%. Clearly, although the Eastern markets are likely to be a significant source of export growth (as shown above), the absolute level of these sales will continue to be dwarfed in the medium run by sales to Western Europe. The EFTA-6 are projected to be, on average, much more dependent on Eastern markets. The CEEC-12 and FSR-4 are forecast to account for 8% and 5%, respectively. Again the EFTAns that are likely to accede to the EU are projected to be more dependent on Eastern markets than the EFTA-6 average.

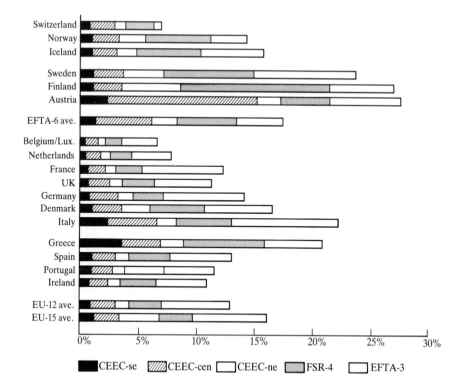

Figure 3.2 Pattern of potential West European exports to non-EU-15 nations, 1989. EU-15 = EU-12 + Austria, Finland and Sweden; CEEC-se = Albania, Bulgaria, Croatia and Romania; CEEC-cen = Slovenia, the Czech Republic, Slovakia and Hungary; CEEC-ne = Estonia, Latvia, Lithuania and Poland; FSR-4 = Russia, Ukraine, Moldova and Belarus; EFTA-3 = Iceland, Norway and Switzerland–Liechtenstein

It is worth noting that the poor-four in the EU-12 are not projected to be systematically more or less dependent on the Eastern markets in the medium term.

Figure 3.2 shows a more detailed picture of Western Europe's projected, medium-run export pattern to Eastern markets. The bars show details for five markets: three groupings of the CEEC-12 (South-east, Central and North-east), the FSR-4 and the EFTA-3 (Iceland, Norway and Switzerland). The CEEC South-east consists of Albania, Bulgaria, Croatia, and Romania. The CEEC Central countries are Slovenia, the Czech Republic, Hungary and Slovakia. The North-east CEECs are Poland and the three Baltic States. Generally, the pattern of trade with the East reflects geographic proximity. A very large share of Austria's trade with Eastern markets is projected to be with the Central European nations surrounding it. Indeed, considering only geography, Austria itself is a Central European nation. For Finland and Sweden, trade with the North-east CEECs and the FSR-4 is important. Italy is close to both the Central and South-east CEECs, and this is reflected in its shares.

A notable fact is the change in the EU's Eastern export share that will occur when (if) Austria, Finland and Sweden join. This enlargement would raise the average share from about 7% to about 10%. Moreover, it would double the number of EU members that are projected to depend on the Eastern markets for more than 10% of their European exports. Since mercantilism drives trade politics, the so-called FANS enlargement is likely to make the Council of Ministers more forward-looking when it comes to trade with the East.

Export Pattern Results for Eastern Economies

Figure 3.3 shows the export pattern for the CEECs. The European export market is divided into six areas: the three regional groupings of the CEEC-12, the FSR-4, the EFTA-3 (Iceland, Norway and Switzerland) and the EU-15 (EU-12 plus Sweden, Austria and Finland). Comparing these figures with the previous ones clearly shows that exporters based in Eastern economies are likely to be more dependent on Eastern markets than exporters based in Western economies. Nevertheless, the EU-15 will account for most of the sales in the medium term. For the CEEC-12 as a whole, sales to the EU 'hub' will account for a little more than 70% of total European exports.

There is variation among the regional groupings. The Central Europeans are projected to depend most heavily on the EU market. The FSR-4 and the North-east CEECs are forecast to depend more than average on the FSR-4 market.

3.2.2   Trade Potentials with Partial Income Catch-up

The second scenario reported involves the same gravity equation. The incomes of the Easterners, however, are increased to reflect the income catch-up that is hoped will occur during the coming decades. As should be clear from inspection of the gravity equation, growth in the East will stimulate Eastern imports and exports. To keep the projections as clear as possible, we assume zero population growth.

The growth prospects of the various Eastern economies would appear to vary greatly. The transition to market economies is firmly under way in several CEECs. However, others appear to have trouble finding a domestic

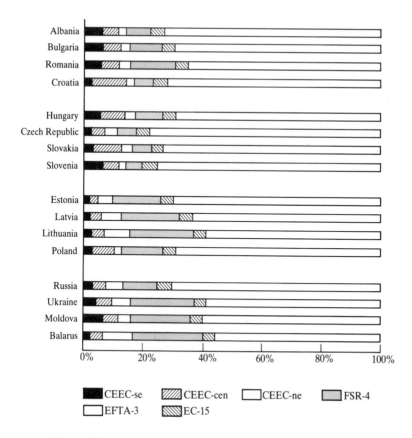

Figure 3.3 Potential export patterns for Eastern economies, 1989

political consensus concerning market reforms. In these, delays in establishing property rights and confronting firms with hard budget constraints are likely to delay the reallocation of resources that is necessary to transform Stalinized economies into modern industrial states. Adding to these problems, many Eastern nations face political instability and governments that are unable to stabilize the macroeconomic environment. All these factors will inhibit aggregate growth. The reason is simple. Growth requires investment by domestic and foreign firms. Macroeconomic and political instability and lack of private property rights make investment a difficult and risky proposition.

In the catch-up scenario, we roughly guess the level of Western incomes to which the various Eastern economies will catch up. Specifically, it is assumed that the Czech Republic, Hungary, Estonia, Latvia, Slovakia and Lithuania catch up to the per capita income of Spain. Slovenia is already

Table 3.5 Implied growth rates for the Eastern economies, income catch-up scenario

Countries catching up to the 'EU poor-3'	Implied annual average growth rate (%)	Countries catching up to Spain (Slovenia catches Austria)	Implied annual average growth rate (%)
Albania	11.1	Slovenia	3.0
Bulgaria	3.3	Hungary	4.8
Croatia	2.3	Czech Republic	3.3
Romania	5.8	Slovakia	4.1
Poland	4.4	Estonia	4.7
Belarus	3.1	Latvia	4.3
Russia	3.2	Lithuania	5.0
Ukraine	4.3		
Moldova	5.3		

richer than Spain, so it is assumed to catch up to neighbouring Austria. All the other CEECs and the FSR-4 are assumed to catch up to the average of Ireland, Greece and Portugal. This degree of catch-up is likely to take decades, so one cannot ignore Western growth. In particular, we assumed that all Western economies grow at 2% per annum during this period.

Table 3.5 shows the implied growth rates for the Eastern economies, that is, the rate of growth that would be necessary to attain the target by 2010 starting at 1989 income levels. The differences among the countries reflect the different initial income levels and the different catch-up targets. The implied growth rates are high but would certainly not be unprecedented. For instance, Asia experienced real income growth rates during the 1970s and 1980s that averaged well over 5% per annum. Nevertheless, it is clear that this catch-up scenario reflects quite optimistic assumptions. It should be envisaged what might happen if all went well. Of course, the most likely outcome is that some Eastern economies will perform even better than this but some will do much worse. The choice of the exact catch-up year is somewhat arbitrary. The year 2010 was taken, since this produced implied growth rates in the CEECs that were close to, but less than, 5% per annum. We considered 2005, 2015 and 2020 as alternatives, but each of these led to implied growth rates of the CEECs that were too high or too low.

To obtain an idea of what Europe (including the EU, EFTA, the CEEC-12 and the FSR-4) would look like if the partial income catch-up occurred, consider how the catch-up would change Western Europe's share of European GDP. The relative economic weight of Western Europe is diminished by the Eastern income growth, but the shift is far from radical. The share of Western Europe in European GDP falls from about three-quarters in 1989 to about two-thirds in 2010. The FSR-4 and the CEEC-12 are projected to account for one-fifth and one-eighth (respectively) of European GDP in 2010. The relatively high level of per capita income in the West can be seen by noting that Western Europe accounted for 52% of Europe's population in 1989. All populations are assumed constant.

Table 3.6 Projected export growth rates for Western Europe with partial catch-up of Eastern incomes (percentage annual average rates)

	EU + EFTA	CEEC-se	CEEC-cen	CEEC-ne	FSR-4
Austria	5	15	13	12	10
Finland	5	19	11	22	4
Iceland	5	29	14	7	7
Norway	5	26	15	16	15
Sweden	5	16	8	15	16
Switzerland	5	14	10	14	11
Belgium/Lux.	5	16	11	14	12
Germany	5	12	7	11	7
Denmark	5	20	14	15	15
Spain	5	23	17	22	15
France	5	17	13	17	12
Greece	5	13	10	18	14
Ireland	5	20	10	18	14
Italy	5	18	10	16	10
Netherlands	5	15	10	14	12
Portugal	5	22	19	28	13
UK	5	18	14	18	14
EFTA-6	5	16	12	15	9
EU-12	5	16	10	14	11
EU-15	5	16	10	14	10

Note: Exporters are listed down the left-hand side, importers across the top.

Results for West European Exports

If the incomes in the East manage to catch up as assumed, West European exports to the East should rise at double-digit rates. The actual projections are shown in Table 3.6 in which exporters are listed on the right-hand side. The table paints a very rosy picture for West European exports over the next couple of decades. The first column shows the growth for intra-West European trade. These numbers are all identical since we have assumed that all Western economies grow at 2% and we ignore population growth.[9] There is much information in the table, but here we focus only on the aggregate numbers shown in the bottom rows. The projected growth rates for exports to the four Eastern regions are all fairly similar, ranging between 10% and 15%. The only difference worth noting is between the rate for EFTA and the EU-12 in the FSR-4 market. The lower rate for EFTA reflects the fact that several EFTAns were already more closely integrated with the USSR than was the average EU-12 economy.

Figure 3.4 shows that this projected export growth will alter the pattern of West Europe's trade. The top set of bars shows the export pattern for the EU and EFTA economies in the catch-up year. The bottom set shows the pattern for two aggregates of Western nations: the EFTA-6 and the EU-12. For comparison, the actual 1989 pattern is shown. It is clear from the bottom set of bars that the importance of Eastern markets for West

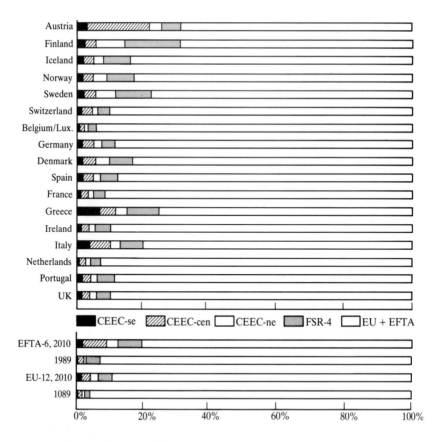

Figure 3.4 Potential export patterns of Western Europe with partial income catch-up in the East

European exporters will increase substantially, but Western Europe will remain the dominant market by far

Results for East European Exports

Figure 3.5 shows how the export pattern of several Central and East European countries would change between 1989 and 2010 under the catch-up scenario.[10] There are two salient features of the figure: (1) in all cases the importance of the West European markets increases substantially, and (2) in all cases the Eastern markets remain important. The most extreme case is that of Czechoslovakia. In 1989, Western markets accounted for only about 35% of its exports. It is projected that this should increase to more than 70% by 2010 under the long-term scenario. Even in

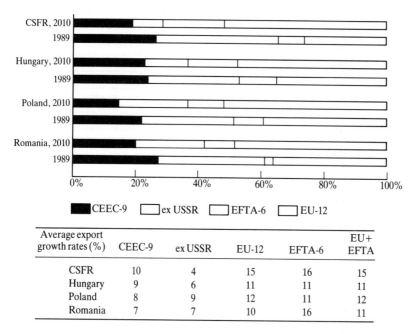

Average export growth rates (%)	CEEC-9	ex USSR	EU-12	EFTA-6	EU+ EFTA
CSFR	10	4	15	16	15
Hungary	9	6	11	11	11
Poland	8	9	12	11	12
Romania	7	7	10	16	11

Figure 3.5 Export patterns and growth of selected CEECs in 2010 versus 1989, income catch-up scenario

Czechoslovakia, which has the lowest share, the East accounts for about 30% of its European export sales. Thus, it is clear that trade among the CEEC-12 and FSR-4 will remain important, although the West European market will have the largest share.

The table in Figure 3.5 shows projected annual average growth of exports by the listed CEECs to the five regions. These growth figures reflect the removal of three distinct sets of trade barriers: of East–West barriers, of the CMEA trade-diverting measures and of the central planning that stifled income growth in the East. As is easily seen, growth of East–East trade is projected to be significantly lower than East–West trade, although both sets of rates are fairly high. More precisely, exports from the CEECs to the FSR-4 should grow at a rate of from 4% to 7%, while intra-CEEC exports should grow from 7% to 10%. Exports to the West are projected to grow at almost twice the FSR-4 rate, with estimates ranging from 10% to 16%.

The long-run potential export patterns for all the CEEC-12 and the FSR-4 are shown in Figure 3.6. As before, two clear facts emerge. Western Europe will account for most of the CEECs' exports, even when the CEECs and FSR-4 have partially caught up to Western income levels. Nevertheless, trade among the Eastern economies will not be negligible.

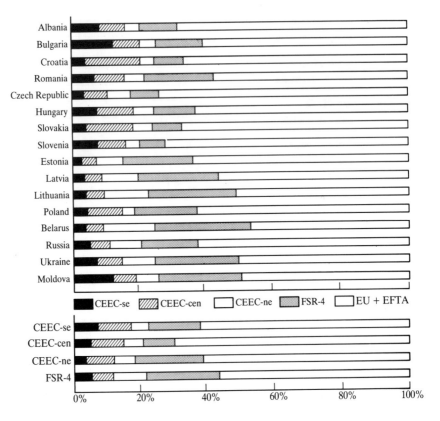

Figure 3.6 Easterners' potential export pattern with partial income catch-up

3.3 Review of Previous Studies

This section compares the results presented above with those of previous studies. The two most important previous studies of the trade potential of Eastern and Central Europe are Wang and Winters (1991) and Collins and Rodrik (1991).[11] Both studies attempt to estimate a model of how a 'normal' country's geographic trade pattern is related to various characteristics, as described above. The next step is to assume that the CEECs' trade patterns will fit this mould once they complete their transitions to market economies. The two difficulties that each study must face are: (1) the choice and estimation of the model of the trade pattern, and (2) the estimation of what the CEECs' own characteristics will be once they get through their transitions.

Table 3.7 Wang–Winters regression estimates

C	GDP_i	Pop_i	GDP_x	POP_x	$Dist_{xi}$
−12.49	1.02	−0.22	1.17	−0.38	−0.75
(32.4)	(42.8)	(8.2)	(58.2)	(15.7)	(22.3)

$R^2 = 0.7$
Number of observations = 4320
All variables in logs.

3.3.1   *Wang and Winters*

Wang and Winters (1991) estimate a gravity model using data for 76 non-CEEC countries averaged over the 1984–6 period. The dummy variables that they include are for adjacency and mutual membership in preferential trade areas. Some of the bilateral flows in their sample were zero, thus making it difficult to take logs of the left-hand-side variable. The authors tried two ways of dealing with zero recorded trade flows: substitution of small values, and simple exclusion of such flows. The two approaches yield similar point estimates of the betas, but the errors from the regression with substituted data are non-normal. The results of their regression with the omitted data are reported in Table 3.7. Note that the variables for both the importing and exporting countries have approximately the same size.

Projecting CEEC Trade Potential   The gravity model, which was estimated on data that do not include Central and East European countries, gives the relationship between GDP, population, distance and bilateral trade flows in a 'normal' country, i.e. one that is as integrated into the world trade system as the average of their 76-country sample. This allows Wang and Winters to predict what the CEECs' trade pattern will be once they also become 'normal' countries. That is, once they complete their transitions to market economies and are integrated with the world trading system. The mechanics of the projection are simple. Estimates for the CEECs' GDP, population and distance are simply inserted into the equation and this together with the data for the other 76 countries generate an import and export pattern for all the CEECs with each of the 76 countries. Wang and Winters focus on the aggregate potential trade flows predicted by their model using the Summers–Heston estimates of the CEECs' GDPs in 1985. The distance variables used were rail, road and marine distances as appropriate.

Estimated Trade Potential   The Wang-Winters results for the base year of 1985 are shown in Table 3.8. Two facts dominate the results. In 1985, the amount of East–West trade was only a fraction of what it would have been in an integrated Europe. Second, East–East trade was too large in 1985. As

Table 3.8 Wang and Winters' model for potential versus actual trade, East European exports, 1985 (millions of US dollars)

	EC	EFTA	Other industrial nations	Less-developed nations	CEECs
Bulgaria	402	61	71	582	9 855
	2 521	602	1 741	742	2 652
CSFR	1 532	596	201	1 998	12 541
	15 221	2 198	4 175	1 707	7 411
Hungary	1 326	749	262	892	4 464
	6 505	923	2 364	1 204	4 103
Poland	2 502	688	344	1 356	5 998
	12 653	2 630	5 922	2 004	9 154
Romania	2 595	302	778	1 942	4 018
	5 247	1 282	3 105	1 506	4 361

Note: First line for each country shows actual trade, second line shows potential.

Source: Wang and Winters (1991), Table 4.

noted by Rodrik (1992), trade among the ex-CMEA countries collapsed in the early 1990s. Although much of this was a disruption of trade between the former USSR and the CEECs, intra-CEEC trade also fell.

Baldwin's Extension of the Wang–Winters Results Baldwin (1993) uses the Wang–Winters estimated coefficients to investigate the potential for trade between EFTA member states and the CEEC-12. The main contribution is to extend the projects to a much wider range of countries and to update the base year of the model to 1989. The results are very much in line with the findings presented in Section 3.2.

3.3.2 *Collins and Rodrik*

The Collins–Rodrik methodology, which differs substantially from the gravity model approach, is discussed in Appendix 3.2 at the end of this chapter. The results of the Collins–Rodrik studies are broadly similar to those of Wang and Winters (1991). Although the authors do not explicitly report actual and potential trade numbers, these can be found by combining information on the trade shares and aggregate CEEC exports. Table 3.9 reports the findings of these calculations. The CEECs' potential exports to the EU-12 are substantially larger than the actual trade in 1988. The magnitudes of the potential–actual gaps are broadly similar to those of Wang and Winters.

Estimated Long-run Potential Trade Collins and Rodrik also examine how large trade would be if the incomes of the CEECs caught up to the EU

Table 3.9 Collins and Rodrik's medium-run results, EFTA potential and actual exports to CEECs, 1988 (US$ billion)

1988 Eastern exports to EU-12	CSFR	Hungary	Poland	Romania	Bulgaria
Actual	3.8	2.4	4.3	2.2	1.3
Potential	12.6	5.9	20.1	9.0	6.7
Potential/actual	3.3	2.5	4.7	4.1	5.2

Source: Calculated from Collins and Rodrik (1991), Tables 2.3 and 2.4.

average, but the trade shares remained at their 1989 levels. This exercise points up the shortcomings of the pragmatic approach to trade shares adopted by the authors. If the incomes of the 110 million citizens in the CEECs caught up with the average EC country, the economic structure of Europe would be fundamentally altered. It is hard to believe that such a radical change in the output and income pattern in Europe would have no effect on the import and export shares of the CEECs. Since the Collins–Rodrik method of estimating the 1989 shares is not based on a theoretical model, they cannot calculate how their assumed growth of CEEC output would affect the CEECs' trade pattern.

To calculate trade with catch-up, the authors repeat the two steps for obtaining aggregate exports. That is, they use the estimates of their openness regression to see how the assumed increase in GNP and log of GNP would increase the export to GNP ratios, and then they multiply this ratio by the GNP figure. The resulting increase in total exports of the CEECs is 180%. Trade figures are not reported explicitly by Collins and Rodrik, but can be calculated from shares as above. The results of these calculations for trade between EFTA and various CEECs are summarized in Table 3.10.

The estimated potential exports to the CEECs are large. These would involve an approximate fourfold increase in EFTAns exports to the CSFR and Hungary, an approximately ninefold increase to Poland and an extraordinary seventy-sixfold and fifty-sixfold increases in exports to Romania and Bulgaria. The radical sizes of the estimates for Romania and Bulgaria stem from the very large growth it would take for these countries to catch up with the EC average as assumed.

3.3.3   *Pre-Second World War European Trade Patterns*

Predicting the effects of changes as massive as the transformation of Eastern Europe is an uncertain endeavour. History provides some guidance. Figure 3.7 displays League of Nations'.data on 1928 exports

Table 3.10   Collins and Rodrik (1991) results. EFTA long-run potential and 1988 actual exports to CEECs (US$ billion)

Catch-up	CSFR	Hungary	Poland	Romania	Bulgaria
EFTA actual (1988)	0.85	1.0	0.88	0.07	0.04
EFTA long-run potential	3.41	4.24	7.48	5.34	2.04
Potential/actual	4.0	4.24	8.5	76.3	51.0

Note: Assumes CEECs per capita incomes catch up with EC average.

(bottom scale) and IMF data on 1991 exports (top scale). The year 1928 was chosen since it was the most recent pre-war, pre-Depression year for which data are available. Scaling makes the two patterns as similar as possible, thus highlighting the differences. Before the war the CEECs' trading performance was on a par with that of Western Europe. The exports of Hungary, Poland, Bulgaria and Romania rivalled those of Finland and Ireland. It is striking that Czechoslovakia's 1928 exports exceeded those of all but six European nations and were only 17% lower than those of Italy. To see how different things were in 1928, the League of Nations tables lists Czechoslovakia under 'Industrial Continental Europe' while Denmark, Spain, Norway and Finland are relegated to 'Other Continental Europe'. The comparison with 1991 is marred by the usual CEEC data problems.[12] Nevertheless, the available data indicate that the CEECs' rank among European exporters has fallen since the Second World War.

Data on individual CEECs' share of European exports (not shown in Figure 3.7) reveal that the CEECs' 1991 shares of European exports are much smaller than in 1928. Specifically, their 1991 shares are between one-half and one-fifth of their 1928 shares. The Baltic States' shares of total European exports in 1990 are only a tenth of what they were in 1928. Here it is necessary to note that difficulties in valuing ruble-zone trade poses greater problems for the Baltic States since the great majority of their trade was denominated in rubles.

The analogy with 1928 has its limitations, but it does show that it is not an exaggeration to suggest that the CEECs' trade with Western Europe will expand fivefold in the coming years. This is how much their trade would have to grow simply to restore them to their pre-war trade standing in Europe.

Direction of Trade   Figure 3.8 compares the 1928 and 1991 pattern of CEEC-5 exports. It shows the fraction of CEEC exports going to the EC, EFTA, and the CEECs excluding the Baltic States, the USSR and the Rest of the World.[13] Note that the shares of CEEC exports going to EEA nations (EC plus EFTA) have fallen substantially between 1928 and 1991 in all five CEECs. In all five, much of this decline was due to reduced exports to EFTA, which was in turn largely due to the decline of 'Mitteleuropa' and the attendant drop in Austria's trade with other Central European nations.

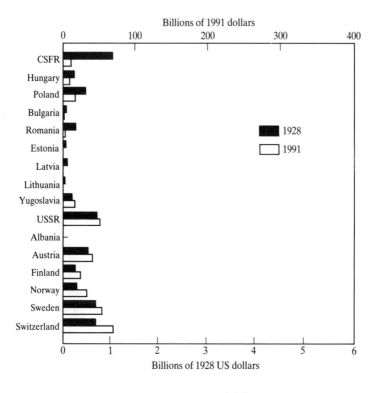

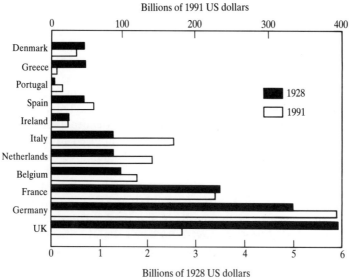

Figure 3.7   Volumes of European exports, 1928 and 1991. (Note the different scales used for these years.) (*Sources:* League of Nations and the IMF)

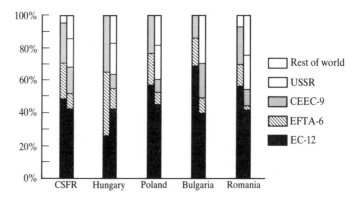

Figure 3.8 CEEC-5 export pattern, 1928 versus 1991. Left bar = 1928, right bar = 1991. (*Sources:* League of Nations and the IMF)

(Recall that the Austro-Hungarian Empire, which included Austria, Hungary, Czechoslovakia, Slovenia, Croatia and a large area of Romania, existed until 1918.) The second part of the decline in Eastern Europe/Western Europe trade came from the diminished importance of the EC-12 as a trading partner for four of the five large CEECs. Also note that in all but Bulgaria, intra-CEEC trade was more important in 1928 than it is now; however, given insurmountable data problems concerning East–East trade in 1991, these numbers should be viewed with caution. The USSR's share of CEEC exports expanded greatly between the two periods, reflecting rapid Soviet growth as well as trading preferences in the Soviet trading bloc, CMEA. Finally, the 'rest of world' share has grown significantly. In 1928 this consisted largely of shipments to North America, while in 1991 it was mostly shipments to LDCs. The level of LDC imports of CEEC goods has reduced by about 20% since 1989.

The pattern of trade for the Baltic States has changed even more since 1928. During the inter-war period these were basically market economies that were heavily dependent on agriculture. Soviet occupation turned them into heavily industrialized economies that imported raw materials from other Soviet republics in exchange for manufactured goods.[14] In 1990, approximately 95% of the Baltic States' trade was with other republics of the former USSR (including themselves). This contrasts sharply with the situation in 1928, when 80–90% of the Baltic States' trade was with the EEA countries, especially Germany and the United Kingdom. In 1928, exports to the USSR amounted to 5.2%, 9.4% and 2.3% of total Estonian, Latvian and Lithuanian exports; intra-Baltic States trade amounted to about 5.2%, 3.5% and 7%, respectively.

Commercial Importance of CEECs to Western Europe in 1928 Few firms in Western Europe currently consider the East a major market. This was not

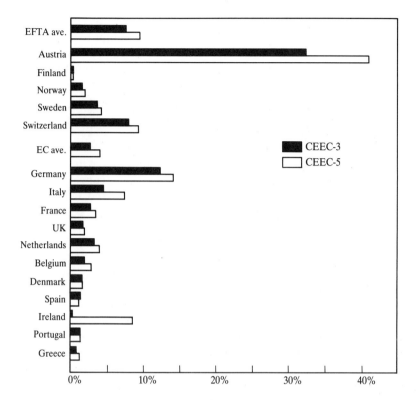

Figure 3.9 Importance of CEEC markets to Western Europe, 1928.
Exports to CEECs as share of exports to all Eastern countries. CEEC-
3 = Czechoslovakia, Hungary and Poland; CEEC-5 = CEEC-
3 + Bulgaria and Romania. (*Source:* League of Nations)

always the case. In 1928, the CEEC markets were quite important to the
exporters of many West European nations. Prior to the imposition of
central planning, some of the CEECs (notably Hungary and Czechoslovakia) were among the richest nations in Europe.

Figure 3.9 presents the importance of the CEEC markets to West
European exporters in 1928. The top bar shows each Western country's
exports to the CEEC-3 markets (Czechoslovakia, Hungary and Poland) as
a percentage of their exports to all of Europe (excluding the USSR). The
bottom bar shows the importance of the CEEC-5 markets (CEEC-3 plus
Bulgaria and Romania). Clearly, markets in Eastern and especially Central
Europe were of critical importance to some Western nations. Austria is the
extreme case, with the East accounting for over 40% of its total exports to
Europe. For Germany, the figure reaches almost 15%, and for Switzerland
it is almost 10%. In contrast, the CEECs were relatively unimportant to

many of the current EU members such as Greece, Portugal and Spain. For the EU-12 as a whole the share of European exports going to the CEEC-5 in 1928 was just over 4%. Note that the markets of the CEEC-3 accounted for most of the exports, reflecting the relative poverty of Bulgaria and Romania.

3.3.4   *Other Studies*

Two other recent studies have looked at how trade flows of the CEECs were affected by central planning. Biessen (1991) estimates an openness equation that is similar to, but simpler than, that of Collins and Rodrik (1991). Specifically, he regresses export/GDP ratios on a constant, per capita GDP and population, using data from 1980 that were adjusted to reflect a series of misvaluations of the CEECs' trade flows. Biessen finds that the CEECs are not outliers in this regression. Thus, he concludes that the CEECs' total trade was not obviously repressed. To investigate whether central planning distorted the direction of the CEECs' trade, he estimates a gravity model using data on EU countries, EFTA countries, six CEECs and the USSR. The estimating equation is similar to that of Wang and Winters, but he includes East–West and West–East dummies, and uses distances 'as the crow flies' between capital cities as a measure of distance (instead of the more commonly used transport-based distance measures). His main point estimates are fairly close to those of Wang and Winters (1991). Since both East–West dummies turn out to be negative and highly significant, he concludes that central planning and Western restrictions greatly reduced East–West trade in Europe. Although the author does not perform the calculation, it is possible to eliminate the degree of East–West trade repression from his estimates. Thus actual Western exports to the East were only one sixth of the level that the model predicts would have occurred with the CEECs, if they had been as integrated as the Western European countries. In other words, an opening up of the CEECs would result, on average, in a sixfold expansion of Western exports to the East.

Van Bergeijk and Oldersma (1990) estimate a gravity model for 49 countries (including six CEECs) involving the usual population, income and distance variables plus a dummy for East–West and East–East trade. As in Biessen (1991), the East–West dummy is estimated to be negative and highly significant. The estimates of the dummies indicate that all bilateral trade flows in 1985 between the East and West were about one-eighth as large as the gravity model would predict based solely on income, population and distance. Unlike Biessen (1991), Van Bergeijk and Oldersma (1990) find that East–East trade was also below the norm defined by the model by about 50%.

Appendix 3.1: Projected Trade Matrices

Medium-run potential trade: Eastern markets. Thousands of US dollars, 1985 prices

Exporter	ALB	BGR	CRO	ROM	SLN	HUN	CZR	SLK	EST	LAT	LIT	POL	BELO	RSFSR	UKR	MOLD
GNP/Pop.	1106	5053	6292	3053	11079	5407	7301	6318	5522	5964	5203	4044	5274	5141	4159	3389
Population	3170	8990	4690	23140	1950	10580	10380	5260	1580	2680	3710	38060	10230	147720	51770	4350
Austria	11307	162164	448394	177240	437925	864300	1067082	1858879	29456	59047	73699	541394	159014	797752	406955	49731
Finland	3532	55074	48534	68879	48282	87728	137881	62497	257823	115704	79543	255218	155404	1343538	277267	24327
Iceland	205	2941	2706	3371	2774	4280	6959	3116	1201	1914	1948	9016	4179	29985	9983	1053
Norway	2899	42954	42551	50888	43635	72060	131462	53888	28964	45373	40946	186012	81076	490995	167926	16613
Sweden	5802	88449	84253	107921	85010	149972	259505	110116	103842	150527	112946	443195	211212	1191181	393391	36687
Switzerland	10756	137942	199436	143940	236242	246425	474346	199445	30204	56000	63772	376743	136608	790714	343547	40454
Albania	0	10408	4825	6696	4238	6594	6402	4086	582	1101	1358	7668	3127	18755	9516	1390
Bulgaria	9320	0	54750	217866	47642	91962	82222	53536	8142	15612	19794	110262	46625	275660	152595	25273
Croatia	4302	54514	0	53132	266866	182490	127209	103211	13962	13962	17193	111298	38056	205852	103844	13527
Czech Republic	5590	80179	124585	90261	134933	214662	0	286783	20158	40419	48405	479525	100431	499287	236702	26870
Estonia	531	8304	7350	10424	7306	13406	21082	9550	0	27974	13072	40216	24832	199354	42580	3700
Hungary	5866	91357	182073	135789	111654	0	218684	352707	13059	26382	34248	246581	76364	377760	278928	27638
Latvia	993	15724	14123	20010	13945	26747	41746	19011	27626	0	52649	93692	81048	335910	86408	7253
Lithuania	1230	20012	17458	26293	16987	34857	50187	24132	12960	52852	0	186266	192774	294213	129474	10011
Poland	6819	109498	111005	139771	107595	246496	488341	234692	391161	92380	182953	0	354274	953244	674089	48971
Romania	6105	221800	54326	0	48226	139158	94233	60221	10406	20226	26475	143288	64210	371770	310744	66039
Slovakia	3636	53203	103013	58784	94011	352834	292260	0	9306	18758	23720	234857	51528	255365	177000	16487
Slovenia	3693	46369	46369	46104	0	109390	134674	92072	6973	13476	16352	105450	35837	195223	95418	12089
Belarus	2788	46413	38047	62784	36653	76520	102522	51615	24238	80105	189799	354274	0	986322	501052	25322
Russia	16109	264408	198304	350268	192397	364742	491113	246476	187497	319904	279117	920712	950385	0	2322567	135399
Ukraine	8410	150598	102929	301237	96756	277103	239559	175779	41205	84670	126383	669909	496756	2389721	0	158977
Moldova	1290	26189	14077	67217	12871	28829	28553	17191	3760	7462	10260	51099	26359	146274	166919	0
Belgium/Lux.	8053	109628	134128	120226	147845	194016	410943	154637	32801	59343	64394	364062	134749	787439	320122	35637
Germany	39636	543786	700977	598708	779363	1022197	3204369	837310	161441	298246	326626	2553014	679168	3836935	1598346	177887
Denmark	4367	64470	70490	76002	73068	121848	262047	95047	33127	62613	61679	337219	118764	619980	242779	24516
Spain	12296	158251	158712	165860	167440	219337	342462	161046	36021	63440	70507	369930	154294	1004836	400764	46919
France	31583	420237	505653	452745	558373	703290	1298100	550406	113671	204241	223952	1245453	475143	2855510	1161539	131760
Greece	11754	123414	50793	102952	47027	77309	83373	49105	9151	16974	20734	108823	48521	315627	153397	22439
Ireland	1214	16794	17422	18684	18391	26223	46747	19768	5737	9766	10233	52075	21657	139020	51740	5643
Italy	67931	703085	892084	645853	1233384	944957	1193762	675506	92848	173185	205311	1182853	457164	2733773	1263146	162935
Netherlands	9661	133937	159476	149128	173210	239579	519551	190570	44491	80264	85628	479727	177203	1026771	411137	44947
Portugal	2305	30283	28901	32192	30133	41139	63571	29960	7305	12699	14003	71704	71704	205216	79650	9224
UK	24934	340681	382664	375175	412288	562070	1075415	434134	107676	189188	201722	1081540	424585	2596504	1013196	111921

Notes: ALB = Albania, BGR = Bulgaria, CRO = Croatia, ROM = Romania, SLN = Slovenia, HUN = Hungary, CZR = Czech Republic, SLK = Slovakia, EST = Estonia, LAT = Latvia, LIT = Lithuania, POL = Poland, BELO = Belarus, RSFSR = Russia, UKR = Ukraine, MOLD = Moldova.
In this and the following tables exporters are listed on the left and markets are listed across the top. GNP per capita (US$) and population (thousands) are given in the top two rows.

Medium-run potential trade: Western markets. Thousands of US dollars, 1985 prices

	FIN	ICE	NOR	SWE	SWI	AUT	BL	D	DK	E	F	GR	IRL	I	NL	P	UK
GNP/Pop.	13648	13020	12971	14032	18511	13483	13681	15317	13413	9610	14494	6264	7375	13265	13016	6729	13249
Population	4960	250	4230	8490	6720	7620	10320	62060	5130	38890	56160	10030	3520	57530	14850	9790	57240
>Pot'l '89 <<	353961	17198	309970	63504	1662266	0	941400	7060175	554994	951065	3434100	263587	111163	5427719	1157213	168736	2667280
Austria	0	14628	361767	167238	378037	355899	406850	2059861	397570	450188	1455098	107878	68598	1174526	553207	87831	1377604
Finland	15321	0	16936	27013	26357	18111	30605	138328	17397	43180	119506	6401	8447	77364	40201	9286	125927
Iceland	363762	16260	0	133560	390242	313386	490356	2426485	563396	452071	1655995	85639	86622	1061548	714637	87746	1718869
Norway	1661032	25547	1318985	0	695315	633023	794358	4058688	986714	788062	2743929	172208	130032	2017314	1115116	152284	2661675
Sweden	369249	24580	379080	0	0	1632514	2145067	14536119	622966	1854937	12792125	274506	195389	2150721	299644	152284	5443628
Switzerland	163233	4191	84693	223877	146906	0	811831	4057561	805606	1025010	3004904	307337	134702	2861849	1052718	200656	2717745
Albania	4162	231	3398	2002	12977	13397	9592	48800	5143	14603	38694	13325	1369	82795	11532	2625	30385
Bulgaria	58113	2963	45076	94123	149018	172049	116930	599127	67987	168300	461043	125287	16965	767348	143166	30870	371764
Croatia	50991	2714	44460	89675	214520	473675	142446	769499	74014	168063	552360	51342	17523	969423	169179	29335	415777
Czech Repub.	141873	6836	134526	112315	499696	1103989	427422	3445023	269472	355156	1388750	82535	46049	1270489	541547	63193	1144366
Estonia	277446	1234	30997	157711	33277	31872	35680	181521	35627	39069	127183	9474	5911	103344	48500	7594	119831
Hungary	91959	4283	75122	161504	264457	910945	205577	1119555	127648	231728	766499	77965	26315	1024534	254401	41661	609313
Latvia	122964	1942	47956	121149	60930	63096	63750	331176	66501	67952	225680	17356	9936	190370	86410	13039	207930
Lithuania	84860	1985	43444	46358	69654	79055	69442	364088	65762	75814	248414	21281	10452	226554	92540	14432	222561
Poland	267435	9021	193847	117343	404173	570416	385622	2795209	353148	390695	1356922	109709	52241	1282023	509229	72588	1172041
Romania	73992	3457	54366	117343	158306	191441	130550	672000	81595	179578	505678	106402	19215	717615	162283	33409	416800
Slovakia	65535	3120	56197	116574	214117	1959907	163911	917388	99607	170206	600091	49540	19845	732656	202432	30351	470793
Slovenia	49585	2720	44566	88039	248389	452201	153478	836286	74993	173313	596219	46464	18082	1310138	180197	29896	437880
Belarus	163233	4191	84693	223877	146906	167939	143070	745379	124671	173313	518908	49033	21778	496679	188551	31150	461215
Russia	1359804	28976	494214	121747	819334	811831	805606	4057561	627107	1025010	3004904	307337	134702	2861849	1052718	200656	2717745
Ukraine	288737	9926	173914	413489	366274	426112	336977	1739123	252670	420635	1257650	153686	51582	1360557	433714	80132	1091170
Moldova	26600	1099	18065	40098	45285	54674	39388	203225	26789	51706	149790	23604	5907	184269	49784	9743	126556
Belgium/Lux.	402490	28908	482440	793870	2172583	936410	0	31197466	795764	1620795	19647101	220385	282915	3610115	8727541	281318	11199538
Germany	1971439	126403	2309589	392164	14243257	6794110	30181760	0	5595886	6853427	61322508	1064946	1088340	17522736	33214973	1195534	34745528
Denmark	397810	16620	560644	996763	638178	558370	804870	5850392	0	618155	2529989	123162	106508	1626065	1211820	115648	2445529
Spain	446666	40905	446074	789784	1884226	948790	1625535	7104783	612948	0	10667624	364835	301549	5853028	1834941	2044425	6238729
France	1399495	109741	1583980	2664150	12596133	3320961	19101058	61624530	2431846	10340901	0	868230	1115003	19923425	11721564	1286046	42112066
Greece	112129	6352	88525	180708	292115	275474	231551	1156559	127939	382202	938299	0	35535	1580041	281456	71084	759800
Ireland	71654	8424	89985	137025	208952	116751	298720	1187813	111186	317467	1210949	35711	0	506960	382583	62353	1749543
Italy	1135545	71414	1020688	1960840	7701251	5276315	3528113	17701016	1571151	5703401	20027492	1469686	469231	0	4048394	949006	10923844
Netherlands	546104	37890	701592	111140	2173637	1148610	8708819	34259106	1195540	1825665	12030785	267308	361563	4133602	0	326570	12725126
Portugal	90915	9177	90328	159040	317545	175616	294349	1293009	119636	2132887	1384084	70790	61789	1016044	342432	0	1167496
UK	1332081	116259	1652954	2598670	5389023	2593263	10946774	35104254	2363292	6080146	42338325	706838	1619577	10925468	12464671	1090628	0

Notes: FIN = Finland, ICE = Iceland, NOR = Norway, SWE = Sweden, SWI = Switzerland, AUT = Austria, BL = Belgium/Luxembourg, D = Germany, DK = Denmark, E = Spain, F = France, GR = Greece, IRL = Ireland, I = Italy, NL = Netherlands, P = Portugal.

Potential trade with income catch-up: Eastern markets. Thousands of US dollars, 1985 prices

>Pot'l 2010 <<	ALB	BGR	CRO	ROM	SLN	HUN	CZR	SLK	EST	LAT	LIT	POL	BELO	RSFSR	UKR	MOLD
GNP/Pop.	10044	10044	10044	10044	20436	14566	14566	14566	14566	14566	14566	10044	10044	10044	10044	10044
Population	3170	8990	4690	23140	1950	10580	10380	5260	1580	2680	3710	38060	10230	147720	51770	4350
Austria	268706	605510	1281747	1222688	1492838	4674289	4002820	8315250	155270	283354	417649	2651639	563545	2916410	1926224	302062
Finland	83939	205643	138735	475160	164589	474451	517219	279566	152675	555234	450770	1250006	550752	4911686	1312375	147762
Iceland	4876	10982	7735	23253	9455	23145	26103	13938	6333	9184	11041	44160	14812	109619	47254	6393
Norway	68902	160387	121634	351052	148747	389716	493139	241054	152675	217736	232042	911048	287333	1794973	794837	100907
Sweden	137873	330263	240841	744493	289789	811077	973451	492577	547373	722342	640063	2170684	748535	4354700	1862022	222836
Switzerland	255612	515066	570094	992967	805321	1332708	1779360	892170	159214	268729	361395	1845211	484140	2890681	1626096	245715
Albania		307560	109167	365604	114328	282240	190056	327582	144664	24264	60908	297247	87714	542646	356491	66840
Bulgaria	302946		214080	2055849	222154	680315	421898	490175	58710	102477	153437	738713	226027	1378491	987984	209979
Croatia	108549	216110		389143	965840	1047830	506622	81040	40158	71133	103442	578746	143191	798979	521847	87229
Czech Rep.	182508	411313	489277	855459	631945	1594976		1762481	145987	266477	376868	3226713	489001	2507719	1539255	224228
Estonia	23945	58821	39856	136420	47249	137543	150027	133803		254662	140535	373666	166953	1382575	382339	42639
Hungary	270957	663064	1011670	1820821	739836		1594535	3066812	133803	246083	377262	2347523	526053	2684389	2566268	326303
Latvia	40941	101887	70060	239554	82498	251032	271761	147583	252718		515339	796349	498467	2131099	7097768	76453
Lithuania	59368	151836	101402	368549	117659	383038	382532	219345	138806	515339		1853708	1388186	2185484	1245227	123546
Poland	286726	723417	561440	1706032	648964	2358724	3241212	1857538	365238	784375	1834465		2216208	6165962	5645383	982149
Romania	355216	2027858	380241		402534	1842757	865525	659598	134309	237660	367364	1718386	557192	3327843	3601397	982149
Slovakia	140295	322527	478079	658384	520305	3098046	1779939		79639	146147	218237	648006	296483	1515683	1360191	162579
Slovenia	110119	217233	935575	399050		742268	633847	516753	46115	81137	116265	648006	159350	895456	566661	92126
Belarus	86237	225604	141581	563826	162655	538729	500646	300566	166326	500414	400198	2258833		4694000	3087357	200223
Russia	513246	1323661	759995	3239584	879318	2644677	2469937	1478206	1325078	2058182	2120683	6045898	4515745		14738877	1102600
Ukraine	342342	963219	503989	3559591	564974	2567036	1539290	1346881	372053	695984	1226815	5620255	3015615	14964669		1654013
Moldova	66534	212201	87324	1006243	95210	338335	232431	166875	43009	77709	126170	543098	202721	1160424	1714490	
Belgium/Lux.	191368	409342	383410	829375	503987	1049274	1541524	691733	172900	284772	364920	1783104	477550	2878708	1515218	216458
Germany	941896	2030461	2003765	4130171	2656761	5528226	12020174	3745504	174620	1431210	1850988	12504155	2406971	10427007	7565383	1080467
Denmark	103788	240729	201498	524296	249079	658975	982987	425171	174620	300463	349532	1651631	420898	2266512	1149135	148905
Spain	292202	590897	453683	1144183	570783	1186213	1284637	720401	189876	304432	399565	1811843	546818	3673425	1896920	284981
France	750524	1569136	1445423	3123249	1903432	3803520	4869410	2462110	599187	980100	1269135	6099982	1683908	10439129	5497865	800294
Greece	279315	460821	145194	710215	160309	418099	312749	219660	48237	81456	117498	532993	171960	1153865	726066	136291
Ireland	28846	62706	49800	128893	62695	141819	175357	88427	30243	46864	57992	255054	76752	508226	244898	34276
Italy	1614310	2625273	2550049	4455401	4204469	5110498	4478019	3021714	489422	831074	1163497	5793379	1620190	9994084	5978795	989651
Netherlands	229586	500113	455866	1028757	590455	1295688	1948931	852469	234525	385169	485255	2349606	628007	3753654	1946016	273004
Portugal	54787	113073	82615	222079	102719	222490	238465	134018	38504	60941	79354	351194	108790	750224	377003	56023
UK	592517	1272080	1093855	2588139	1405444	3039777	4034080	1941992	567585	907867	1143159	5297169	1504729	9492258	4795719	679797

Potential trade with income catch-up: Western markets. Thousands of US dollars, 1985 prices

>Pot'l '89 <<	FIN	ICE	NOR	SVE	SWI	AUT	BL	D	DK	E	F	GR	IRL	I	NL	P	UK
GNP/Pop.	13648	13020	12971	14032	18511	13483	13681	15317	13413	9610	14494	6264	7375	13265	13106	6729	13249
Population	4960	250	4230	8490	6720	7620	10320	62060	5130	38890	56160	10030	3520	57530	14850	9790	57240
Austria	353961	17198	309970	635604	1662266		941400	7060175	554994	951065	3434100	263587	111163	5427719	1157213	168736	2667280
Finland	0	14628	361767	167938	378037	355899	406850	2059861	397570	450188	1455098	107878	68598	1174526	553207	87831	1377604
Iceland	15321	0	16936	27013	26357	18111	30605	138328	17397	43180	119506	6401	8447	77364	40201	9286	125927
Norway	363762	16260		1330960	390242	26357	490356	2426485	563396	452071	1655995	85639	86622	1061548	714637	87746	1718869
Sweden	1661032	25547	1318985		695315	313386	794358	4058688	986714	788062	2743929	172208	130032	2017314	1115116	152284	2661675
Switzerland	369249	24580	379080	685054		633023	2145067	14536119	622966	1854937	12792125	274506	195389	7780440	2150721	299644	5443628
Albania	4162	231	3398	6702	12977	13397	9592	48800	5143	14603	38694	13325	1369	82795	11532	2625	30385
Bulgaria	58113	2963	45076	96023	149018	172049	116930	599527	67987	168300	461043	125287	16965	767348	143166	30870	371764
Croatia	50991	2714	44460	85767	214520	473675	142446	769499	74014	168063	552360	51342	17523	969423	169729	29335	415777
Czech Repub.	141873	6836	134526	262575	499696	1103989	427422	3445023	269472	355156	1388750	82535	46049	1270489	541547	63193	1144366
Estonia	277446	1234	30997	112915	33277	31872	35680	181521	35627	39069	127183	9474	5911	103344	48500	7594	119831
Hungary	91959	4283	75122	158711	264457	910945	205577	1119555	127648	231728	766499	77965	26315	1024534	254401	41661	609313
Latvia	122964	1942	47956	161504	60930	63096	63750	331176	66501	67952	225680	17356	9936	190370	86410	13039	207930
Lithuania	84860	1985	43444	121549	69654	79055	69442	364088	65762	75814	288414	21281	10452	226554	92540	14432	222561
Poland	267435	9021	193847	460558	404173	570416	385622	2795209	353148	390695	1356922	109709	52241	1282023	509229	72588	1172041
Romania	73992	3457	54366	117143	158306	191441	130550	672000	81595	179578	505678	106402	19215	717615	162283	33409	416800
Slovakia	65535	3120	56197	112574	214117	1959907	163911	917388	99607	170206	600091	49540	19845	732656	202432	30351	470793
Slovenia	49585	2720	44566	88139	248389	452201	153478	836286	74993	173313	596219	46464	18082	1310138	180197	29896	437880
Belarus	163233	4191	84693	222977	146906	167939	143070	745379	124671	163345	518908	49033	21778	496679	188551	31150	461215
Russia	1359804	28976	494214	121747	819334	811831	805606	4057561	627107	1025010	3004904	307337	134702	2861849	1052718	200656	2717745
Ukraine	288737	9926	173914	415589	366274	426112	336977	1739123	252670	420635	1257650	153686	51582	1360557	433714	80132	1091170
Moldova	26600	1099	18065	42498	45285	54674	39388	203225	26789	51706	149790	23604	5907	184269	49784	9743	126556
Belgium/Lux.	402490	28908	482440	793870	2172583	936410		31197466	795764	1620795	19647101	220385	282915	3610115	8727541	281318	11199538
Germany	1971439	126403	2309589	3921564	14243257	6794110	30181760		5595886	6853427	61322508	1064946	1088340	17522736	33214973	1195534	34745528
Denmark	397810	16620	560644	995763	638178	558370	804870	5850392		618155	2529989	123162	106508	1626065	1211820	115648	2445529
Spain	446666	40905	446074	783584	1884226	948790	1625535	7104783	612948		10667624	364835	301549	5853028	1834941	2044425	6238729
France	1399495	109741	1583980	2664550	12596133	3320961	19101058	61624530	2431846	10340901		868230	1115003	19923425	11721564	1286046	42112066
Greece	112129	6352	88525	182708	292115	275474	231551	1156559	127939	382202	938299		35535	1580041	281456	71084	759800
Ireland	71654	8424	89985	137125	208952	116751	298720	1187813	111186	317467	1210949	35711		506960	382583	62353	1749543
Italy	1135545	71414	1020688	196040	7701251	5276315	3528113	17701016	1571151	5703401	20027492	1469686	469231		4048394	949006	10923844
Netherlands	546104	37890	701592	1111340	2173637	1148610	8708819	34259106	1195540	1825665	12030785	267308	361563	4048394		326570	12725126
Portugal	90915	9177	90328	153740	317545	175616	294349	1293009	119636	2132887	1384084	70790	61789	1016044	342432		1167496
UK	1332081	116259	1652954	2593367	5389023	2593263	10946774	35104254	2363292	6080146	42338325	706838	1619577	10925468	12464671	1090628	0

Appendix 3.2: The Collins–Rodrik Methodology

Collins and Rodrik (1991) estimate the potential for trade in Europe using a methodology that is not based on an integrated procedure or model such as the gravity model. Their approach, which has never been previously attempted, is pragmatic and based on a number of empirical regularities and plausible conjectures. The technique breaks down the trade pattern into an aggregate export figure and country-specific trade shares. Thus instead of directly estimating the exports of, say, Hungary to Sweden and Norway, the Collins–Rodrik technique first estimates total Hungarian exports and then separately estimates the shares of the total that go to Sweden and to Norway. We address these two procedures in order.

Aggregate Exports

The first step of the Collins–Rodrik methodology is itself composed of two intermediate steps: first, they estimate what the CEECs' export to GDP ratios should be if they were normal market economies, then they multiply this ratio by an estimate of the CEECs' GDP to obtain aggregate exports. Aggregate imports are assumed to equal aggregate exports.

To estimate what the CEECs' normal export-to-GDP ratio should be, the authors rely on the well-known empirical regularity that the richer a country becomes, the more open it is. In other words, export-to-GDP ratios are positively correlated with per capita GDP. Reasons for this regularity abound. Some focus on how high incomes tend to be associated with a high relative demand for imported goods. Others reverse the causality, asserting that openness increases per capita income. To capture this relationship quantitatively, Collins and Rodrik take a pragmatic approach. Using data from 1988, they regress the openness ratio (exports to GDP) of a cross-section of 91 countries (no CEECs are included) on GNP, the log of GNP, the log of population, and a series of dummies including, notably, a dummy for countries whose export-to-GNP ratio exceeds 40%. The results are reproduced in Table 3.11.[15] Note that the R^2 statistic is quite high for a cross-section regression. The point estimates suggest that a country tends to become more open as its per capita income rises but less open as its population rises.

Apart from its lack of theoretical justification, the estimated equation is rather usual in several respects. For instance, no constant term is included, GNP *and* the log of GNP enter both on the right-hand side, and the dependent variable is measured in percentage points rather than the log of percentage points. Moreover, it is not usual to include a dummy, such as D40, which depends upon the realization of the dependent variable. The

Table 3.11   The Collins–Rodrik model of a 'normal' export/GDP ratio

GNP	lnGNP	lnPOP	D40	DMIDE	DDD	DLA	DSA
$-4*10^{-6}$	4.3	-6.6	29.7	-11.3	-9.1	-7.9	-5.0
(-3.1)	(11.9)	(-7.8)	(12.1)	(-3.5)	(-3.3)	(-3.3)	(-2.7)

Notes: Dummy variables: D40 = countries where dependent variable is over 40%, DMIDE = Middle East countries, DDD = Developed countries, DLA = Latin America, DSA = Sub-Saharan Africa.
$R^2 = 0.79$. Mean of dependent variable = 21.7. 1988 data.

problem is that such a variable is correlated with the error term by construction.

Finally, to obtain forecast 1988 trade flows the authors insert estimates of the CEECs' current GNPs and populations into the estimated openness equation. This generates an export/GNP ratio. The 1988 GDP estimates used are those of *Planecon*.

Trade Shares

Estimating the trade share is more problematic since it is hard to know what the CEECs' trade patterns would have been if they had been part of the West since the Second World War. To avoid this, Collins and Rodrik base their predictions of the CEECs' trade shares on their 1928 trade shares, updated to reflect changes in the relative economic importance of certain nations between 1928 and 1991.

Specifically, the 1928 trade shares come from a League of Nations survey that was published in the 1940s. The authors argue that these trade shares reflect the CEECs' normal trade pattern in that year in the sense that trade was not yet systematically distorted by planned economy mechanisms or war. As Collins and Rodrik point out, it is obvious that one should not expect the CEECs' 1928 pattern to re-emerge in the post-transition period, if for no other reason than the changes that have taken place in the Western countries. For instance, in 1928, the United Kingdom was the clear leader in world trade. Since 1928, however, the UK role in world trade has fallen sharply relative to that of the United States and Germany, *inter alia.* Consequently, we should expect that the United Kingdom's shares of the CEECs' trade will be systematically lower after the CEECs complete their transitions. The authors attempt to correct for this change in the importance of various market economies since 1928 by examining how the trade patterns of six Western countries changed between 1928 and 1989.

The procedure for updating the relative importance of the various Western partners of the CEECs is based on a pragmatic approach. The authors examine how the trade shares of six 'comparator' countries shifted

Table 3.12 Collins and Rodrik's import share regressions

Variable	Estimate	t-statistic
Constant	0.009	3.2
s^{28}	0.266	5.3
US dummy	0.015	1.2
Japan–South Korea–Taiwan dummy	0.053	4.8
Belgium–Luxembourg dummy	0.022	2.0
France dummy	0.072169	6.3
Germany dummy	0.169	11.7
Italy dummy	0.069	5.8
Netherlands dummy	0.033	3.1
Spain dummy	0.030	2.5
Soviet Union dummy	0.020	1.8
Eastern Europe dummy	−0.009	−1.9

Notes: $R^2 = 0.71$. Number of observations = 192. 1989 data.

between 1928 and 1989 with 33 partner countries. The 33 partners include the six comparators themselves, six of the CEECs (CSFR, Hungary, Poland, Bulgaria, Romania and Yugoslavia) and the Soviet Union. Some countries, such as Japan, South Korea and Taiwan, were combined and treated as a single partner. The six comparator countries, chosen on the basis of the authors' introspection, were Austria, Finland, Germany, Italy, Portugal and Spain. The shift is quantified by regression analysis. Namely, the 1989 shares of the six comparator countries with 33 partner countries were regressed on a constant, the 1928 share and a dummy for each partner country. That is, the estimating equation is:

$$s_{ix}^{89} = \beta_0 C + B_1 s_{ix}^{28} + \sum_j \beta_j (D_j) \tag{3.2}$$

where the D_j are dummies for each partner, with a single dummy for all CEECs. Note that this is estimated on cross-sectional data that contain 192 observations ($6 \times 533 - 6$). The idea behind this estimating equation is that the 1989 shares should be related to the 1928 shares and partner-specific shifts captured by the dummies. It may be useful to think of this regression as measuring how the trade shares of the comparator countries changed, on average, between 1928 and 1989.

This procedure is somewhat difficult to understand at first, so it is worth illustrating the point. Consider the US share of imports of the six comparator countries in 1989. These 1989 share data will constitute six of 192 observations on the dependent variable. The fitted value for each of the six observations will depend only on the US 1928 share for each of the six comparator countries and the common US dummy. Heuristically, the US dummy is estimated on only six observations. The results of the Collins and Rodrik least squares regression for import shares are reported in Table 3.12. Note that dummies with a *t*-statistic of less than one were dropped.

The results for the export shares are qualitatively similar, but the coefficient on the 1928 share is almost twice as large as the coefficient on the 1928 import share. This apparently indicates that the import patterns of the comparator countries have changed much more than the export patterns. Collins and Rodrik use the estimates from the regressions on the comparator countries to update the CEECs' 1928 trade shares. That is, they assume that the trade shares of the CEECs will change in the same way as the shares did, on average, for the comparator countries. For instance, to obtain a forecast of Hungary's post-transition trade share with Germany, they take Hungary's 1928 German import share, multiply it by 0.266, add 0.009 (i.e. the constant in the comparator country regression) and then add 0.169 (i.e. the German constant). In this way, Collins and Rodrik assume that the 1928 and modern trade patterns of the CEECs will change in the same way as the six comparator countries' pattern changed on average.

Finally, to obtain aggregate bilateral trade flows for 1988, Collins and Rodrik multiply each forecasted 1989 import and export share by the forecasted aggregate import and export totals for 1988.

Comparing Gravity Model and Collins–Rodrik

The Collins–Rodrik methodology is not based on a unified analytic framework. Nevertheless, their results are quite similar to those derived from the gravity model. Although there may be many reasons for this, a likely one is that the authors had a gravity-like model in mind when they designed their methodology. This showed in two of the choices they made in their pragmatic approach.

First, they presume that the CEECs' trade pattern in the 1990s would be related to their 1928 trade pattern. If one did not have a structural model in mind – such as the gravity model – this would seem to be a very implausible assumption. Data from 1928 would shed very little light on most aspects of the post-transformation economies in the East. For example, the relationship between money and prices in 1928 would tell us virtually nothing about what the link would look like in the 1990s since the entire monetary system and financial technology have changed. However, in trade patterns, the changes in technology are unlikely to change significantly the relative ease of trading with various partners. For instance, in 1928 it was probably much easier for a Hungarian to sell to Germany than to Ireland. Six decades of advances in communications, transportation and market integration have made it easier for a Hungarian to sell to both Ireland and Germany, but it is probably safe to say that Germany is still more accessible to Hungarians.

The second gravity-like assumption made by Collins and Rodrik shows in their choice of comparator countries. To see this, let us suppose that one believed that physical geography was only a minor determinant of trade patterns. In this case, one might have chosen comparator countries that shared similar economic structures with the CEECs, such as middle-income LDCs that have recently undergone significant transformations. Instead, the authors chose countries that are a long way from being similar to the CEECs in terms of economic structure (e.g. Germany and Austria) but are quite close geographically. Determining exactly why the Collins–Rodrik results parallel those of the gravity model would require more in-depth empirical work, but it would appear that the very strong and very stable correlation between physical distance and trade is the underpinning of both the gravity model and the Collins–Rodrik methodologies.

Notes

1. The gravitational attraction between two bodies depends upon the mass of each body and the distance separating them. An analogy with the law of gravity yields the name 'gravity model'. As we shall see, the gravity model predicts bilateral trade increases with the economic mass of the countries, but decreases with the distance that separates them.
2. Note that the tradablity of goods is itself endogenous, so this reasoning should be thought of as indicative.
3. This assumes that the right-hand-side variables are non-stochastic.
4. The easiest trade costs to think of are transport costs. However, see Chapter 2 on location effects for a more complete description of trade costs.
5. Sophie Huang did most of the actual data manipulation and all the estimations for this model.
6. The random-effects estimator is a standard panel data technique. It allows for a stochastic constant term for each bilateral trade flow.
7. Unfortunately, it was not possible to extract 1989 actual numbers for the Baltic States. However, before the dissolution of the USSR, the Baltic States engaged in very little trade with the West, so assuming that this was zero is probably not too incorrect.
8. For 'actual', the countries included are Czechoslovakia, Hungary, Poland, Romania, Yugoslavia, Albania, Bulgaria, East Germany, the USSR and other European countries not specified elsewhere. For 'potential', we take the former USSR to be the FSR-4 and the Baltic States. The 'CEECs' category consists of the Visegrad-4 plus Bulgaria, Romania, Slovenia, Croatia and Albania.
9. The actual figure is 5.14%, which is 2% times the sum of the two estimated coefficients on per capita income in the gravity model.
10. All countries for which the necessary 1989 data were available in the IMF's *Direction of Trade Statistics Yearbook* are shown.
11. The well-known Hamilton and Winters (1992) study contains estimates of East–West trade that are based on the Wang and Winters (1991) paper.
12. East–East exports, which account for 10–30% of CEECs' exports, were probably underestimated in 1991 due to under-reporting and valuation problems.
13. Bulgaria reported no trade with the USSR in 1928 or 1991.
14. See the IMF's Economic Reviews, April 1992.
15. The regression results were not reported in the Collins–Rodrik study.

PART 2

The Problem

4

The Current System

Europe's trade arrangements are evolving so rapidly that the description of them in this chapter may be out of date by the time this book is published. The changes, however, are likely to concern the extent of CEEC–CEEC free trade agreements and the number of bilateral EU–CEEC and EFTA–CEEC agreements. These developments should not affect the major thrust of the critique of the system.

4.1   Description

The current pan-European trade arrangements can be divided into West European, East–West and CEEC–CEEC. Arrangements in the western part of the continent are simple. Those in the eastern part are much more complicated.

4.1.1   *West European Trade Arrangements*

A schematic diagram of pan-European trade arrangements in early 1994 is presented in Figure 4.1. Western Europe has a 'concentric circles' trade arrangement (Figure 4.2 illustrates this term). The outer circle delimits a free trade zone for industrial goods. All countries that are encompassed by the outer circle grant duty-free status to the industrial goods of all other countries inside the outer circles. This duty-free zone did not emerge as part of a grand scheme; it is created by the joint functioning of three sets of agreements. Those governing the European Free Trade Association (EFTA) ensure duty-free trade among EFTA nations (the countries

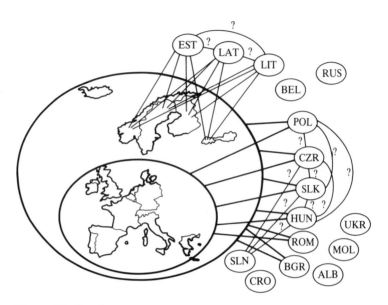

Figure 4.1 Pan-European trade arrangements in early 1994

between the inner and outer circles). The Treaty of Rome guarantees it among members of the European Union (the inner-circle countries). The bilateral free trade agreements between each EFTA nation and the EU ensure it between the two groups.

The inner circle represents the European Union (EU). Countries in this circle are integrated in ways that go far beyond duty-free treatment for industrial goods. The depth of this inner-circle integration is discussed at length in Chapter 6.

4.1.2 East–West Arrangements

East–West arrangements are dominated by the EU–ĊEEC Association Agreements, called the Europe Agreements. (See CEPR, 1992 and Rollo and Smith, 1993, for detailed critiques.) These arrangements, which comprise written agreements and modest bilateral institutional frame-works, form a very solid foundation for pan-European integration. As they stand, however, the Europe Agreements are bilateral deals. They are not an integral part of a larger scheme. When this book went to press, six CEECs had signed Association Agreements with the EU (Bulgaria, the Czech Republic, Hungary, Poland, Romania and Slovakia). Negotiations for an Association Agreement with Slovenia are to start in 1994. The EU decided

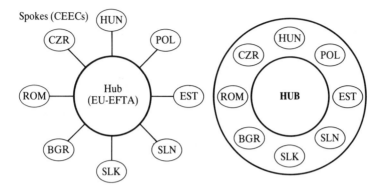

Figure 4.2 Concentric circles and hub-and-spoke trade arrangements

at its summer summit meeting in Copenhagen to negotiate free trade deals with the Baltic States and eventually offer them Europe Agreements.

The entry into force of the Europe Agreements was substantially delayed by the slow action of the parliaments of EU member states. For instance, the Europe Agreements with Hungary and Poland were signed in December 1991, but they came into force only in February 1994. Among others factors, the lack of a grand vision of Europe and of high-level political engagement in many EU member states contributed to the long delay. Meanwhile, trade between the CEECs and EU was governed by so-called Interim Agreements. The Interim Agreements can be thought of as Europe Agreements minus the political provisions. Note that a form of political dialogue was started even before the Europe Agreements came into force.

The Europe Agreements

The Europe Agreements (EAs) are evolutionary in nature. They establish frameworks for the bilateral economic and political integration of the CEECs into the European Union, including eventual EU membership. The European Council (the highest decision-making body in the EU made up of the EU heads of government) decided at their 1993 Copenhagen meeting that 'the associated countries in Central and Eastern Europe that so desire shall become members of the European Union'. This modifies the Europe Agreements that only recognize that the final objective of the CEECs is to become EU members. The Copenhagen meeting also sped up the opening of EU markets' exports from the associated countries. The six EAs are similar to each other, but are not identical. It is useful to consider the political and economic provisions of a typical Agreement separately.

Political Provisions   No timetables or explicit eligibility criteria for EU membership have been announced. The only practical political step is to open a so-called political dialogue, established by Article 2 of the EAs. This provision is quite uneven in its treatment of means and ends. On 'means', the EAs are extremely vague. It stipulates only that 'appropriate contacts, exchanges and consultations' should occur. The level of contact is quite high, involving meetings at the ministerial level, the political director for the CEECs and President of the European Council and the Commission for the EU. Meetings at the Parliamentary level are also foreseen. The EAs are much more explicit about the goals.

For the 'ends', the EAs are quite ambitious, but are still fairly short on specifics. The dialogue is meant:

1.   To accompany and consolidate the *rapprochement* of the relevant CEEC and the EU.
2.   To support the new political orders in the CEECs.
3.   To facilitate full integration of the CEEC into the 'community of democratic nations'.
4.   To bring about better mutual understanding and increasing convergence of positions on international issues.
5.   To enable the signatories to consider each other's position and interests in their internal decision-making process.
6.   To contribute to the *rapprochement* of the signatories' position on security issues.
7.   To enhance security and stability in the whole of Europe.

The political dialogue was supposed to have started only with the adoption of the Europe Agreements. At the insistence of the CEECs, a political dialogue already began under the Interim Agreements. It is particularly worth noting that the dialogue involves meetings with all six EA countries as a group despite the fact that the Europe Agreements mention only bilateral dialogues.

Economic Provisions   The EAs aim to establish bilateral free trade areas between the EU and the individual CEECs covering substantially all trade. The EU promises to remove tariffs and quantitative restrictions on most industrial products by the end of 1994. The CEECs are allowed to remove tariffs more slowly. While considerable liberalization will occur, substantial protection will remain for a group of 'sensitive' industrial products including some textiles, and some coal and steel products. All duties on steel and coal should be phased out by 1 January 1996 and those on textiles by the end of 1996. Remaining quantitive restrictions on textiles should be eliminated by the end of 1997.

Agricultural trade is mostly excluded from liberalization. Provisions in the EAs explicitly state that the Agreements 'shall not restrict in any way' the agricultural policies of the EU or the CEECs. This permits the EU to insulate the CAP from any potential impact the EAs might have.

Zero-tariff status for industrial products does not mean free access. The EU has a long history of imposing contingent protection such as anti-dumping duties and 'voluntary' export restraints (VERs). These measures are permitted under the Agreements and the EU has already imposed them on some CEEC exports. Some EFTA nations have introduced similar measures. There is a danger that without a high-level political commitment to market opening, the grand vision could be muddied by piecemeal contingent protection.

Beyond the liberalization of most industrial goods, a further goal is 'to make progress towards realizing between them the other economic freedoms on which the Community is based'. To this end, the EAs contain provisions governing the movement of services, capital and people. The Agreements progressively liberalize trade in services. They also provide for mutual 'rights of establishment' for firms as well as for mutual national treatment of establishments. The EAs open EU government procurement to CEEC firms under the same conditions as EU companies. Limited free movement of capital is guaranteed by the EAs. In particular, payments arising from the movement of goods, services and persons between the parties must be allowed (in convertible currencies). Capital transfers concerning direct investments and repatriated profits from such investments must be authorized. The movement of CEEC workers is to be governed by existing laws, although there is some imprecise language about EU members improving access of CEEC workers to their labour markets.

A very important element of the Europe Agreements is the commitment of the CEECs to adopt laws on economic and related issues that approximate the EU laws. This includes competition rules and limits on state aid to industries.

The protection of intellectual, industrial and commercial property is provided for at the same standard as applies to the Union. Economic, financial and cultural cooperation is also foreseen in the EAs. This arrangement of bilateral deals is called a 'hub-and-spoke' system (Figure 4.2 illustrates the term).

Trade Agreements with EFTA

EFTA has followed a policy of 'parallelism', that is, shadowing the EU's moves with respect to the CEECs. This policy, adopted primarily at the insistence of Sweden, is presumably intended to avoid creating even the most minor difficulties for its accession talks. The six CEECs with Europe

Agreements have signed bilateral free trade deals with EFTA nations as a whole. Other CEECs have signed such agreements with individual EFTA nations. The EFTA agreements are fairly similar to the Europe Agreements in terms of economic integration.

Due to disagreements in EFTA over the pace of market opening to the East (it would be more accurate to say 'to the south and west' for some EFTAns), several EFTAns have signed bilateral deals with several CEECs. These are shown in Figure 4.1.

4.1.3   CEEC–CEEC Agreements

There are many free trade agreements (FTAs) among the CEECs themselves and the list is growing. These CEEC–CEEC deals exist for a variety of reasons. Nonetheless, it is probably fair to say that most of them would not have been signed were it not for political pressure from EU and EFTA nations. Thus, they are in some sense rather artificial.

It is a matter of history that most FTAs among developing countries never come to fruition.[1] An IMF study by De la Torre and Kelly (1992) analyses regional trade arrangements and reviews several factors leading to the low implementation rate of FTAs among poor countries. Chapter 5 complements that with an explanation in terms of political economy on why FTAs between such countries usually fail. Whatever the reason, these CEEC–CEEC FTAs would appear to lack credibility (indicated by question marks in Figure 4.1).

The last notable aspect of Eastern trade arrangements is that some Eastern economices have no Association Agreements or bilateral FTAs, as yet. These include Slovenia, the Baltic States and Albania. In early 1994, EU relations with these countries were governed by 'Trade and Economic Cooperation Agreements' (signed with the four in May 1992). These extend MFN treatment (with GSP status), abolish specific quantitive restrictions and promote commercial and economic cooperation.

4.1.4   Arrangements with the FSR-4

For political and economic reasons, EU and EFTA trade relations with Russia, the Ukraine, Moldova and Belarus are much more limited. 'Partnership and Cooperation Agreements' are what will govern trade with these nations. There is some possibility that they will involve into free trade agreements. These links are not shown in the diagram.

4.1.5 *What's Wrong With This Picture?*

The current pan-European trade arrangement is far from the worst possible. The trade liberalization that has already been promised, especially the bilateral deals between the CEECs and the EU, constitutes an important step towards reintegrating the eastern and western parts of the European continent. These Association Agreements (also known as the Europe Agreements) are the foundation of Europe's post-Communist trade system. Nevertheless, the current pan-European trade system has three significant shortcomings.

1. Some Eastern nations have not yet been included.
2. Hub-and-spoke bilateralism is an inferior means of organizing trade relations.
3. The steps to closer integration are extremely uneven.

The first shortcoming is a problem for the not-yet-included nations. In the 1950s and 1960s, duty-free status in Western Europe provided an important preference. Now, zero tariffs on manufactured goods in Europe is the norm. For instance, more than 80% of Germany's imports of manufactured goods come from countries which have a duty-free status. Accordingly, it is more accurate to view European free trade agreements as levelling the playing field rather than providing preferential access. Firms that are without duty-free privileges suffer from an artificial disadvantage. This is quite important since Western Europe is the major market for the CEEC-based firms. The decision of the 1993 Copenhagen meeting of the European Council commits the EU to remedying this shortcoming, so this book devotes no further space to the issue. The second two shortcoming are discussed in the following chapters.

Note

1. Approximately 130 FTAs have been notified to the GATT (as is required by GATT Article XXIV). Of these, only a handful have been successful in any meaningful sense.

5

Hub-and-spoke Bilateralism

The Europe Agreements and the EFTA Association Agreements constitute a hub-and-spoke trade arrangement. This chapter examines the effects of such a system. It argues that such an arrangement is better than no liberalization all, but that it marginalizes the 'spoke' economies. To put the point more colloquially, this chapter points out that a hub-and-spoke arrangement is a half-empty glass. Perceptive readers, however, will understand that this admits that the glass is already half-full. The chapter concludes with an analysis of the political economy forces that tend to support hub-and-spoke bilateralism.

5.1   Economic Effects

As a general operating principle, more trade liberalization is better than less. The East–West liberalization that Europe is currently experiencing is a very positive development. The market opening promised in the Europe Agreements and EFTA–CEEC trade agreements allow market forces to operate more freely, thereby resulting in positive allocation and accumulation effects. The general logic of these effects was explored in more detail in Chapter 2, so they are not repeated here. One point, however, which deserves to be stressed is that liberalization between large and small economies typically benefits a small economy proportionately more than the large one. This section focuses on the gains that are lost by having a hub-and-spoke arrangement instead of a more general liberalization of all trade flows in Europe.

5.1.1 *Allocation Effects*

As we saw in Chapter 2, a country that lowers tariffs on imports from some of its trade partners but not on others provides an artificial incentive for domestic residents to switch their purchases away from the non-favoured trade partner. This may be harmful to the country since it may involve diverting trade from low- to high-cost producers. By favouring imports from the hub a hub-and-spoke trade arrangement may lead to this sort of trade diversion. Joining together in a regional free trade area decreases this possibility since it reduces the fraction of trade that is divertable.

Rules of Origin Costs

A web of trade deals can create a nightmarish tangle of administrative procedures that raise costs for enterprises and for governments. Most costly of all are those dealing with 'rules of origin'. These involve proving that a product was actually made in a country benefiting from a preferential trade arrangement. For example, the Europe Agreements mean that Poland charges lower tariffs (eventually zero tariffs) on goods made in Germany than on those made in, say, Lithuania. This provides importers with an incentive to buy Lithuanian goods and repackage them as German ones before importing them into Poland. To foil this, preferential trade agreements have rules on how to decide where a good comes from. The problem is that it is expensive for private firms and governments to verify the origins of all imports. In the CEECs, public and private administration of manifold rules of origin would siphon off skilled labour. It would also open the door to corruption, since switching the country of origin on products to import them under a lower tariff rate can save importers millions of dollars a year. Unscrupulous importers may be tempted to share profits with customs officers. These problems exist with any preferential trade arrangement, but problems grow as the web of FTAs becomes more complex.

The costs of 'rules of origin' can be further minimized if the CEECs adopted external tariff rates that equalled those of the EC. This would lessen the need for the EC to control goods arriving from CEECs, since there would be no incentive to route third-country goods through the CEECs to avoid EC tariffs.

Restricted Pro-competitive Effect

An additional allocation effect of a hub-and-spoke agreements is to restrict competition from CEEC-based firms. For the most part, competition from EU-based firms would provide all the competition that is needed. However, in certain industries, CEEC-based firms will be more competitive. For instance, in labour-intensive industries such as textiles, clothing and shoes, intra-CEEC may be an important source of competition. Similarly, in some service industries that are labour-intensive, such as construction, intra-CEEC competition could play an important role in stimulating CEEC firms.

5.1.2   *Investment-deterring Effect*

The physical geography of the CEECs (especially the Visegrad group and Slovenia) highly favours integration with Western Europe. An important goal of policy should be to translate this favourable physical geography into favourable economic geography. Here we argue that the hub-and-spoke trade arrangements negotiated by the CEECs exert a marginalizing effect on them. The argument requires an understanding of the theory of 'economic geography' discussed in Chapter 2.

The marginalizing tendencies of hub-and-spoke FTAs can be illustrated with a numerical example. Figure 5.1 shows a hypothetical example, which intentionally puts to the side several important issues. Let us imagine there are three locations being considered as the site for a new manufacturing facility: Germany and two East European sites, one in Hungary and one in Poland. For simplicity, assume that the division of sales among markets is fixed irrespective of costs, with 75% sold in the EU and 12.5% sold in each Eastern country. (This simplification allows us to separate cost considerations from those of demand.) Let us assume that the unit production costs would be 10 if the plant is located in the EU, 8 if the plant is located in Hungary or Poland and 15 if three separate plants must be built. Economies of scale explain the high cost of separating production; lower CEEC wages explain why the EU location means higher production costs.

To start that analysis, let us assume initially that there are no FTAs, so unit trade costs amounted to 6 for the two East–West bilateral trade flows as well as for East–East trade. Unit trade costs within any of the three markets are normalized to zero. The simplified problem facing the potential manufacturer is to choose the location with the lowest costs. Without FTAs, the cost-minimizing location for the plant is the EU. The average cost in Hungary or Poland is 13.25 – 8 for production plus an average trade cost of (3/4)*6 plus (1/8)*0 plus (1/8)*6. This surpasses the EU costs of 11.5. The high unit production cost in the EU is more than offset by the lower average trade cost.

Let us envision the impact of hub-and-spoke bilateralism on this outcome and presume that EU–Hungary and EU–Poland FTAs take effect, cutting the unit cost of East–West trade to 3. East–East trade costs remain at 6. Arithmetic shows that the average unit cost of locating the

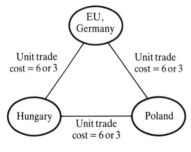

Unit production costs:
10 in EU, 8 in Eastern Europe

Figure 5.1 Numerical example of investment-deterring effects of hub-and-spoke trade arrangements

plant in the EU is still lower (10.75) than doing so in Hungary or Poland (11). Although the FTAs lower East–West trade costs, trade costs within the EU are lower yet, so there is still some market size effect favouring the EU location. Location in the EU confers preferential access to all three markets, not just two.

Finally, let us consider the impact of turning the hub-and-spoke FTAs into a free trade zone by implementation of a Hungary-Poland FTA. Here we see that the total unit costs of locating in Hungary or Poland are lower (10.625) than doing so in the EU (10.75). Although location in the EU implies zero trade costs for 75% of the manufacturer's sales, the lower East European production costs finally become the dominant issue.

Of course, this simple illustration is not general, and we do not mean that filling the gaps between 'spokes' will lead to a tidal wave of foreign investment into the CEECs. Nevertheless, the basic message is clear. Hub-and-spoke FTAs tend to marginalize the 'spoke' economies, since factories in the 'spokes' have artificially lower market access than factories in the hub. Consequently hub-and-spoke FTAs render an artificial deterrent to investment in the outer economies. Filling the gaps with spoke–spoke FTAs removes this policy-induced investment deterrent.

It may seem natural to consider a production cost differential that was much larger than the 8–10 since wages in the East are so much lower than EU wages. The reader can work out that a larger production cost advantage would change the results, making the CEEC location always cheaper. There are two responses to this. What matters for location are relative wages corrected for productivity. Thus, while Eastern wages may be a small fraction of those in Western Europe, the productivity of facilities located in the East also tend to be low. An extreme example serves to illustrate the point. If low wages were the key to low-cost manufacturing, Bangladesh would be an industrial powerhouse. The second response is that, whatever the average production cost differential, this investment-deterring effect would operate on the margin. That is, there will always be some marginal investment deterred by the existence of CEEC–CEEC barriers.

Hub-and-spoke FTAs make the Eastern economies even smaller than they need be. Another way of saying this is that signing bilateral trade deals with the hub, without signing deals with the spokes, is self-inflicted peripherality. By making small economies smaller than they need be, a hub-and-spoke system reinforces firms' tendency to locate in the central market, i.e. the EU.

5.1.3 Negative Impact on EU Firms

The other side of the investment-deterring effect is lower profits for EU firms doing business in the East. That is, trade barriers between CEECs – and the possibility that such barriers may be erected in the future – inhibit many normal commercial practices. For instance, current or future East–East barriers would constrain Western firms that wished to supply several CEECs from manufacturing, servicing or storage facilities that were concentrated in one country in the region. In the numerical example, the costs faced by the EU firm in supplying the two Eastern markets are higher with the hub-and-spoke arrangement than with the free trade one. Thus, the EU firms should also support the extension of free trade between the CEECs.

5.1.4 Hysteresis in Location

A key lesson from the literature on the 'new' location is that the location of economic activity is marked by multiple outcomes. That is, there is not a single constellation of economic concentrations towards which Europe is inevitably heading. There is uncertainty about what it will look like. Moreover, once a particular location gets a head-start, it may be extremely difficult for other regions to catch up. The import of all this is that the temporary investment-deterring effects of the current hub-and-spoke system may have consequences that last far beyond the termination of that system. In other words, bad policies – even when they are only temporary – may have very long-lived harmful consequences.

For example, let us suppose that a large Central European market emerges around Austria, Germany, Slovenia, Poland, Hungary, the Czech Republic and Slovakia. The location of the new industrial concentrations in this area is not determined. Yet once a location gets a head-start, it will be difficult for others to catch up (see Chapter 2 for further details). The importance of all this should be clear. Since hub-and-spoke bilateralism favours location in the 'hub', five or ten years of hub-and-spoke bilateralism will give German and Austrian locations a head-start on CEEC locations. Thus, much of the new industry may eventually locate in Germany and Austria. Given the logic of economic geography, even EU membership in ten years might not be enough to offset the initial head-start. The circular causality will continue to favour regions that do have a head-start. The effect of a bad policy may be felt long after the policy is reversed.

5.1.5 *Accumulation Effects*

Chapter 2 explained how trade liberalization may stimulate investment in the medium run, thereby raising growth in that period. Viewing a hub-and-spoke system as an incomplete liberalization, we can apply Chapter 2's arguments to say that the hub-and-spoke system will increase growth less than would a more complete liberalization. The same is true for long-term growth effects, since the incentives for local accumulation of human capital and knowledge capital are similar to those encouraging physical capital accumulation.

5.1.6 *Political Marginalization*

At the moment, countries as diverse as the United States, Germany and Iceland are opening their markets to CEEC goods. This extension of favourable market access, however, has been based largely on sentiment and foreign policy reasons instead of on Western commercial interests. Unfortunately, the West's 'honeymoon' sentiment towards the CEECs is likely to fade well before they have completed the transition to market economies and have attained Western income levels. To lock-in market access gains, and secure further market access, it is important that access to the CEECs' own markets attracts a good deal of commercial interest from Western firms. As argued above, it is in the interests of domestic firms to gain access to a foreign market that leads a government to engage in an exchange of market access. From the political (not economic) point of view a trade negotiation involves 'buying' foreign market access with the currency of domestic market access. The individual CEECs are likely to become much more interesting commercially as they grow in the coming years, but individually they will remain small.

An interesting example of the too-small-to-matter syndrome can be found in the plight of Switzerland. When it became clear that the EU's

Single Market programme threatened EFTA-based industries with a loss of relative competitiveness, EFTAn governments approached the Community and requested negotiations. The aim was essentially to relevel the playing field by allowing the EFTAns to participate in the Single Market. Although all the EFTA economies are individually small, together they constitute an important market for EU exporters. Accordingly, the EFTAns persuaded EU leaders to focus on the issue. The result was the European Economic Area (EEA) agreement (see Baldwin et al., 1992, for the details of this reasoning). As history would have it, Swiss voters rejected the EEA agreement in December 1992. Since then, the Swiss government has attempted to negotiate with the EU to relevel the playing field by another means. The results to date have been negligible. The main problem is that Switzerland is just too small to matter. Mercantilism's 'law of the jungle' means that small countries acting on their own are often ignored. In this case, the political benefits that EU leaders might gain by engaging in market-opening discussions with Switzerland are negligible, so protectionist forces in the EU triumph. Additionally, the commercial gains may be considered too insignificant to be worth serious attention by EU leaders.

Several CEECs now have FTAs with Western Europe. However, these agreements are not ironclad. In the modern world, barriers to trade go much deeper than tariffs, so CEECs cannot be content to remain with whatever FTAs they manage to negotiate during the honeymoon. Moreover, the EC has a long history of imposing contingent protection such as arbitrary anti-subsidy and anti-dumping duties, as well as 'voluntary' export restraints (VERs) on small countries that have successfully expanded exports to the EC. Many newly industrializing countries in Asia have had their export booms hindered by just such policies. The same protectionist interests are likely to attempt to block the CEECs' rapid export growth. Countering such developments will require bargaining power.

A slightly different problem could eventually arise concerning CEEC trade with the former Soviet republics. As these republics start to develop, they may face pressures to raise barriers against the CEECs' exports. This would harm CEEC exporters since, in the long run, these markets will be one of the CEECs' natural trading partners.

5.1.7 *Artificial Discouragement of CEEC–CEEC Trade*

The intra-CEEC trade barriers retard the development of East–East trade. This is particularly harmful to exporters based in these countries since the CEECs might the fastest-growing markets in Europe. Chapter 3 shows that trade among the CEECs has the potential to account for 20–30% of their European exports.

In addition to these harmful economic effects, the current system of hub-and-spoke bilateralism is an aberration in Western Europe's post-Second World War history. This point is discussed in more detail in Chapter 1.

5.2   Political Economy of Hub-and-spoke Bilateralism

Section 2.5 argued that the political economy of trade negotiation is a happy coincidence of mistakes.[1] From a political perspective, exports are good and imports are bad. A more subtle expression of this idea is that trade is good because trade creates jobs. No matter how it is expressed, this idea is nonsense from the medium- or long-run economic perspective (see Section 2.5 for more detail). However, the important fact is that this mistaken reasoning points governments in the right direction. It leads them to conduct trade negotiations based on an exchange of market access. Specifically, since exports are good and imports bad, if country A wants better access to country's B's markets, then country A is expected to 'pay' for this market access by opening its own market to B's exports.[2]

Usually, the market openings that result from this mistaken reasoning are good for all nations involved. A drawback of this mechanism, however, is that it may create a law of the jungle. That is, with market access as the currency of exchange, large countries are rich and small ones are poor. The rules of the GATT correct this imbalance with the principle of most-favoured-nations (MFN) treatment. However, when negotiating regional trade arrangements, the MFN does not apply, so the law of the jungle may prevail.

Political economy forces created by an application of this law of the jungle support hub-and-spoke bilateralism. Let us take a country like the Czech Republic. On the pro-liberalization side, Czech exporters have a large interest in the EU market, but only a minor interest in the market of, say, Estonia. On the anti-liberalization side, Czech import-competing industries dislike imports whether they come from the EU, Estonia or elsewhere. Now let us consider the political forces inside the Czech Republic. Czech exporters are willing to fight quite hard for market opening with the large EU market. They are willing to fight much less hard for market opening with Estonia. In other words, there are strong political forces backing market opening with the 'hub' but very little support for it with other 'spokes'. Since Czech protectionists simply want to reduce import competition from any source, they are likely to win in blocking spoke–spoke liberalization, although they may lose in hub–spoke liberalization.

An interesting additional effect may occur if foreign investment from the hub is important in the spoke economies. To attract foreign investors, the spoke governments may promise protection from imports. Moreover, given a credible trade agreement with the hub, it is much easier for the spoke government to promise long-term protection against imports from other spoke economies. If this sort of pandering-for-investment protectionism becomes quite common, the spoke economies may eventually be 'Balkanized'. That is, foreign multinationals may be enticed into locating inefficiently small production facilities in each spoke economy. Having done this, the multinationals may become a new anti-liberalization force. Companies from the hub that have invested in inefficiently small facilities in several spoke economies may resist efforts to liberalize spoke–spoke trade. This may make the hub governments more reluctant to take any initiative in redressing hub-and-spoke bilateralism.

5.2.1 *Why FTAs between Developing Nations Usually Fail*

If some unusual event creates a great wave of enthusiasm for brotherhood among the spoke economies, politicians in these countries may sign agreements promising to open spoke–spoke trade. Yet once the headlines fade and the enthusiasm wanes, the drab politics of protectionism usually reasserts itself. Promises are broken, or never fulfilled, and the expected liberalization never appears. Moreover, since protectionist forces reappear in both spoke economies, the broken promises are generally accepted without protest. Note how different the situation is for spoke–hub trade arrangements. Exporters in both the hub and the spoke (but especially those in the spoke economies) care a good deal about access to each others' markets. Accordingly, exporters would raise their voices if promises were not kept. That is, the same sort of backsliding that is common in spoke–spoke agreements will not be tolerated in hub–spoke trade deals.

5.2.2 *The 'Passing Parade' Pandering Problem*

Some competition among CEEC governments for foreign direct investment is probably a healthy thing for all parties. Inward investment is promoted by policies such as guaranteed profit remittances, property rights assurances (especially for intellectual property rights) and an absence of trade-related investment measures such as export requirements and local content rules. Although this is well understood, governments throughout the world often do not adopt such policies, for domestic political reasons. Competition among CEECs for Western foreign direct investment (FDI) is an effective way of ensuring that they adhere to FDI policies that are in their best interest in any case.

However, too much competition among CEEC policy makers could lead to an inferior, non-cooperative outcome. The basic problem can be exemplified with the so-called 'passing parade' parable. Let us imagine that a crowd gathers to watch a parade. As the parade passes, people in the front stand on their toes to see better, thus forcing all those behind them also to stand on their toes. In the end, most see no better than before, but all have to stand on their toes.

In the CEECs, potential investors, foreign and domestic alike, have an incentive to ask for import protection as a condition for making their investments. If, however, all CEECs succumb to this pandering and erect trade barriers to attract investment or retain jobs, they could all eventually be 'standing on their toes' without results. This destructive competition could backfire. Each country's uncoordinated pandering to foreign investors could lead to trade barriers that lower the overall attractiveness of the region, thus resulting in less investment in each country. Of course, given the political power of EU exporters, it will be much more difficult for the CEEC governments to promise protection against imports from the EU. But a hub-and-spoke system allows a free hand to erect barriers against imports from other CEECs.

Notes

1. This is just a convenient way of expressing the notion that the politics and economics of trade negotiations are mismatched. Governments are not mistaken, they are simply interested in maximizing political support rather than national welfare. The happy coincidence is that higher national welfare is a byproduct of the political optimization.
2. Note that import liberalizations are called 'concessions' by trade negotiators. This is absurd from the point of view of national welfare, since the 'concession' benefits the welfare of the conceding nation. Indeed, it may help the conceding nation more than the country that wins the 'concession'.

6

No Intermediate Steps

At present, Eastern nations face three steps towards closer integration. The first two – GATT membership and Association Agreements with the EU and EFTA – are relatively easy. The third step – EU membership – is extremely difficult for EU incumbents and the CEECs alike.

6.1   Three Uneven Steps to EU Membership

It took the EU nations 35 years to work their way up to their current degree of integration. A series of stages was involved, namely the Common Market, the Single European Act, and the Treaty on European Union. As it stands, these sub-steps are combined into one large step – EU membership. No new EU entrant has ever taken as large a step as is currently being contemplated by the CEECs.

6.1.1   Description of the Three Steps

This point is shown schematically in Figure 6.1. The diagram necessarily glosses over many details, but it reflects the major stages of economic integration. The first step is GATT membership. The second is duty-free trade in industrial goods. The third step in the diagram consists of three sub-steps that are referred to as sub-steps one, two and three. Sub-step one is the Treaty of Rome. This extended free trade to all products and opened up labour mobility to a large extent. This included free trade in agricultural goods and the common agricultural policy (CAP). Moreover, it entailed a common external tariff and supranational institutions with real power. The

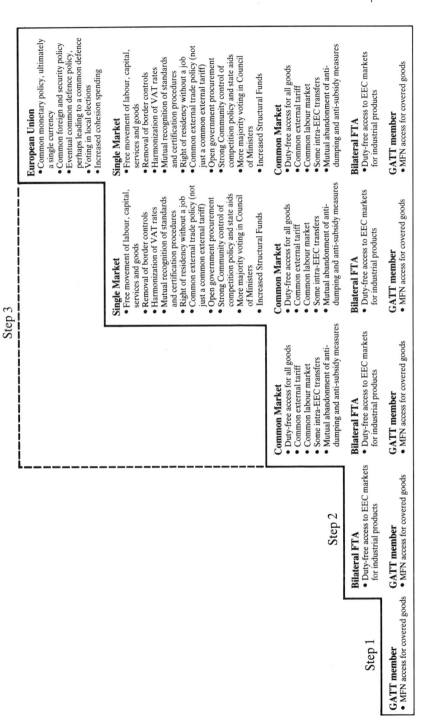

Figure 6.1 The three uneven steps to integration

most important of these are the Council of Ministers and the European Court of Justice.

Sub-step two is the 1992 Single Market programme, formally called the Single European Act. The Single Market re-enforced the free movement of labour and goods and secured the free movement of capital and services. This included guaranteeing the right of establishment for EU firms in all EU countries and it opened all the purchases of EU governments to competition from any EU-based firm. The 1992 programme also instituted mutual recognition of health and safety standards and the certification procedures of all member states (with some exceptions), substantially harmonized value-added taxes (VAT), and strengthened supranational control of competition policy and national subsidies. Finally, Structural Fund spending was doubled and qualified majority voting was adopted for many issues in the Council of Ministers.

It is easy to forget just how radical the 1992 programme was. It constituted a quantum leap in economic integration for the EU. For several years after its adoption many wondered whether the economies of Western Europe could tolerate such a shock. In fact, the changes necessary to implement the Single European Act are so radical that many of the EU-12 have not yet passed all the legislation that was supposed to have been in place at the end of 1992. EU businesses are still in the midst of adjusting to the new laws and practices.

Sub-step three is the Treaty on European Union, widely known by the name of the town in which it was signed, Maastricht. The Treaty commits members to another significant deepening of integration, although most of the integration is scheduled to occur several years in the future. On the economic side, Maastricht commits EU members to a monetary union, ultimately including a single currency. On the political side, it promises common security and defence policies, leading perhaps to a common defence. It also increases the powers of the European Parliament and creates EU citizenship. Most of this has been agreed but not yet implemented. Despite this, Maastricht is relevant to the current restructuring of trade arrangements in Europe. Much more progress will have been made on the Maastricht promises by the time EU membership is a serious issue for the CEECs. Additionally, EU membership for the CEECs will affect the extent to which the Treaty is implemented. Most CEECs are more integrationist than many EU incumbents, at least as far as common foreign, security and defence policies are concerned.

6.2   Historical Widening and Deepening of the EU

The lessons of previous EU enlargements are widely misunderstood. Many, for instance, take the case of Greece as an inspiration since it entered just

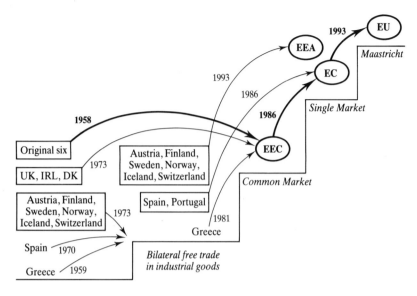

Figure 6.2   Historical widening and deepening of the EU

seven years after democracy was restored in that country. This chapter argues that the 1980s enlargement of the EU has almost no relevance for the CEECs. The point is that the Community that Greece, Portugal and Spain joined no longer exists – their accession irrevocably altered it.[1] Furthermore, this section shows that the unevenness of the steps now facing the CEECs is not at all in line with the EU's historical experience. Winters (1993) provides a more thorough description and analysis of EU enlargements.

6.2.1   *Early Years of the Common Market*

Figure 6.2 summarizes the major steps that are described in this section. The current EU was formed when the Treaty of Rome went into effect in 1958. At that time six countries joined. Although it was often called the Common Market, the EEC of the 1950s and 1960s did not live up to its name. It was not until 1968 that all tariffs were removed on intra-EEC trade.

In 1961, the EEC signed an Association Agreement with Greece. In 1970 it signed one with Spain. Thus, Greece and Spain took their first step towards eventual membership – the step of bilateral free trade in industrial goods – 20 years and 16 years before their respective accessions.

6.2.2   *North-west Enlargement in the 1970s*

Negotiations concerning the first enlargement started in 1970 soon after the EEC had accomplished its goal of removing all internal tariffs and quotas. Four north-west European countries were involved.[2] This enlargement was not easy. These same countries had applied almost ten years early, only to be denied entry. Their re-application in 1966 and 1967 was essentially ignored by the Community until the end of the decade. It was not until December 1969 that the EEC-6 decided to open accession negotiations with the four applicants. The accession treaties were signed in January 1972. Interestingly, the delays and the first refusal were due to doubts about the United Kingdom's 'Europeanness'. To quote Owen and Dynes (1989), 'the British application was vetoed by de Gaulle – the first French "non" – in 1963, on the grounds that Britain's ties were transatlantic rather than European'.

When the United Kingdom, Ireland and Denmark joined, the EEC was not much more than a free trade zone with common external tariffs and some harmonization of sectoral policies. The most important of these was the Common Agriculture Policy and the Coal and Steel Community. The Treaty of Rome did allow for a common labour market.

The countries in this enlargement consisted of three fairly prosperous nations (the United Kingdom, Denmark and Norway) and one poor but very small country (Ireland, with 3.5 million people) that had close trade ties with another entrant (the United Kingdom). Clearly, this enlargement did not significantly increase the economic diversity of the EEC. The EEC-6 consisted of three powerhouse economies (West Germany, France and Italy) and three small, rich countries (Luxembourg, Belgium and the Netherlands). The EEC-9 was made up of four large economies, four small, rich economies and one very small, poor one. Ireland's per capita GDP was about 50% of the EEC-6 average upon accession.

This enlargement, however, did greatly increase the political diversity of the EEC. It introduced one of the great schisms that marks European politics. The original 'Six' form the core of the 'deepeners' (nations devoted to deep integration, eventually leading to political union) while the United Kingdom and Denmark form the core of the 'wideners' (nations preferring shallow integration limited to economics).

The economic changes implied by this first enlargement were not substantial. The most important was the lowering of tariffs in a geographically discriminatory manner. All the EEC-9 economies were heavily regulated by today's standards. In particular, capital mobility was very limited. As noted above, when the United Kingdom, Denmark and Ireland joined the EEC, the remaining six EFTAns signed bilateral free trade agreements with the EEC. These changes are summarized by the leftmost set of arrows in Figure 6.2.

6.2.3   *Southern Enlargement in the 1980s*

Democracy was restored in Portugal, Greece and Spain in 1974, 1975 and 1977, respectively, although the political situation in Portugal remained unstable for several years. Greece applied for EEC membership in 1975 and Portugal and Spain followed two years later. Their returns to democracy were critical in allowing these countries to proceed with applications for membership in the EEC. While democracy is a good thing in its own right, it is critical for membership in a body like the EEC. The point here is that member states must be able to make credible commitments to long-run policies. Authoritarian governments cannot do this. The government that follows their eventual downfall usually feels no obligation to carry out the promises made by the dictator. Of course, this is a problem even in well-functioning democracies, but it is much less severe.

Greece was admitted six years after it had tendered its application. The Community it joined bears little resemblance to today's EU-12. The EEC-9 had a population in excess of 250 million. There was also only one poor country among the incumbents. Moreover, although Greece was poor (its per capita income was only 80% that of Ireland and only 41% of the EEC-9 average), it had only 10 million citizens. Thus, as with Ireland, Greece seemed to pose only a minor burden on the incumbents. The EEC-9's desire to lock-in democratic reforms in the 'cradle of European democracy' played a large part in the decision to admit Greece.

Compared with the degree of integration implied by the Maastricht Treaty, membership did not involve a big step for Greece. The Single European Act (i.e. the 1992 programme) had not yet been conceived. As noted above, the EEC at the time was very little more than a Customs Union and a Common Agricultural Policy.

Five years later Spain and Portugal joined. This brought the EEC up to its current strength of twelve. These countries joined knowing that they would have to comply with the Single European Act. Since this Act stipulated an extremely large increase in the integration of all Community nations, Spain and Portugal faced a considerable step to membership. However, this was not the first stage in either country's integration with Europe. Spain had had a free trade agreement with the Community since 1970; Portugal was a former EFTAn.

Political Changes

The accession of the Iberians created a group of countries – the 'poor-four' – that favours redistributive policies in the Community. This drastically altered EU politics. For instance, at each of the major steps towards closer integration taken since the poor-four (the Single European Act and Maastricht), the amount of transfers was greatly increased.

It is important to point out the implications of this change for future enlargements of the EU. It appears that many in Central Europe take heart from the accession of Greece, Portugal and Spain. After all, the reasoning goes, if Greece can do it, so can we. *The simple fact that Greece and the Iberians entered the EU is almost entirely moot for the CEECs. The Community that Greece, Portugal and Spain joined no longer exists. Their accession fundamentally altered it.* In particular, by creating a group of countries that benefit greatly from EC largesse, the Southern enlargement of the EC created a group of countries that will oppose the accession of more poor ones.

When Greece joined, Ireland was the only other poor country. When Spain and Portugal joined, the Greeks and Irish together accounted for only about 5% of the EEC population. Now the poor-four account for about one-fifth of the EU's population. More to the point, they are very close to having a blocking minority in the Council of Ministers, so their political power outstrips their numbers (see Chapter 7 for more details).

6.2.4   *North-east Enlargement in the 1990s*

The most recent enlargement exercise began in 1992. It has gone smoothly and rapidly by all accounts (compared with previous enlargements). As it looks now, the accession treaties for Finland, Austria, Norway and Sweden (the 'FANS') will probably be ready in 1994 or 1995.[3] Given Europe's general economic malaise and the tarnishing of the EU's image by the Maastricht muddle and the EMS crises, it is less certain that the electorates of these four will allow their leaders to join the Union. Nevertheless, the economic climate in Europe appears to be recovering as the recession ends, so membership should look a better economic prospect. The political uncertainties in Russia are also likely to play an important role. The fear of what might happen if authoritarianism returns to Russia might persuade Austrians, Finns and Swedes to vote 'yes'. Such arguments will carry less weight with Norwegians. Norway is already a NATO member.

The continuing FANS enlargement is a straightforward affair. The acceding nations are rich, small and have agricultural sectors that are even more protected than those of the EU. Accordingly, their entry threatens neither of the two most powerful special interests in the Community: the poor-four and the farmers. On the contrary, both groups would probably be helped. The EFTAns entry would help incumbent EU farmers to hold on to their beloved CAP because the new members would be net importers at the current CAP prices.[4] The poor-four would be helped since the rich taxpayers in the FANS will increase the EU's coffers.

The FANS enlargement is comparatively easy. The reason is that the great majority of the policy changes necessary to bring the FANS policies into line with the EU's were already accomplished in the EEA agreement talks. The FANS had already agreed to accept almost all the *Acquis communautaire* pertaining to the Single Market. This is shown in Figure 6.2 where an arrow takes the EFTAns into the EEA. The most difficult issues in the FANS accession talks involve special payments to remote regions of the FANS, special payments to Arctic and Alpine farmers, and several specific issues such as fish, environment standards and health and public regulations.

6.2.5   *Summarizing the Historical Steps towards Integration*

In guessing how soon the CEECs will be ready for EU membership it is easy to overlook just how hard it was for the incumbents to reach their current degree of integration. Moreover, the EU has committed itself to a radical deepening of its economic integration in the past ten years. This deepening has been so extreme that many incumbents have not been able to implement it. For instance, the Single European Act was supposed to have been fully implemented by the end of 1992, yet some member states have yet to pass all the necessary legislation. The final stage of economic integration, Economic and Monetary Union, is foreseen for 1996 or 1999, according to the Maastricht Treaty. Few analysts believe that a majority of EU members can meet the convergence criteria by the earlier date. This is just too large a step for many West European economies to take in such a short time. There are a growing number of economists and government officials who view even the 1999 target as premature. To them, the degree of economic and political integration that would be necessary to support a monetary union is not likely to be possible for quite some time.

Table 6.1 shows the number of years each EU member spent at the major steps towards integration. The entrants are listed in reverse chronological order. The three rightmost columns require some speculation since the EU is in the midst of a substantial widening and a large deepening that involves much uncertainty.

The FANS Enlargement

Let us turn first to the ongoing FANS enlargement. These countries had bilateral duty-free industrial trade with the EU for two decades before taking the next step towards integration. The European Economic Area (EEA) is the Single Market stage for the acceding EFTAns (see Chapter 1 for more details on the EEA). This came into being in 1993. It is possible that the FANS will not be able to join before 1996, although the official target of January 1995 may still be met. This means that the FANS

Table 6.1 Number of years spent at each integration step (including transition periods)

	Bilateral free trade in industrial products	Common Market (1958–86)	Single Market (1986–93)	Economic and Monetary Union (1993–99?)	Total years for four steps
Austria, Sweden, Finland, Norway	20	Skip	3	3	26
Spain	16	Skip	7	6	29
Portugal	13	Skip	7	6	26
Greece	20	5	7	6	38
Ireland, Denmark, United Kingdom	Skip	13	7	6	26
Original six	Skip	28	7	6	41
CEECs (optimistic scenario)	8–10	Skip	Skip	Skip	8–10

Notes: The table assumes that Austria, Sweden, Finland and Norway will accede to the EU in 1996 and that monetary union occurs in 1999 for all EU members.
NB: Single Market step is EEA for EFTAns.

will spend two or three years at the Single Market stage. Indeed, since the FANS started adopting the *Acquis communautaire* in 1992, it might be more accurate to think of them having at least three or four years to adjust to the radical changes implied by adherence to the Union's economic laws. The move to a monetary union is supposed to occur by the end of the decade at the latest. Table 6.1 assumes that all EU members will achieve this level of integration by 1999. Based on these assumptions, it will have taken the FANS 26 years to climb the integration steps that lead from a market economy to the European Union.

Spain

Spain spent 16 years at the equivalent of the Association Agreements stage. It skipped the Common Market stage jumping straight up to the Single Market step. Note, however, that this jump up to the Single Market was very difficult for Spain. Evidence for this can be found in the fact that it was granted long transition periods (up to 15 years) for many Single Market measures. Moreover, the pain of the radical economic changes that were necessary for them to integrate with the comparatively liberal EU was eased by very large transfers from EU coffers. In particular, the European Regional Development Fund was substantially increased as part of the accession of Spain and Portugal. This is interesting, since although Spain's economy was heavily regulated by Western standards, Spain in the mid-1980s was very market-oriented compared with the CEECs of just five years ago. Spain is in fairly good shape as far as meeting the EMU criteria is concerned, so there is some hope that it would actually complete that in 1999. On this assumption, it will have taken Spain 29 years to climb the European integration ladder.

Portugal

Portugal joined the EU when Spain did, but since it is a former EFTAn it has had bilateral free trade in manufactures only since 1973. Thus, Portugal spent 16 years at the first step. Like Spain, it skipped straight to the Single Market but did so with the help of long transition periods and massive transfers. The full climb will have taken Portugal 26 years, if it joins the EMU in 1999. It is not at all certain, however, that Portugal will be ready for monetary union by that date.

Greece

Greece had an Association Agreement for 20 years before it joined the Community. It had five years of experience with the Common Market before adoption of the Single European Act. Its parliament has still not adopted all the Single European Act measures. Virtually everyone agrees that Greece will not be ready to take the final step to EMU by the end of this decade. Greece has not participated in the discipline of the European Monetary System's Exchange Rate Mechanism. Its debt to GDP ratio is approaching 100% and in 1991 it ran a public sector deficit that was more than 15% of its GDP. Given the poor state of its public finances, it is no surprise that Greek inflation and interest rates are far above what would be required to meet the EMU convergence criteria. If, by some miracle, Greece does manage to join the EMU in 1999, it will have taken 38 years to reach Economic and Monetary Union.

Ireland, Denmark, United Kingdom

Ireland, Denmark and the United Kingdom joined in 1973, skipping the bilateral free trade step. They spent 13 years at the Common Market stage and seven years at the Single Market stage. Ireland and Denmark have received massive transfers from the Structural Funds and the CAP. Ireland faces a serious problem in getting its debt/GDP ratio down to acceptable levels by 1999, but its low current deficit and inflation rate provide a positive signal. Twenty-six years will have elapsed between these countries' first steps toward integration and participation in the EMU in 1999.

The original EEC-6 nations spent almost three decades at the Common Market stage, seven years at the Single Market one and six years getting to the EMU stage.

Optimistic Case for the CEECs

To illustrate the contrast, the last row of Table 6.1 shows the optimistic scenario for the most advanced CEECs. Some analysts assume that accession talks with the Visegrad group will begin soon after the FANS enlargement is completed in 1995 or 1996. Given the usual delays involved, even the most optimistic scenario envisions membership for the CEECs around the turn of the century. This would give the CEECs 8–10 years (depending upon whether one counts from the Interim Agreements or the Europe Agreements) at the bilateral free trade stage. They would skip the Common Market and the Single Market directly to Economic and Monetary Union. All this would take no more than a decade.

The lessons of history are vague, since so many factors affect major political and economic events. Moreover, there is no good reason to think that the number of years taken by previous EU entrants has any implications for how long it will take the CEECs to enter. One point, however, is indisputable. If the Visegrad nations manage to take the very large step to membership within a decade, they will be breaking all historical speed records.

Of course, the current leaders of the CEECs are quite used to breaking records. In a few short years they saw their entire world order demolished. In a single year, the political and economic chains between Eastern Europe and the USSR were broken. The political and economic strength of the Soviet Union was decimated and the mighty USSR broke up into a large number small countries. It might be worth recalling, however, that it is much easier to set speed records in pulling down old structures than it is in building new ones.

6.3   A Long Wait on the Association Agreement Step

Encouraging all Eastern nations to take the third step to EU membership would create a pan-European trade arrangement that might be best from a long-run economic perspective. It would provide obvious benefits for the CEECs. It would also help the EU incumbents economically, if for no other reason than that it would bankrupt the CAP and thereby force reform of that massively inefficient programme. However, an Eastern enlargement of the EU that involved more than one or two of the small CEECs is improbable for decades. Chapter 7 presents this argument in detail, but the basic problem is that the CEECs are far too different from the average EU incumbent. To mention just two differences, the Visegrad-4 are two and a half times more agricultural and less than one third as rich as the EU-12. They could not enter the EU without threatening two powerful special-interest groups – incumbent farmers and poor regions – during the decades they will need to catch up. Enlargements that included Eastern nations beyond the Visegrad-4 are even less likely to occur in the foreseeable future.

Given this logic, it should be clear why the lack of an intermediate step is a shortcoming. Without a midway integration stage, most or all Eastern countries will be stalled for decades at the Association Agreement step. Even if a political or military imperative permits early accession of the Visegrad-4, there will still be many CEECs stalled at the Association Agreement stage. Allowing the pan-European integration process to be delayed at the bilateral free-trade stage would frustrate the aspirations of millions of Central and East Europeans for decades. This might pose a political problem for Western Europe. Moreover, this outcome would miss the important economic gains that closer integration could bring to the continent.

Of course, the future is full of surprises. Extreme political events could convince West European voters to open their pocket books and admit the CEECs.

Notes

1. Similarly, accession by the Visegrad CEECs would irrevocably alter the current EU. This is explored at length in Chapter 7.
2. Only three, the United Kingdom, Ireland and Denmark, joined. However, when thinking about future enlargements, one should focus on countries that EEC incumbents found acceptable for membership rather than those that actually joined.
3. Given the opposition of Norway's parliament to EU membership, and the fact that its referendum will be non-binding, it is highly probable that Norway will not accede in this round of EU enlargement. Thus perhaps instead of the FANS enlargement, one should speak of the SAF (read 'safe') enlargement.
4. Protectionist policies in the FANS have raised their domestic food prices even further above world prices than those of the EU.

PART 3

Some Solutions

7

EU Enlargement

An enlargement of the European Union to the East is now certain. Its timing is not. The 'Conclusions of the Presidency' (issued after the June 1993 meeting of the EU heads of government in Copenhagen) commits the EU to admitting all the CEECs with Association Agreements. The wording of the commitment is diplomatic:

> The European Council today agreed that the associated countries in Central and Eastern Europe that so desire shall become members of the European Union. Accession will take place as soon as an associated country is able to assume the obligations of membership by satisfying the economic and political conditions required.
>
> Membership requires that the candidate country has achieved stability of institutions guaranteeing democracy, the rule of law, human rights and respect for and protection of minorities, the existence of a functioning market economy as well as the capacity to cope with competitive pressure and market forces within the Union. Membership presupposes the candidate's ability to take on the obligations of membership including adherence to the aims of political, economic and monetary union.
>
> The Union's capacity to absorb new members, while maintaining the momentum of European integration, is also an important consideration in the general interest of both the Union and the candidate countries.

Although this statement confirmed what many thought was inevitable, the Copenhagen summit may prove to be a turning point in Europe's post-war history.

The reference to 'the Union's capacity to absorb new members' should not be overlooked. It indicates that the incumbents will not allow an Eastern enlargement to delay the drive towards deeper integration. Two aspects of the Union are critical to further deepening of European integration: the transfers involved in the Common Agricultural Policy and the Structural and Cohesion Funds, and smooth functioning of the Union's main decision-making mechanism, the Council of Ministers. Thus the capacity-to-absorb proviso could be interpreted as saying that an Eastern enlargement cannot happen if it would overwhelm the Union's spending programmes or impede the Council of Ministers. In less diplomatic language the Conclusions of the Presidency might be rendered as: 'The CEEC and the EU are now engaged, but the wedding date has not been set and the bride's price could pose a problem.'

Who Gets in First?

For political and economic reasons, the promises of membership for the CEECs cannot be fulfilled all at once. This raises the unanswerable question: Who will be in the first wave? The current received wisdom is that the first entrants will be drawn from the Visegrád group (the Czech Republic, Hungary, Poland, Slovakia) and perhaps Slovenia. The Visegraders are a very uneven group in terms of populations and economics. Poland, in particular, is about four times larger and much poorer than the Czech Republic, Hungary, or Slovenia. Slovakia is significantly poorer than Poland and its transformation has been less successful. Slovenia is richer and less agricultural than Portugal and Greece.

Despite this economic diversity, the Visegrád countries are very strongly linked in the minds of important EU policy makers. The reasons for this are never written down explicitly, so it is interesting to speculate. If EU politics is the engine behind an Eastern enlargement, economics is the brake. EU incumbents that strongly favour enlargement are primarily concerned about instability in Central Europe. Germany, in particular, wants stable, secure and prosperous neighbours on its Eastern borders. It is probably fair to say that there is almost no chance that the first Eastern enlargement would occur without Poland (barring any serious reversal or stagnation of the Polish transformation). A glance at the map goes a long way towards explaining Poland's status. Insisting that Poland be included in the first wave will probably hasten Poland's entry. If an Eastern enlargement were simply a matter of economics, Poland might not be included. If, however, economics were all that mattered, an Eastern enlargement might not occur for a very long time. In other words, excluding Poland would remove much of the impetus for – as well as the economic difficulties of – the first Eastern enlargement. It would seem that the substitution of Slovenia for Slovakia would not be constrained by this reasoning.

The status of the Czech Republic is important for the same geopolitical reasons. Slovenia borders Italy to the east and Slovakia will be part of the

EU's eastern border once Austria is a member. The queue becomes even more disorderly when considering enlargements beyond the first wave.

What Next?

Whether the first enlargement occurs in 6, 16 or 26 years, the problems of current pan-European trade arrangement will remain for the non-acceding CEECs. Hub-and-spoke bilateralism and the lack of intermediate steps would continue to mar the integration of a greater Europe. In particular, it would not solve the problems of the three Baltic States and the two south-east nations (Bulgaria and Romania); nor would it help eventually to integrate Albania. The issue of EU membership for the other Balkan States and former Soviet republics is best thought of as a question for futurologists. It could take generations to heal the scars in the other Balkan States. For very different reasons, EU membership for the former Soviet republics (Belarus, Ukraine, Moldova and perhaps Russia) is a remote possibility.

Plan of Chapter

This chapter looks at the benefits and difficulties of an Eastern EU enlargement. Section 7.1 examines the benefits of EU enlargement. Section 7.2 describes six major difficulties posed by enlargement: the effects on Structural Funds, the CAP budget, Council of Ministers voting, migration, the deepeners-versus-wideners schism, and security guarantees for the CEECs.

To summarize, the chapter shows that the massive liberalization entailed by EU enlargement would probably bring large long-run economic benefits to all Europe. However, the Eastern economies are currently too populous, too poor and too agricultural to enter the EU without radically altering the Union itself. Consequently, a significant enlargement of the EU to the East is unlikely to occur until the Easterners are much richer and much less agricultural. This is likely to take at least two decades for most of the CEECs.

7.1   The Benefits of an Eastern EU Enlargement

EU membership for the CEECs would involve a massive and radical liberalization of barriers to trade in goods and factors. Furthermore, according to Copenhagen decision, CEEC 'Membership presupposes the candidate's ability to take on the obligations of membership including adherence to the aims of political, economic and monetary union'. According to plans agreed upon by all member states (and all the EFTA member states negotiating accession), the CEECs would join a European Union that involves:

- Free movement of goods, services, people and capital
- A common external trade policy
- A supranational appellate system (the European Court of Justice) to enforce consistent application of Community law throughout the Union
- Open government procurement
- A common agricultural policy
- A common competition policy for undertakings affecting intra-Union trade
- A common policy on state aids affecting intra-Union trade
- A common policy on public undertakings of a commercial nature
- A common policy promoting the development of disadvantaged regions by structural spending
- Substantial harmonization of industrial, health, safety and environmental standards
- Mutual recognition of national standards and professional qualifications
- Monetary union
- European citizenship
- A common foreign and security policy of some sort
- A framing of a common defence policy, which may in time lead to a common defence.

This list is not exhaustive.

7.1.1   *Political Benefits*

Politics is the driving force behind Eastern nations' desire to join and incumbents' desires to have them. These considerations – political anchorage and security guarantees – are intrinsically vague, since they are based on fears of future developments. The CEECs recently freed themselves from foreign domination, embraced democracy and switched to market economics. These changes are not irreversible. Internal and external forces could turn back the clock. It is hoped that EU membership would prevent this. The incumbent EU members that favour an early Eastern enlargement are also motivated chiefly by political and security matters. Germany, for instance, is very concerned about the consequences of serious political and/or economic turmoil on its eastern border.

It is quite clear that EU membership would provide the CEECs with a safeguard against internal opponents of democracy and capitalism. It acted in this way for Greece, Portugal and Spain, as Winters (1993) points out. In contrast, it is not entirely clear how EU membership would help with security, at least as far as military security is concerned. Any observer of EU behaviour in the conflict in the former Yugoslavia and the Gulf War should be very doubtful about the willingness of most EU member states to send their soldiers to die in foreign lands. Furthermore, this tendency is likely to become stronger after the current EFTA enlargement. By 1996, the EU is likely to consist of four large rich economies (France, Italy, United Kingdom, Germany), seven small, rich countries (three Benelux nations, two Nordic nations and Austria), three small, poor ones (Ireland, Portugal and Greece), and one large, poor one (Spain). It would seem difficult to get these nations to agree on any joint military action. Nevertheless, EU membership is likely to reinforce security in a more diffuse manner. For instance, one can imagine that a return of an authoritarian government to Russia might force the 'Finlandization' of the Baltic States if they are not part of the European Community.

7.1.2   *Economic Gains*

An Eastern EU enlargement would free market forces. This would lead to large net economic benefits, although it would involve a redistribution of incomes, especially in incumbent member states. Chapter 2 describes these effects at some length and they are merely summarized here. The effects of market opening can be classified into three types: allocation, accumulation and location.

Allocation effects concern the efficiency with which an economy's resources are allocated among various sectors. Freely determined market prices are the invisible hand that guides resource allocation in a market economy. Barriers that hinder competition and/or interfere with the market determination of prices tend to distort the price-based communication between consumers and producers; distorted prices are translated into a confused and inefficient allocation of resources. Barriers to the international exchanges of goods, services and productive factors are a prime example of such interference. By removing such barriers an Eastern enlargement of the EU would improve that efficiency with which the European resources are allocated. Very frequently, a primary effect of removing such barriers is to lead to a convergence of the prices of goods, services and factors. While this convergence usually results in a net gain in welfare, it also implies large redistribution of income.

Accumulation effects – better known as growth effects – concern the rate at which productive factors accumulate. Sustained growth in output requires the sustained accumulation of some factor or factors of production (here we take a broad definition of factors that includes knowledge). That is, to continually increase the amount of output per capita, an economy must continually accumulate human capital, physical capital and/or knowledge capital. In a market economy this ceaseless accumulation is the result of innumerable investment decisions made primarily by self-interested private agents. For instance, students invest (time and money) in their own education and training primarily to increase their own incomes. Firms train their workers to raise profits by lowering costs or increasing output. They also continually develop new products and new production processes, again mainly to increase profits. The net result of these private decisions is a rate of accumulation that results in a rate of GDP growth. Many policies that improve the efficiency with which existing resources are allocated also tend to improve the investment climate. Consequently, the massive and radical liberalization of markets implied by an Eastern EU enlargement is very likely to increase growth throughout Europe.

Location effects involve the geographical allocation of existing resources. In general, the recent literature on these effects focuses on the distribution of economic activity. One robust conclusion is that the relationship between concentration and liberalization is complex. At one extreme, prohibitive barriers lead to the total decentralization of production. At this extreme, liberalization is clearly accompanied by increased concentration of production in large markets. At the other extreme, location of production is evenly spread when there are no costs to trading, so liberalization near this extreme is accompanied by a decrease in concentration. Beyond this rather vacuous result, it is difficult to say much about the location effects of an EU enlargement. One thing is certain: many CEECs are closer to Europe's economic centre of gravity than are many EU incumbents. Furthermore, as the average incomes of CEEC citizens catch up with Western levels, the economic centre of Europe will move substantially eastwards. To understand this, one only needs to recall how important *Mitteleuropa* was to the European economy before the imposition of central planning. This would suggest that any further concentration of activity might well be to the benefit of the CEECs.

Economic Effects on Members of the European Union

A large share of the total net gains discussed above would accrue to the current members of the EU. One set of gains would come from standard comparative advantage sources. Given the abundance of labour in the CEECs compared with the current EU members and the existence of systematic trade barriers in such goods (clothing, textiles, shoes, agricultural goods, etc.), enlargement would stimulate production of labour-intensive goods in the East and discourage it in the West. This would free resources in the West, allowing them to be employed in more productive activities. Since this increased specialization would allow nations to focus their resources on what they do relatively best, the pan-European allocation of resources would improve, increasing output per capita throughout the region.

An Eastern enlargement of the European Union would increase Europe's economic importance in the world. Expanding to the CEEC-10 alone would increase the EU's population by roughly a third.

Economic Effects on the East

All the effects discussed in Chapter 2 are relevant to the analysis of the impact that an EU enlargement would have on the East. Several points, however, are worth highlighting.

When economically large and small areas integrate, the benefits typically accrue more than proportionally to the small areas. For example, analysis of the EEA agreement by Haaland and Norman (1992) shows that the small EFTA economies would gain considerably more (in terms of percentage increase in their GDP) than would the EU. It is easy to understand this asymmetry. The economic gains depend essentially on the way in which integration increases opportunities for consumers and producers to arrange their affairs more efficiently. The integration of a large and a small economy increases the opportunities facing firms and consumers in the small economy by more than it does for those located in the large one. It is therefore natural that small areas gain more in relation to their pre-integration incomes.

It is widely believed that capital and technology are relatively scarce in the economies in the eastern part of Europe. Consequently, integration with the West should be expected systematically to lower the price of goods that are intensive in these factors. Moreover, standard comparative advantage theory suggests that in the short and medium run integration would result in a fall in the proportion of resources devoted to the production of technology- and capital-intensive goods. Furthermore, since the infrastructures in the CEECs are extremely underdeveloped compared with those of the EU, structural spending is likely to be productive in the East.

7.2 Difficulties of an Eastern EU Enlargement

7.2.1 *Direct Budgetary Costs*

Any enlargement of the EU to the East would have important effects on the Union's budget. This section attempts to quantify this statement roughly.

Table 7.1 The EU's 1992 budget (billions of ECU)

Revenue		Spending	
VAT	58.0%	CAP	53.7%
Tariffs	18.9%	Structural Funds	31.6%
Agricultural levies	3.3%	R&D, energy and technology	3.3%
GNP based	13.9%	Administration	4.7%
Other	5.8%	Foreign aid	3.5%
		Other	1.3%
Total Billion ECU	59.7	Total Billion ECU	58.1

Source: Courchene et al. (1993).

Before turning to projections, we briefly cover the salient features of the EU's budget.[1]

The EU Budget: A Primer

Table 7.1 shows that two items dominate the spending side of the EU budget – the Structural Funds and the Common Agricultural Policy (CAP). Together these two programmes account for over 80% of all EU spending. The importance of these items in the budget accurately reflects their importance in the Community. By providing the means to help various regions and groups adjust to changes induced by integration, these programmes play a critical role in allowing the EU to be much more than a free trade area. In a sense, these expenditures are the weight that counterbalances the centrifugal forces pulling the twelve very different nations apart.

On the revenue side, there are four main sources. The most important by far is based on national VAT receipts. According to agreed rules, a slice of each member's national VAT revenue is paid to the Community.[2] In 1988 the slice was capped at 1.4%. The second and third sources, namely tariff revenue and agricultural levies (variable tariffs) collected on imports from non-EC countries, are quite straightforward. Under EU rules, all revenues collected on imports from non-EC states accrue to the EU directly. The fourth major income source has a simple name – 'the fourth resource'. The revenue that members pay is based on their GNPs. The amount varies according to budgetary needs. This is the component of the budget that is relied on to 'top-up' revenue in order to balance accounts. (The EU budget must be balanced each year.)

Evolution of Spending and Revenue Various political and economic pressures have forced the EU budget to change rapidly. It is important to keep this in mind, since some of the budget projections below are based on 1990 spending and revenue practices.

On the revenue side, tariff liberalization due to the Tokyo Round GATT agreement has greatly cut into the EU's revenue from customs duties. Changing world food prices have similarly reduced receipts from the EU's system of variable agricultural levies on food imports. In 1977, more than 60% of the EU budget was financed by these two items. Courchene et al. (1993), in a report for the EC Commission, project that by 1994 this figure will have fallen to about 20%. Tariff cuts and agricultural liberalizations promised in the Uruguay round will continue to diminish the importance of this politically painless source of revenue. Contributions from members' VAT receipts have been the most important replacement for falling income from trade taxes. However, since the VAT base is larger in the poorer EU nations, dependence on the VAT component built a degree of regressivity into Union financing. Objections to this feature led to calls for reform, which essentially involve placing more emphasis on the fourth resource and less on the VAT-based resource. According to the 1988 budget agreement the maximum slice of the VAT base collected by the Union will fall in equal steps from 1.4% to 1% in 1999. The limit on the EU budget is set to climb from 1.2% in 1994 to 1.27% in 1999.

On the spending side, total EU expenditures more than doubled in real terms from 1973 to 1988 (Franklin, 1992). This is due mainly to the increasing cost of CAP price supports, the creation and expansion of the Structural Funds and the southern enlargement of the Community. As a share of EU GDP, the budget has risen from about three-tenths of 1% in 1971 to almost 1.2% in 1992. On the whole, the EU budget is progressive in that it transfers resources to the poorer countries, but certain anomalies exist. As Franklin (1992) shows, some rich countries, Denmark and Luxembourg, are net recipients, while the United Kingdom (whose per capita income puts it at the EU average) is the second largest net contributor.

A very important shift in EU spending priorities was set in the 1988 'Delors Package'. Spending on agriculture must grow more slowly than the EU GDP. Its share of EU expenditure must fall from about 65% in 1988 to less than 50% in the coming years. The 1988 budget deal doubled Structural Funds spending. In 1993 these accounted for between a quarter and a third of expenditures. Agreements surrounding the Maastricht Treaty and the Edinburgh summit agreement imply that this share will rise to 35–40% of EU outlays by 1999. See Courchene et al. (1993) for more details.

Structural Funds   The Structural Funds are large transfers to the poorer member states and regions. The funds are explicitly aimed at encouraging greater economic and social 'cohesion'. Cohesion is generally taken to mean convergence of per capita income levels.

Table 7.2 Structural Funds spending
1989–93 (in billion ECU)

Spending by objective	
1: Low-income regions	38.3
2: Declining-industry regions	7.2
3, 4: Long-term unemployment and youth training	7.5
5a: Agricultural structural adjustment regions	3.4
5b: Rural areas	2.8
Other	
Total	60.3

Source: Eurostat (1992).

Spending on cohesion is classified by the nature of the problem at which it is aimed. The regions or groups that are the focus of these aims are given the rather unpoetic names of Objectives 1–5b (Table 7.2 shows historical spending by objective). 'Objective 1' regions are defined as regions with per capita incomes that are less than 75% of the EU average. Over 20% of the current EU population is eligible under this objective. The spending of these regions is aimed at improving infrastructure and local training. This includes all of Greece, Ireland, Northern Ireland and Portugal as well as Corsica, large parts of Spain and Southern Italy. 'Objective 2' regions are those that suffer from a decline in traditional industries such as coal and steel. Over 45 million of the EU's 340 million citizens live in these regions. The spending under this objective is aimed at creating jobs, improving the environment, developing R&D and renovating land and buildings. 'Objective 5b' regions are rural areas, such as the Highlands of Scotland. Other people eligible for structural funds are the long-term unemployed (Objective 3), unemployed youth (Objective 4); backward farms (Objective 5a) and the Eastern States of Germany (Regulation No. 3575/90).

For our present purpose, the most important aspect of these expenditures is their close link with per capita incomes. This is highly pertinent to the question of projecting the budgetary cost of an Eastern EU enlargement, since incomes are low in the Eastern nations of Europe.

In 1990 and 1991, the EU spent 12.5 and 14.4 billion ECU, respectively (about a quarter of its budget in both years) on these transfers. Plans have been put forward that significantly expand this type of Community expenditure. For instance, a new category (creatively named Objective 6) would provide funds to regions that are heavily dependent on the fishing industry. Also a special Cohesion Fund was agreed by heads of state at the Maastricht meeting where the Treaty on European Union was also agreed. This fund should have an annual budget of 1.5 billion ECU in 1994 rising to 2.5 billion by 1997. It is to be used to fund projects exclusively in the four poorest EU states: Greece, Ireland, Portugal and Spain. Many commentators view this new fund as a 'sweetener' to persuade the poor EU states to agree to the tighter integration implied by the Maastricht Treaty. As such, it is an excellent example of the EU's rich-North/poor-South politics. When the rich EU nations want something that does not directly benefit the poorer states, the poorer states demand generous transfers in exchange for acquiescence.

Common Agricultural Policy The CAP is a very complicated and very expensive set of policies aimed at raising the incomes and output of the EU farm sector. More than half the support is paid for directly by consumers via the 'hidden tax' of protectionism (import barriers keep prices above free trade prices thereby transferring income from consumers to producers) (OECD, 1992). The rest is paid for by the European Agriculture Guidance and Guarantee Fund (EAGGF). This Fund accounted for almost 60% of the 1991 EU budget. The guarantee section of the Fund finances price floors for most food products by buying food in EU markets, restricting imports, subsidizing exports and, to some extent, limiting production. The guidance section finances the improvement in the structure of the Community's agricultural sector.

How Poor, Populous and Agricultural are the CEECs?

More than 80% of EU money is spent on farmers and poor regions. The critical data for determining the budgetary impact of the CEECs are per capita incomes and the size of their agricultural sectors.

Visegrad Countries Table 7.3 shows the populations, GDP per capita and agriculture share of GDP for the Visegrad-4 and Slovenia. The data are from the World Bank's World Development Report (WDR) and the table is based on the data from the International Comparison Programme and World Bank staff calculations. The WDR does not report data separately for the Czech Republic and Slovakia, so *Planecon* data were used to establish the ratio of income levels in the two states. This ratio was applied to the WDR data for the CSFR. Data for several incumbent EU members are included for comparison. The use of 1991 data is a severe limitation, since incomes and agriculture share has been changing rapidly in the region.

Looking first at averages, we see that the Visegrad-4 are two and half times more agricultural than the average EU-12 nation and less than one-third as rich. Slovakia is by far the poorest (22% of EU-12 average income) and Slovenia much the richest (64% of EU-12 average income). Poland accounts for almost two-thirds of the Visegrad's 64 million people. According to 1991 figures, the average Pole produces less than one-quarter

Table 7.3 Visegrad income, population and agriculture shares, 1991

	Population (millions)	GDP per capita (US$)	Agriculture share of GDP (%)
Czech Republic	10.4	7570	8
Hungary	10.3	6080	10
Slovakia	5.2	3790	8
Poland	38.2	4720	7
Visegrad average	64.1	5325	8
Slovenia[a]	2.0	10800	5
Visegrad '5' average	66.1	5491	8
EU-12 average	**346**	**16800**	**3**
Portugal	9.9	9450	9
Greece	10.3	7680	17
Ireland	3.5	11430	11
Spain	39.0	12670	5
Germany	79.1	19770	2

Note: [a] Data from *Planecon*.

Source: World Bank (1993).

of what the average German does. Hungary is the most agricultural of the four in terms of GDP shares. However, given Poland's large land area (313, 000 square kilometres) Polish agriculture accounts for by far the largest part of Visegrad agriculture. All the Visegrad countries are less agricultural than Ireland and Greece.

One fact that continually dominates analysis of the Visegrad enlargement is the group's large population. If the Visegrad-4 were admitted as a group, it would be the largest single increase in the EU population. The 1973 enlargement is a close second, at 64.0 million. Of course, in terms of percentage increase of the EU population, the 1973 enlargement was greater.

Other CEECs The other Central and Eastern countries are much more agricultural than the Visegrad group, as shown in Table 7.4. They are between four and seven times more agricultural than the EU-12, although Estonia and Bulgaria are less agricultural than Greece. Apart from Romania, they are all quite small. The Baltic States are fairly prosperous but the EU-12 average is still more than twice that of Estonia.

Some Rudimentary Calculations

Before turning to models and estimates, let us consider some simple but instructive calculations. The largest structural spending programme (Objective 1) draws the line at regions with per capita incomes that are less than 75% of the EU average. Consider how many years it would take the Visegrad group to get above this cut-off point, assuming that the EU

Table 7.4   Other CEEC income, population and agriculture shares,
1991

	Population (millions)	GDP per capita (US$)	Agriculture share of GDP (%)
Estonia	1.6	8 090	15
Latvia	2.6	7 540	20
Lithuania	3.7	5 410	20
Bulgaria	9.0	4 980	13
Romania	23.0	6 900	19
EU-12 average	346	16 800	3

Source: World Bank (1993).

average rises at 2% per annum. Table 7.5 shows the results for a range of growth rates.

Few countries have managed to sustain 6% growth for extended periods, but it may be possible for the most successful CEECs. Under this optimistic assumption, it would take two decades for the average income of the Visegrad-4 group to be above the current criteria for structural spending. Taken individually, both Hungary and Poland would take approximately two decades, but the Czech Republic would take only 14 years. Slovakia is an outlier at 26 years (and this assumes that it will average 6% growth between 1991 and 2017). Allowing for more moderate growth rates produces substantially longer catch-up times. At 4% the Visegrad average would take three decades to catch up and at 3% growth four decades would be required. The round numbers for the group average are a coincidence. Reflecting Slovenia's much higher 1991 income level, its catch-up times are much shorter. Note that since the average EU income will rise with the ongoing EFTA enlargement, the number of years in Table 7.5 should be thought of as lower-bound estimates.

The more complicated models that are considered below can be thought of as elaborations of this simple exercise. Indeed, the basic conclusion below confirms the idea that it would take at least two decades (from 1991) for the Visegraders to become rich enough to make their entry inexpensive to incumbent special-interest groups.

These calculations, however, do not take account of agriculture. In what follows we look at some detailed calculations of the impact of the Visegraders on the CAP. Again we perform some simpler exercises to highlight the main points. The landmass of the EU-12 equals 2 368 000 square kilometres; the figure for the Visegrad group equals 534. It is probably fair to say that the Visegrad land is at least as arable as the EU-12 land, on average. On this crude assumption, Visegrad farmland would augment the EU farming area by 22%. If agricultural yields are equalized, then a very rough guess is that EU farm output would rise about 22%. The 64 million Visegraders will raise the EU population by about 19%.

Table 7.5   Years for Visegrad group to catch up to 75% of EU-12 average income

	3% CEEC growth	4% CEEC growth	6% CEEC growth
Czech Republic	28	21	14
Hungary	35	26	18
Slovakia	51	39	26
Poland	44	33	22
Visegrad-4 average	**40**	**30**	**20**
Slovenia	15	11	8

Note: Assumes 2% growth of EU average income.

Assuming that they consume about as much food as the EU average, we have a rudimentary estimate that Visegrad enlargement would expand the current food surplus in the EU. Thus, even if Visegrad farmers are denied CAP subsidies, their exports would still burden the CAP by increasing the cost of maintaining the CAP prices.

Budgetary Impact of the Visegrad-4 Joining the EU

Projecting the receipts and contributions that Eastern nations would make as EU members is an extremely difficult task. It inevitably involves a large amount of guesswork. We discuss the techniques that have already been used in the literature and then propose an extension that allows us to make a crude calculation of the minimum number of years it will take before the CEECs and FSRs would be budget-neutral as EU members.

CAP Costs   Very careful estimates of the cost of allowing the Visegrad-4 (Hungary, the Czech Republic, Slovakia and Poland) access to the CAP are presented by Anderson and Tyers (1993). They consider the effects on farm trade and welfare of a Visegrad enlargement, assuming that the McSharry reforms are fully implemented. The authors use a multicommodity dynamic simulation model of world food markets that is based on 1990 data. The model distinguishes seven commodity groups: wheat, coarse grain, rice, sugar, dairy products, meat of ruminants and meat of non-ruminants. These seven commodity groups exclude edible oils and beverages. This disaggregation provides a large payoff because the distortionary effects of the CAP vary greatly between products. The output composition of various nations' agricultural production also varies greatly. The model is global in coverage, so changes in Europe feed into world prices. It also allows production and consumption cross-effects in the interdependent markets for grains, livestock products and sugar. It is dynamic in the sense that it incorporates effects of income, population and productivity changes for each year through to 2010. The model was developed as part of an IFPRI project (Tyers, 1993).

The results reported are for the year 2000. The scenario undertaken by the authors supposes that there are no changes in the CAP beyond the McSharry reforms, so farmers and consumers in the incumbent EU nations are unaffected. Eastern consumers, however, would face higher prices. This would cost them an extra US $15.9 billion annually. Visegrad farmers would be better off by US $52.5 billion. Thus, allowing the Visegrad countries into the CAP would involve a massive transfer from incumbent EU taxpayers and Visegrad consumers to Visegrad farmers.

Absorbing Visegrad food production into the CAP would be costly for several reasons. First, the CAP food prices and production subsidies would stimulate Visegrad agricultural production. The Visegrad group's combined output of farm products would be almost US $10 billion higher than under the non-membership scenario. The production increase would be concentrated in the livestock sectors. After full adjustment, the annual Visegrad output of pig and poultry meat would rise by one third, that of beef by a half and that of dairy by two-thirds. To maintain EU food prices, all this would have to be exported to third countries. Thus apart from production subsidies, the EU would have to provide large export subsidies for the excess food. Of course, dumping this extra food on the world market would further depress world food prices. Apart from any international trade ramifications, the lower prices would make it also more expensive to subside the export of EU incumbents' surplus food.

Anderson and Tyers (1993) estimate that the total extra cost to the EU budget would amount to US $47 billion each year. This figure amounts to 37.6 billion ECU using an exchange rate of 1.25. Quite simply, the extra cost of Visegrad membership would bankrupt the CAP. For comparison, total CAP spending levels in 1991, 1992 and 1993 are 31.0 billion, 31.2 billion and 35.1 billion ECU respectively.

Structural Spending Costs A recent study for the EC Commission by an independent group of economists (Courchene et al., 1993) projects the budgetary impact of enlargement to the East. The methodology projects cohesion spending and CAP spending for the CEECs separately. The study asserts that Portugal and Greece are likely to receive about 400 ECU per capita after the Edinburgh agreement increases are carried out by 1999. Currently these countries receive approximately half this figure. To project the total cost, the study argues that 'an ECU 400 transfer per head in their favour would seem, on current policy, a minimum in view of their relative backwardness and evident lack of modern infrastructure'. *Using this assumption, the Visegrad-4 would receive 26 billion ECU in Structural Funds.* For comparison, note that in 1993 the incumbent poor-four received about 16 billion ECU.

The Courchene et al. study draws on Brenton and Gros (1993) for its

Table 7.6 Budgetary cost of admitting Visegrad-4 in 2000 (ECU billion)

	CAP cost	Structural Funds cost	Contribution	Net budget cost
Visegrad-4	37.6	26	5.5	58.1

Notes: CAP costs from Anderson and Tyers (1993); Structural Funds costs from EC Commission (1993). See text for explanation of contribution.

estimates of the CAP cost of a Visegrad enlargement. That study, which is not based on an explicit model of the food market, concludes that the CAP costs would rise by 17 billion ECU. Brenton and Gros (1993) rely on more *ad hoc* assumptions than the Anderson–Tyers model and Brenton and Gros do not allow for an impact of Visegrad production on world prices. For these reasons, the Anderson–Tyers numbers are preferred.

National Contributions by the CEECs   Currently, the EU budget amounts to about 1.2% of the Union's total GDP. This fraction is set to rise to about 1.3% by the year 2000. Each EU member pays about 1.2% of its GDP to finance the Union's expenditures.

Using the 1.3% contribution figure, it is straightforward to calculate the contribution the Visegrad group would make as members in 2000. According to World Bank figures, the Visegrad GDP was about US $340 billion in 1991. Assuming a 4% real growth rate yields a 2000 Visegrad GDP of US $482 billion; a 6% real growth rate produces a figure of US $573 billion. Thus, the gross contribution of the new entrants would be between US $6.3 and US $7.5 billion. Using an exchange rate of 1.25, contributions would be between 5 and 6 billion ECU. Table 7.6 shows the overall implications taking the midpoint of the contribution estimates.

According to the EC Commission (Courchene et al., 1993), the EU's total budget in 1999 is projected to be about 86 billion ECU. Thus, given these estimates, the Visegrad enlargement, with no change in expenditure policies, would force an increase in the EU budget of 74%. Taking account of the budgetary contributions of the CEECs, the net increase in revenues or decrease in spending would amount to 58.1 billion ECU, which would be 68% of the projected 1999 budget.

Cost of Further Eastern Enlargements

The CAP accounts for about a half of EU spending, so the accuracy of any estimate of budget costs relies heavily on its CAP cost figure. The estimate of the CAP cost discussed above was from a very detailed study. Unfortunately, this sort of high-quality estimate is not available for the other CEECs. To examine the budgetary impact of enlargements that go beyond the Visegrad-4, we are forced to turn to cruder methods. As a

Table 7.7 The Begg model data

	1989 pop. (millions)	1989 GNP per cap. (US$)	Ag. share of GDP (%)	(ECUs per capital received, 1990)		
				Structural Funds receipts	CAP (EAGGF) receipts	Sum of receipts
Belgium	10.0	15.5	2	15	55	70
Denmark	5.1	15.2	4	15	192	207
France	56.2	16.4	3	22	82	104
Germany	62.0	17.3	2	12	60	72
Greece	10.0	7.1	16	116	170	286
Ireland	3.5	8.3	11	209	306	515
Italy	57.5	15.0	4	28	78	106
Netherlands	14.8	14.7	4	10	234	244
Portugal	10.3	7.6	9	103	17	120
Spain	38.8	10.9	5	73	48	121
UK	57.2	15.0	2	19	31	50

Source: Baldwin et al. (1992), Tables 3.2.2–3.2.4 (with typos corrected).

consequence, the estimates are much rougher and less reliable. Nevertheless, it is worth considering these less solid estimates to obtain an idea of how much further enlargements would cost.

The Begg Model   David Begg presents an approach that involves estimating a model of EU receipts and contributions using data for the current EU incumbents (see Chapter 3 in Baldwin et al., 1992). (The data are shown in Table 7.7.) The estimated model is then applied to data for the Eastern countries to obtain projected receipts and contributions for five of the CEECs. The results are approximate, however, since the assumptions of the model necessarily gloss over important details of EU expenditures. While it would be possible to estimate a more detailed model of EU expenditures, the constraint of Eastern data availability rules this out. Nevertheless, the approach has the merit of being understandable and therefore transparent.

Begg's model separates EU expenditures into Structural Funds and CAP disbursements. His model of cohesion spending exploits the close correlation between per capita income, the share of agriculture in GDP and per capita receipts of Structural Funds. His cross-section regression fits the data very well. For receipts of CAP spending (more specifically, the European Agricultural Guidance and Guarantee Fund), Begg estimates an equation involving national agriculture output and an intercept dummy for the Netherlands. This equation fits more poorly than the Structural Funds equation, since different types of food products receive very different levels of support. The main message of the estimates, however, is that CAP receipts rise in proportion with agricultural output, with the factor of proportionality averaging 15%. Finally, for contributions made by the member states to the EU budget, Begg regresses the 1990 contributions by

Table 7.8 Begg's budget projections at 1989 income levels

	(Millions of 1989 ECU)			
	Contributions	Receipts		Net
		Structural		budgetary
	Gross	Funds	CAP	cost
Poland	817	4 600	1 409	5 192
Hungary	341	1 255	544	1 458
CSFR	617	1 360	446	1 189
Bulgaria	263	1 205	516	1 458
Romania	396	3 190	809	3 603
				Total 12 900

	(1989 ECU per capita)	
	Total	Net
	receipts	cost
Poland	157	136
Hungary	173	140
CSFR	116	76
Bulgaria	191	162
Romania	172	155

Source: Baldwin et al. (1992), Table 3.2.5 and author's calculations.

the EU-12 (measured in millions of ECU) on their national GDPs. This equation fits the data very well. It suggests that contributions should rise by 9% for every 10% rise in real national output.

Projected Eastern Receipts   The next step is to gather data for the CEECs and use the regression results to project receipts and contributions for the CEECs. Begg's results are reproduced in Table 7.8. Note that although the complete cost of admitting the five CEECs mentioned in the table is large, the amount is not intolerable. In 1989 this would have amounted to roughly a quarter of the EU budget, and roughly one quarter of 1% of the EU-12's GDP. Thus, if there were some dire necessity or overwhelming political will to admit the five CEECs, this calculation suggests that it would be economically possible. However, given the titanic battles that currently occur in the Council of Ministers over a few billion ECU, the idea of paying as little as 13 billion ECU to newcomers may be beyond the range of politically likely outcomes.

Begg also calculates the budgetary cost of an Eastern enlargement allowing for a doubling of the Eastern income levels. He finds, however, that this does not lower the budgetary cost. It raises it. The reason for this surprising result is that he assumes that agriculture would remain a constant fraction of total GDP. Thus rising incomes lead to lower Structural Funds transfers and higher contributions. However, it also leads to higher agricultural output and thus more CAP receipts. Given the higher agriculture shares in these economies, the latter outweighs the former. Below we consider allowing the agriculture shares to vary.

The Discrepancy with the Anderson–Tyers Numbers

The large discrepancy between the Begg and Anderson–Tyers numbers for CAP costs is simple to account for with two facts. The CAP heavily favours farm products that are typical of north European agriculture and the Visegrad group (especially Poland) has farmland that is amenable to exactly this sort of food production. Consequently, the Anderson–Tyers methodology (which takes account of these differences) produces a much higher and much more accurate estimate than the Begg method, which does not distinguish among different types of farm output.

To see this more carefully, consider the pattern of CAP costs among the EU incumbents. The CAP is complex, but its effects can be seen by translating its various policies into an implied ratio of domestic prices to world prices. To take the example of a dairy, this ratio was 4 in 1990 (Anderson and Tyers, 1993, Table 1). This means that if all the subsidies and price supports provided to the EU dairy products were forced onto the price, then those products would be four times more expensive than those on the world market. The numbers for wheat, rice and non-ruminant meat are 1.75, 2.78 and 1.54, respectively. Clearly, the CAP does not support all forms of food production equally. The second fact is that the composition of farm output varies greatly across EU countries due to differences in climate and soil conditions. For instance, Denmark, Ireland and the Netherlands are large exporters of cheese and butter, while France's exports focus on wheat. The combination of these two fact means that the CAP is heavily biased towards northern European farm output (especially dairy). Table 7.9 confirms this directly. It shows the amount of CAP subsidy (i.e., EAGGF Guarantee Funds) per unit of farm output in the various EU incumbent nations. The highest ratios by far are for the Netherlands and Ireland. Four of the six nations that receive above-average subsidization are clearly northern European. Greece is an important exception. Italy's above-average receipt is due largely to its rice production (rice is the next most distorted sector after dairy products).

Note also that the Begg numbers assume that the current level of structural spending will continue. This ignores the doubling of structural spending that was promised at the Edinburgh meeting of the EU heads of government.

Updating and Extending the Begg Model

The budget projections reported above cover a limited range of Eastern nations and are based on 1989 income data. The track records of the CEECs have been quite varied over the past few years. While all suffered a decline in measured incomes, some suffered much more than others. To account for more recent information and to expand to country coverage, a

Table 7.9   CAP receipts per ECU of agricultural value added for EU incumbents

	CAP receipts	Value added in agriculture	Receipts/ ag. value added
Belgium	0.546	2.82	0.19
Denmark	0.977	3.55	0.28
Germany	3.700	16.66	0.22
Greece	1.700	5.82	0.29
Spain	1.850	16.57	0.11
France	4.606	28.25	0.16
Ireland	1.071	3.00	0.36
Italy	4.506	17.82	0.25
Netherlands	3.469	8.36	0.42
Portugal	0.175	3.74	0.05
UK	1.797	13.09	0.14
Average			0.21

Note: All figures are billions of ECU except the ratio. 1989 data.

Sources: Data taken from Table 3.2.3 of Baldwin et al. (1992). World Bank and *Official Journal of the European Communities* were the original sources.

modified version on the Begg model is estimated. These new regressions for contributions and receipts are used to project budgetary costs for entry by the nine CEECs using a similar procedure to the one mentioned above.

A very thorough source of GDP per capita data on Eastern and Western European nations is the World Bank Development Report. The Report presents data that have been corrected for price differences. It is based on the International Comparison Programme data (see Summers and Heston, 1988), but updated and expanded by the Bank's staff using various methods (see Table 30, World Bank, 1993, and relevant notes). To use these data for the Easterners, we needed regression estimates of the EU-12 that were based on the same information. This meant rerunning the above regressions for the EU member states using the World Bank GDP figures for 1991. The exact specifications of the regressions were changed slightly to improve the fit with the new data. We found it convenient to express all figures in per capita terms. Specifically, the estimated relationships for CAP receipts, Structural Funds receipts and gross contributions were:

$$CAP/Pop = -44.98 + 0.410(Ag.GDP/Pop)$$
$$- 150(Portgl + \text{Spain dummy})$$
$$Struct. \ Funds/Pop = 209.25 - 0.015(GDP/Pop) \qquad \textbf{(7.1)}$$
$$+ 114.7(\text{Irish dummy})$$
$$Contribution/Pop = 0.012(GDP/Pop)$$

The t-statistics on all coefficients were quite high and the R^2 statistics for the three were 0.75, 0.99 and 0.65, respectively. The idea that the CAP favours north European agriculture (and thus will underestimate the cost of the

Table 7.10 Budget costs at 1991 incomes and agriculture shares

	ECU (per capita)			ECU (billion)
	Gross receipts	Gross contribution	Net contribution	Total budget cost
Slovenia	209	85	124	0.2
Czech Republic	256	60	196	2.0
Hungary	271	48	223	2.3
sub-total				**4.5**
Poland	209	37	172	6.5
sub-total			0	**11.0**
Estonia	428	64	364	0.6
Latvia	507	59	448	1.2
Lithuania	410	43	367	1.4
sub-total				**14.2**
Slovakia	211	31	180	0.9
Romania	458	54	404	9.3
Bulgaria	293	39	254	2.3
sub-total				**26.7**

Sources: Author's calculations, World Bank GDP and agriculture data for 1991.

northern CEECs) is supported by the negative sign on the Portuguese and Spanish dummy in the CAP regression.

These regressions fit the actual 1989 receipts and contributions fairly well. The fit of the structural spending is very good and there is no systematic bias for, say, rich versus poor members. The fit for the CAP regression is not quite as good. The regression underpredicts receipts for Spain and overpredicts for Portugal, so there is no systematic bias for the poorer member states. It is worth noting that the last regression overpredicts contributions for three of the four poor member states, but the fit is good.

Projected Budget Costs of Enlargement These regressions are used on Eastern data to project receipts and contributions. The results, expressed in 1989 ECU, are shown in Table 7.10. The numbers are larger than Begg's, but not as large as the Anderson–Tyers and Courchene et al. (1993) figures. The estimates are far too low and should be thought of as a lower bound on the true budget cost. In particular, the CAP numbers are underestimated since the model does not allow for differences in the composition of farm products. The structural spending figures are too low since they ignore the promised increase in structural spending. The total cost of the five countries considered by Begg is 21 billion ECU in Table 7.10 compared with Begg's estimate of 12.9 billion ECU. This reflects the fact that 1991 income and agriculture share data are used (and income dropped significantly in these countries between 1989 and 1991), and the fact that the regression coefficients are different. The figures in the table show that the cost of admitting Slovenia, the Czech Republic and Hungary would amount to 4.5

billion ECU. This amount would have been a fairly modest addition to the EU-12's 1991 budgetary outlays of 55.6 billion ECU. The cost of admitting Slovakia and Poland in addition brings the total to almost 12 billion ECU. Adding Bulgaria and Romania increases the cost to 21 billion ECU. This is a very small fraction of the EU-12's GDP, but more than 40% of the 1991 budget. The numbers in the table show that enlargement further east and further south quickly raises the budgetary cost.

Who Pays the Bill?

The calculations in the previous subsections show the total impact of Eastern enlargement on the budget. We could stop at this aggregate-level analysis if the budgetary costs could somehow be evenly spread over all incumbents. This is not likely to be the case. The burden of an Eastern enlargement is likely to fall mainly on the shoulders of the poor and the farmers in the EU. The logic of this statement is elementary. An enlargement by 2000 that included only the Visegrad-4 would require an increase of the EU budget of about 70%. This would force a combination of reduced EU expenditures in the incumbent member states and an increase in revenue contributions from them.

Let us consider revenue-raising possibilities. The member states have demonstrated great resistance to revenue-increasing measures (witness the controversy over the Delors II package). Moreover, each member state has a veto on these fiscal issues. Evidence of the likely reaction of EU taxpayers to revenue-raising proposals can be found in Germany. This is extremely telling, since the same voters overwhelmingly supported unification. Although the German politicians promised that unification would not lead to higher taxes, West Germans will have to pay more. German voters have so far refused the tax increases that are necessary to pay for the budgetary costs of German unification. It is impossible to predict the exact reactions of EU voters in the coming years. It seems reasonable, however, to suggest that tax increases, or increases in national debts, to pay for an Eastern enlargement would not be very popular with the West European voters.

Let us consider the cost-cutting possibilities. EU expenditure consists mainly of subsidies to farmers and poor regions. Accordingly, any substantial savings would reduce the incomes of Western Europe's farmers and/or poor regions. These two groups wield great power in EU politics. It seems, therefore, that a coalition of EU farmers and poor countries would block an Eastern enlargement until the Easterners are much richer and much less agricultural.

Years to Budget Neutrality

The basic message of the preceding analysis is that the budgetary burden on an enlargement is an important obstacle to EU membership for the CEECs.

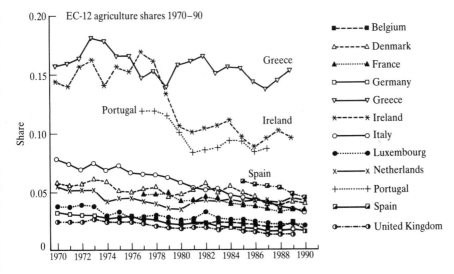

Figure 7.1 EU agriculture shares, 1970–90 (World Bank data)

Since the level of national income is an important determinant of receipts and the national contributions, and many CEECs are expected to grow rapidly in the coming decades, it would be interesting to know how many years would be required for each of the Eastern economies to reach budget neutrality. Unfortunately, the best estimates of the budget costs – Anderson–Tyers and Courchene et al. – are not amenable to this sort of 'what-if' speculation. For this reason, it is necessary to rely on the less satisfactory budget-projection methodologies described above. While it is a simple task to perform these calculations, one quickly runs into the problem that Begg encountered with his income-doubling scenario. Unless Eastern agricultural shares fall as per capita incomes rise, output growth may increase their burden as members.

A slightly less crude method is to take account of the widely observed tendency for agriculture shares to fall as countries become richer. The history of agriculture shares in the EU-12 from 1970 to 1991 is plotted in Figure 7.1. Clearly, the poor-four have seen their agriculture shares fall significantly (except Greece). It is also true that, again except for Greece, the poor-four have grown faster than the EU-12 average. Finally, note that the agriculture shares of the poor-four were similar in 1970 to the current shares of the CEECs.

A Model of Declining Agriculture Shares   To capture coarsely the relationship between rising growth and falling agriculture shares, we run a log-log regression of the poor-four's agriculture shares on their real incomes from 1970 to 1990.[3] This is, of course, a very rudimentary model of a complex

Table 7.11   Underestimate of years to budget neutrality: Visegrad nations

| Agriculture share elasticity → | Assumed average annual growth rates | | | | | | | | Total GDP increase needed (%) |
| | 2% | | 4% | | 6% | | 10% | | |
	Low	High	Low	High	Low	High	Low	High	
Czech Republic	37	31	19	16	13	11	8	7	108
Hungary	41	35	21	18	14	12	9	8	125
Poland	43	38	22	19	15	13	9	8	135
Slovakia	47	41	24	21	16	14	10	10	154
Slovenia	25	21	13	11	9	8	6	5	64

Source: Author's calculations.

phenomenon. Greece is an outlier in this group, so another regression was run excluding Greece. The resulting regressions (performed using the fixed effects estimation technique) fit the data remarkably well. The R^2 was about 90% for both the three- and four-country regressions. The estimated elasticity of agriculture shares with respect to income were minus 0.63 in the four-country case and minus 0.86 in the three-country one (the standard errors were 0.09 and 0.11, respectively). We take these as low and high estimates of the elasticities. Clearly, including all the EU-12 would have resulted in much less negative estimates. In our projections, this would have had the result of greatly increasing the number of years until budget neutrality. However, we stay with data only for the poor-four of the EU since we suspect that the economies of the poor-four in the 1970s and 1980s are better predictors of the CEEC economies in the coming decades than would be the EU-12 taken as a whole.

Projecting Years to Budget Neutrality   With this final link, we have a complete – but extremely crude – model of how the budgetary costs of the Eastern nations will evolve with their incomes. It is important to keep in mind the fact that the model of expenditures that is being used grossly underestimated the cost of the Visegrad accession. Consequently, the resulting projections are clearly an underestimate of the years to budget neutrality.

All that remains to complete the projection is to guess at CEEC growth rates for the coming decades. It is, however, impossible to know them. The most likely outcome is that some CEECs will grow rapidly, others slowly and others not at all. Table 7.11 presents the results for a range of annual growth rate assumptions as well as for the high and low agriculture elasticities. Note that the high elasticity results (this is high in absolute value) always imply a shorter period until budget neutrality. This reflects the fact that CAP receipts fall more rapidly when the agriculture shares fall more rapidly. The years to neutrality are also systematically lower for the high growth rates, since receipts fall and contributions rise as incomes rise.

Results for the Visegrad Group   As the model stands, budget costs depend only on per capita income levels and the elasticity of the agriculture shares. If one chooses either of the two elasticities, it is possible to ask how much richer each CEEC must become before they will be budget neutral. This calculation for the low elasticity is reported in the final column of Table 7.11. *Note that except Slovenia, all the CEECs must at least double their average incomes before they would be budget neutral.* Average incomes in the Czech Republic would have to rise by 108%, those in Hungary by 125%, those in Poland by 135% and those in Slovakia by 154%. Recall, however, that the model on which this is based underestimated the cost of a Visegrad enlargement in the year 2000 by 46 billion ECU (about 80%). The figures in the table should therefore be viewed as underestimates.

For convenience, Table 7.11 shows, for various growth rates, the number of years needed to attain the necessary rise in income for the two different agriculture share elasticities. For instance, an extremely optimistic assumption is that the CEECs will manage a sustained growth of 6% per annum from their 1991 levels (this would approximate South-east Asian growth rates in the 1980s).[4] Adding the optimistic assumption on agriculture share responsiveness to this yields the optimistic underestimate of years to budget neutrality. The table shows that it would take between 10 and 15 years for all Easterners to attain budget neutrality (except Slovenia, which would take nine). At the other extreme, slow growth and a gradually declining agriculture share would postpone the zero-budget-cost date substantially.

To allow for the possibility of truly miraculous growth, the table considers an average growth rate of 10% per annum. In this case, all the CEECs would be budget neutral by the end of the decade. A further implication of the table is that Slovakia is something of an outlier in the Visegrad group, due to its low income and large agriculture share.

Other CEECs   Table 7.12 shows the results of the same calculation for the other CEECs. The mid-range underestimate puts the number of years at around 20. For the poorest and most agricultural more than four decades would be required. As pointed out earlier, these are underestimates of the number of years since the base model underestimates the initial cost.

The table also illustrates another shortcoming of the methodology. Economic performance in the East has bifurcated. Some nations, such as the Czech Republic, Hungary, Slovenia and Poland, have laid the foundations of sustained growth, and in some cases have even started to grow. Others have yet to make significant microeconomic reforms and have not stabilized the macroeconomic environment. Clearly, the table cannot detect this effect.

Table 7.12 Underestimate of years to budget neutrality: other CEECs

Share elasticity →	Assumed average annual growth rates								Total GDP increase needed (%)
	2%		4%		6%		10%		
	Low	High	Low	High	Low	High	Low	High	
Estonia	41	34	21	18	14	12	9	8	125
Latvia	43	36	22	18	15	13	9	8	135
Lithuania	45	38	23	19	16	13	10	8	145
Bulgaria	45	38	23	19	16	13	10	8	145
Romania	44	36	22	19	15	13	9	8	140

Source: Author's calculations.

7.2.2 *Voting Effects*

Giving votes to new members can have important, unexpected and costly effects. The Cohesion Fund is a good example. To win the support of the EU's poor-four (Ireland, Greece, Portugal and Spain) for the Maastricht Treaty, the EU-12 had to agree to double structural expenditure via a new fund (the Cohesion Fund) that can be spent only in the poor-four. It seems clear that without Spain and Portugal, Ireland and Greece would never have managed to force such a large change in EU spending priorities. No one predicted the Cohesion Fund when Spain and Portugal were admitted, but perhaps they should have. Iberian politicians would have acted irresponsibly if they had *not* used their Council position to improve the welfare of the people that elected them.

Who can predict the consequences of granting CEECs the right to vote on Union matters? One thing should be clear. As EU members, the CEECs will use their power to secure benefits for their electorates. France used its power to raise protection and subsidies for her farmers, as did the United Kingdom to get a rebate on its contribution to the EU budget. Why should the CEECs be any different? As full EU members, the CEECs will have the right to vote on issues ranging from a common defence policy to reform of the CAP. Under current practices, members are accorded votes in relation to their populations; small countries have a disproportionate number of votes. Since there are 100 million CEEC citizens (64 million in the Visegrad group) and most of the CEECs are small (eight of the CEEC-10 have 10 million or less, five of them with 5 million or less), the CEECs would have a important number of votes. This would have momentous implications for politics in the Union.

The analysis in this section serves to reinforce the belief that EU voting procedures must be overhauled before any substantial enlargement occurs. Indeed, there is already serious consideration in the current discussions on enlargement of changing the rules.[5] The complications this poses for the analysis are forbidding. For instance, one problem with the current system is that small countries in the EU have a very disproportionate amount of power (this point is documented below). Most CEECs are small nations with populations ranging from 2 to 10 million, so they too would have disproportionate power. It is not easy to know what conclusion to draw from this. The most obvious rule-change might never occur, since reducing the power of small EU nations would require a unanimous vote. If small incumbent nations faced the choice between maintaining their own power and admitting the CEECs into the Union, the CEECs might never get in. In the absence of a better approach, the analysis in this section assumes that the current rules will remain in place.

EU Voting Rules

The voting rules of the Council of Ministers (the main decision-making body of the EU) are fairly complicated (see Box 7.1) and an outline of them is as follows. On very important issues, such as the adoption of the EU fundamental law (e.g. the Maastricht Treaty and the Single European Act), enlargement and fiscal questions, the Council operates on the principle of unanimity. The unanimity principle gives much power to all countries. Essentially it puts every country, even small Luxembourg, in a position to ruin the deal. Accordingly, such issues are packaged with other issues. The package of deals is expanded until everyone is happy with it. With the Single European Act, the poorer EU countries argued that the 1992 programme would benefit the EU-rich more than the EU-poor, so that the package of deals should include 'sweeteners' for the EU-poor. In the case of the Single European Act, the sweetener took the form of a substantial increase in the transfers paid to the EU-poor under the Structural Funds.

Many other issues are decided on a basis of a 71% majority rule. For such issues, a winning coalition does not have to 'buy off' all the opposition, only enough to reach at least 71%. This suggests the very precise definition of power that is the focus of the formal literature on power that is discussed in Chapter 2. Power is the ability of a country to turn a losing coalition into a winning one. This constitutes power, since a country that finds itself in such a pivotal situation can ask for many sweeteners as the price for its vote. The country can request that the coalition members agree to a proposal that provides benefits to its citizens. For instance, if Poland found itself in a pivotal position on a series of votes (or on one crucial vote), the Polish representative could ask for more Structural Funds, or extra protection for its agriculture.[6]

Analysis of the voting effects of an Eastern EU enlargement cannot focus only on the entrants. Adding countries changes the power of

---

Box 7.1   Voting in the Council of Ministers

The Council of Ministers is made up of a representative from each member state, but the number of votes cast by each representative varies according to the size (population) of the country. Currently the votes are as follows:

10 votes:	Germany, France, Italy, United Kingdom
8 votes:	Spain
5 votes:	Belgium, Greece, the Netherlands, Portugal
3 votes:	Denmark, Ireland
2 votes:	Luxembourg.

The total votes of the EU-12 is 76. The countries currently negotiating membership will get votes as follows:

4 votes:	Sweden, Austria
3 votes:	Finland, Norway.

Assuming that Norway will refuse entry, this would bring the total votes in the Council to 87.

Some critical issues, such as fiscal matters and modifications of the Treaty of Rome, require unanimity in the Council. Other less important issues require only a qualified majority of 71%. For the EU-12 this mean 54 votes (on some issues the votes must come from at least eight different members). For the EU-15, the number will be 62 votes.

The representatives on the Council are sent directly by their national governments. The relevant constituencies, therefore, are the national electorates.

---

incumbents. Typically, adding more countries, without changing the number of votes per incumbent, dilutes the power of the incumbents. Let us think about this in terms of how often a particular country might be in the pivotal position described above. The more members there are, the less likely it will be that any one country's votes are critical. As we saw in a sequence of numerical examples in Chapter 2, this dilution of power is not always true.

A final important consideration is that of voting blocs. On certain issues, the Central and Eastern nations that do join the EU are likely to have common views. For instance, if they are admitted while they are still poorer than average, they are likely to be enthusiastic for more structural spending. They are likely to favour a strong common EU defence policy, and since a much larger share of the GDP comes from agriculture (at least at their current levels of income), they are likely to want a shift of CAP resources to their nations.

Does Voting Power Matter?

One tangible ramification of power in the Council of Ministers is the ability of national representatives to secure large financial transfers from the EU, 'to bring the bacon home', as they say in Texas. To show that voting power in the Council of Ministers is an important issue, we compare the correlation between the voting power of incumbents and the net financial transfers that they receive. Before getting down to this task two parenthetical statements are necessary. As Franklin (1992) notes, official figures on net transfers (total receipts minus total contributions) are difficult to obtain since 'the [EU] Commission has always resolutely sought to avoid publishing the net balances of member states'. Here we use Franklin's figures. He states that these come from a *Financial Times* article, which was based on an anonymous source in the EU Commission. The second comment is that the pattern of net transfers in the EU-12 has been considered highly arbitrary. Franklin (1992) states 'the actual transfers between member states have remained haphazard and, chiefly because of the CAP, throw up some real anomalies'. For instance, two of the richest EU countries, Luxembourg and Denmark, receive more transfers from the EU than they pay in contributions.

Figure 7.2 plots the transfer per person figure and the Council votes per million citizens. Countries are listed in order of votes per citizen. Since the units of these two differ, it is somewhat awkward to plot them on the same figure. Let us consider the two extreme member states. Germans have about one-quarter of a Council vote per million citizens while Luxembourgers have more than five per million. Corresponding to this, the Germans on net pay a little more than 100 ECU per year to the EU budget and the Luxembourgers receive on net about 1800 ECU per person from the EU budget. The alignment of vote-per-person and net-spending-per-person is not perfect, but clearly there is a close correlation.

It should be noted that this sort of calculation is definitely misguided from an economic perspective (and perhaps even from a political one). The point is that Franklin's numbers seem to include all EU expenditures. For instance, part of Luxembourg's receipts seem to include the budget for Eurostat, which is located there. This is misleading, since the Eurostat budget is not a gift. It is used to pay productive factors that could have been employed in some other activity. Moreover, it is not possible to deduce causality from correlation. Nonetheless, it is clear that the interpretation of

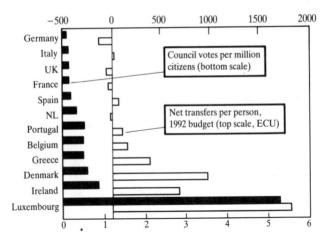

Figure 7.2   Transfers per EU citizen and votes by citizen according to nationality

votes per citizen as a measure of politicians' ability to 'bring home the bacon' is not rejected by the data. Using this measure of power, the actual transfers are anything but haphazard. They accurately reflect the relative power of countries in the Council of Ministers.

In some ways, it is tempting to use this correlation to predict the budgetary cost of an Eastern enlargement. That is, the figure suggests that EU spending is really determined by simple political power in the Council, rather than by rules of the CAP and the Structural Funds. The problem is that a Visegrad enlargement would be like admitting two more Greeces, another Denmark and a Spain. This would significantly dilute the power of the incumbents, so the actual transfers in the figure would change. All this is mere speculation, of course, but it does serve a good purpose. Without doubt, a significant enlargement of the EU to the East would have very important consequences for the balance of power in the Council of Ministers, unless the current rules are fundamentally reformed.

Existing Studies of Voting Power and EU Enlargement

The notion that an Eastern enlargement would dilute the power of incumbent states can be made a little more firm. There are several studies that gauge the impact of the ongoing FANS enlargement. Widgren (1991, 1993) uses a formal measure of power called the Shapley–Shubik Index. Chapter 2 explains this measure in detail. Heuristically, it assesses the probability that a particular country's votes will be pivotal on any randomly selected issue. A higher index indicates more power. The various

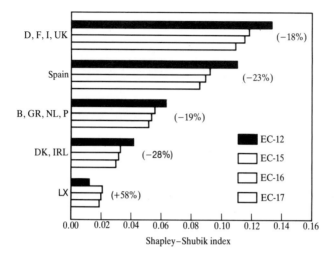

Figure 7.3 Shapley–Shubik indices for EU-12, EU-15, EU-16 and EU-17. Figures in parentheses indicate percentage change in index between EU-12 and EU-17. D = Germany, F = France, I = Italy, B = Belgium, GR = Greece, NL = Netherlands, P = Portugal, DK = Denmark, IRL = Ireland, LX = Luxembourg

enlargement scenarios he considers are shaped by recent events. Accession talks are well under way for Austria, Finland, Norway and Sweden, but many suspect that the Norwegian parliament will reject membership. These facts led Widgren to examine the possibility of an EU-15 (the EU-12 plus Austria, Finland and Sweden) and an EU-16 (EU-15 plus Norway). Initially it was thought that Switzerland might also join, so Widgren also studied the possibility of an EU-17.

With these scenarios before him, the next question was how many votes each entrant would be awarded at the Council of Ministers. His solution is quite ingenious. Widgren noted that the relationship between votes and population fits a logarithmic approximation very well. Using this relationship, the votes that the former EFTAns will get (rounding off to the nearest integer) are equal to four for Austria, Sweden and Switzerland, and three for Norway and Finland. Interestingly, these are the actual numbers that are being discussed in the current accession talks.

Finally, Widgren calculates the SSI power indices for each EU country under the base case (EU-12) and three enlargement scenarios. His results are shown in Figure 7.3. The EU-12 countries are grouped by the actual number of votes they have in the Council of Ministers. The SSI power measures for the base case EU-12 are shown by the top bar in each group of bars. Note that the four large EU countries have the most power by far and that the power indices decrease with the number of votes. The impact of the

Table 7.13   Projected Council of Ministers
votes for CEECs

Country	Population	Projected votes
Czech Republic	10.4	5
Hungary	10.3	5
Slovakia	5.2	4
Poland	38.2	8
Slovenia	2.0	3
Romania	23.0	7
Bulgaria	9.0	5
Estonia	1.6	3
Latvia	2.6	3
Lithuania	3.7	4

Source: Author's calculations.

enlargement on the power of incumbents is quite interesting. Except for Luxembourg, the entry of the EFTAns will reduce the power of all incumbents. Again, except for Luxembourg, the power reduction is smoothly related to the scale of the enlargement, with all the SSIs falling from EU-15 to EU-16 and EU-17.

The loss in power is not proportional. The numbers to the right of the bars show the percentage reduction in the SSI power measures between the EU-12 base case and the EU-17 enlargement scenario. The biggest losers are Denmark and Ireland, who have three votes each. In all the scenarios considered here, the entrants have three or four votes. Heuristically, we can think that the entrants provide the most competition in coalition building with the countries that have a similar number of votes. In some sense, the votes of the new entrants are close substitutes for the incumbents that have the same number of votes. While intuitively appealing, it is certainly not a general result. Indeed, note that Spain with eight votes loses almost as much.

The impact on Luxembourg demonstrates how an enlargement can have a very unusual impact on the power of incumbents. Adding three more medium-sized to small countries greatly increases their power, but the inclusion of two more medium-sized countries reduces it.

Blocking Coalitions and Eastern EU Enlargement

Using the voting–population relationship discussed above, we can roughly project how many votes each CEEC is likely to receive as members under current practice (Table 7.13). Having done this, we examine the implications for blocking coalitions of Easterners. A key premise throughout this analysis is that the qualified majority rule of 71% is maintained. The

Table 7.14 Illustration of blocking coalitions after Eastern enlargement

Eastern EU enlargement scenarios Base Case is EU-15 (EU-12 plus Austria, Finland and Sweden)	Total votes in the Council	Total poor votes	Total Eastern votes	Votes needed for blocking
EU-12	76	21	0	23
EU-15	87	21	0	26
EU-15 + CZR or Hungary	92	26	5	27
EU-15 + CZR and Hungary	97	31	10	29
EU-18 = EU-15 + Czech Republic, Hungary, Poland	105	39	18	31
EU-19 = EU-18 + Slovakia	109	43	22	32
EU-20 = EU-19 + Slovenia	112	46	25	33
EU-23 = EU-20 + Estonia, Latvia, Lithuania	122	56	35	35
EU-25 = EU-23 + Bulgaria, Romania	134	68	47	39

Source: Author's calculation.

voting mechanism and even the entire institutional structure of the EU may be modified before the Easterners are allowed in, so much of the reasoning may be wide of the mark. However, the reasoning using current rules shows how difficult it would be to accommodate several Eastern newcomers without institutional reform.

Analysis of Potential for Eastern Blocking Coalitions　Table 7.14 shows the total Council of Ministers votes, the number of votes for a blocking minority and the number of Eastern and poor votes under a variety of enlargement scenarios. The arithmetic in the table makes a very important point. Any Eastern enlargement could have serious consequences for EU politics.

To illustrate this, let us consider a Visegrad enlargement. The Visegrad-4 would have 22 votes, 11 votes short of a blocking minority. This would mean that that new poor-four had more votes than the old poor-four. Substituting Slovenia for Slovakia would give the first CEEC entrants 21 votes. Once we get to the point where the Visegrad-4 plus Slovenia and the Baltic States were admitted, the Eastern countries would have a blocking coalition. Enlarging even further east and south makes the possibility of blocking coalitions even greater. In the extreme case, the EU-12 plus SAF countries of the FANS enlargement (assuming that Norway says no) plus the CEEC-10 would yield an EU-25. The CEEC-10 would have over one third of the votes on the Council of Ministers.

Analysis of Potential for Poor-country Blocking Coalitions　Analysis of the budgetary cost of an Eastern enlargement suggests that the incumbent poor-four would be in competition with any CEECs that were allowed into the EU. The underlying presumption is that EU revenue is scarce. An alternative scenario is suggested by the column that shows the number of poor-country votes. Since even the richest CEECs are poorer than Spain and they are likely to remain so for many years, the CEECs may join the poor-four in demanding higher transfers. The reversal of Greece's opposition to the Iberian enlargement may have had something to do with exactly this type of reasoning. Let us start with the current situation. In the EU-12, the poor-four have almost enough votes to block. Indeed, the poor-four plus Luxembourg could hold up any piece of EU legislation. The SAF (Sweden, Austria and Finland) enlargement would reduce their power by raising the votes needed for a blocking coalition to 26.

Let us consider how various Eastern enlargements would alter the ability of the EU poor nations to block a qualified majority under current rules. If either Hungary or the Czech Republic were admitted while they were still poor, the poor-country coalition would be only one vote short of a blocking minority. If both Hungary and the Czech Republic entered the Union (and were allocated votes under existing rules), the poor coalition would have enough votes to obstruct all EU legislation. The addition of Poland and Slovakia or Slovenia gives the poor coalition a comfortable margin. Clearly, if ever the political power of the new poor-four were added to that of the old poor-four, the tone of the debate in the Council of Ministers would change considerably.

In the past, higher spending in the EU poor regions has been paid for with a combination of increased revenue contributions and reforms of the CAP. Since many CEECs are also quite agricultural, and they produce the types of food products that are heavily subsidized by the CAP, one might guess that a poor coalition with a significant CEEC component would demand that increased transfers not cut into CAP spending. The only alternative is higher net contributions by the rich countries. Of course, the rich countries do have the right to refuse such increases. If however, the poor coalition promised to hold up all the measures that the rich countries wanted, taxpayers in the EU countries are likely to be asked to pay more. This line of reasoning suggests that the rich EU incumbents might fear a substantial Eastern enlargement. Of course, it cannot be both ways. If an Eastern enlargement strengthened the hand of EU poor countries enough, the poor countries might support it. In this case, the rich EU nations would be certain that an Eastern enlargement would result in higher taxes, so they might oppose it. In contrast, if an Eastern enlargement only slightly increased the power of the poor coalition, the incumbent poor-four might oppose membership for the CEECs. The point is that the increased competition for transfers would not be fully compensated for by an increase in the EU total budget.

As with all the discussion in this section, speculation and conjecture are unavoidable. Nevertheless, the voting implications of an enlargement of the EU to the East are likely to be momentous.

Potential Voting Reforms

To maintain the momentum of European integration, the EU's Council of Ministers must be able to take difficult decisions. Moreover, there is a limit to how often structural spending can be increased to encourage coope- ration. The above reasoning suggests that admitting the Visegrad countries under current EU rules would substantially complicate decision making in the Council of Ministers and the European Council. This might be especially true when finding a common foreign policy. Problems such as Greece's opposition to EU recognition of Macedonia are likely to multiply when several CEECs have a *de jure* veto in the Council.

One of the most important problems with the current EU voting system is the over-representation of EU citizens that happen to live in small nations. This is a problem that might have to be dealt with even without an Eastern enlargement. Various Eastern enlargements will make a solution much more important. At its Copenhagen meeting, the European Council agreed eventually to admit ten CEECs. The six CEECs that already have Europe Agreements, as well as Slovenia and the Baltic States, will eventually be admitted to the EU. Eight of these ten countries have populations of 10 million or less. Five of the ten have populations of 5 million or less. What has so far been the difficulty of small countries could turn into a nightmare of small countries.

The nature of the necessary institutional reform will be heavily influenced by how soon an Eastern enlargement occurs and how far East it reaches. Clearly, the power of small countries must be trimmed. The amount of trimming necessary to make a European Union of 15 members (EU-12 plus Austria, Finland and Sweden) work smoothly is different from that needed to make a EU of 19 or even 25 work smoothly. Moreover, not only are the CEECs small, they will be very poor if admitted quickly. Since the schism of poor versus rich is an important factor that has hindered EU decision making, it would seem that the faster an enlargement occurs, the more severe must be the reform of the voting process.

The thrust of all this is that incumbent small nations in the EU may become reluctant as the wedding of the EU and the CEECs approaches. A focal point for this rethinking may come during the preparation of the institutional reform that is supposed to happen in 1996. At that point, the small incumbent nations may be faced with the choice between reducing their own power and endorsing an early Eastern enlargement.

Any effort to project the voting effects of an Eastern enlargement must come with a 'buyer beware' sticker. A witticism serves this purpose. Three

Finns – Kari, Matti and Petri – go for a week's ice fishing, each carrying a bottle of vodka. As they are cutting the hole in the ice, the issue of what to do with the vodka arises. They decide to settle it democratically. A vote is held and the outcome is two votes against one to drink Kari's bottle first. After Kari's bottle is finished, they vote on what to do next. Sure enough, the outcome is again two votes against one, but this time the decision is that each should drink his own bottle. As the anecdote illustrates, it is impossible to know what will happen if the rules are subject to voting.

7.2.3   *Migration Effects*

Migration tends to equalize wages of comparable labour. Given the current relative-wage situation, opening the EU labour market to Eastern workers may lower Western wages for unskilled workers. Although this would cause considerable political difficulties in Western Europe, it would, in the long run, constitute an economic gain.

Size of Migration Flows

The size of likely East–West migration is extremely difficult to estimate. One approach is to examine Western Europe's experience with South–North migration in the post-war period. Income differences in the EU have been as high as three to one during the 1970s and 1980s. The share of poor nations' populations that have migrated within the EU range from 15% for Ireland to 1.4% for Spain. About 4% of Greeks and more than 9% of Portuguese live in other EU nations according to Eurostat figures.[7] Since East–West income differences are not too far from this three-to-one figure, one could roughly project that 5–10% of Easterners might move West.

Considering only an EU enlargement to Poland, the Czech Republic, Slovakia and Hungary, this 5%–10% range implies that between 3.2 and 6.4 million people would migrate in response to existing East–West wage differentials. This does not appear to be a very large number compared with the EU's current population of 345 million. If the migrants decided to spread themselves evenly over the EU-12, they would pose few problems. Migrants, however, usually move to a handful of urban areas, with particular ethnic groups dominating small locales. Because of this tendency, even a relatively small number of migrants can create very large political problems. The persistence of high unemployment rates compounds these problems. Of course, some of this migration will occur whether the EU enlarges to the East or not.

Table 7.15　Dependency ratios in Europe

	Actual 1990 dependency ratio	Projected 2030 dependency ratio
EU-12	0.4851	0.7133
EFTA-6	0.5064	0.7318
CEEC – north-east	0.5365	0.6153
CEEC – central	0.5169	0.6170
CEEC – south-east	0.5180	0.5809
CEEC-12	0.5251	0.6034
Russia + three FSRs	0.5390	0.6386
Various totals		
Total East	0.5341	0.6264
Total West	0.4869	0.7150
Total East + West	0.5086	0.6702
Various enlargements		
EFTA-3	0.4996	0.7348
EU-15	0.4865	0.7143
EU-15 + CEEC-12	0.4956	0.6846

Note: CEEC – north-east = the Baltic States and Poland; CEEC – central = Hungary; Czech Republic, Slovakia and Slovenia; CEEC – south-east = Bulgaria, Romania, Albania and Croatia; the three FSRs are Ukraine, Belarus and Moldova.

Source: World Bank, *World Population Projections, 1992–1993 Edition*, 1992.

The Ageing of the EU Population

One effect of East–West migration that is often ignored is its impact on the age profile and dependency ratios in Europe. Many have pointed out that Western Europe's dependency ratio, defined as the ratio of non-working-age population (ages 0–14 and over 64) to the working-age population, will rise steeply in the coming decades. Table 7.15 shows that the EU-12's current ratio of 0.49 is projected by the World Bank to rise to 0.71 by 2030. This ageing of the population is extremely important. By reducing the taxable proportion of the population, this trend is likely to cause numerous social and political problems. For instance, the tax burden on the working-age population must grow to provide social services for the non-working population. The table shows that although the dependency ratios are already higher in the East, they will have lower dependency ratios by 2030. This is especially true for the south-east CEECs Bulgaria, Romania, Albania and Croatia. Note that Russia and the other three FSRs are projected to have the highest dependency ratios in the east.

This East–West difference suggests an interesting possibility. An EU enlargement would allow free migration and migrants tend to be fairly young when they move. Thus, East–West migration might ameliorate the problems caused by Western Europe's rising dependency ratio. To put it crudely, young Eastern migrants could help to pay for the retirement benefits of Western Europe's aging population. To evaluate this possibility, dependency ratios are calculated for various combined populations. The data for these calculations are the relevant nations' populations and age profiles in 1990 and projected population and age profiles for 2030. Using these, the dependency ratios are calculated from the combined age profiles. The results, shown in Table 7.15, are not very spectacular. Even if the whole CEEC-12 population was combined with that of the EU-15 (EU-12 plus Austria, Finland and Sweden), the dependency ratio falls from 0.71 to 0.68. This unpolished calculation does tend to overestimate the dependency ratio in Western Europe since the Eastern migrants are likely to be younger than the average Easterner.

The Brain Drain Effect

The final effect is that of the 'brain drain amplified' (Baldwin and Venables, 1994). The basic idea is simple and is based on the widely held concept that the East is relatively rich in skilled labour and relatively poor in capital. The presence of a large pool of skilled labour that is cheap by European standards is one main attraction that the CEECs present to foreign investors. Moreover, the expectation that a good deal of foreign investment will occur in the near future is of great interest to skilled labourers in the East. If the Eastern economies joined the EU, all these skilled labourers would have the right to move to any European Union country. A very likely outcome of this situation is that the best and the brightest from the East would move West. Migration of this type would tend to reduce the incentives for Western investment in the East. Thus, the usual harmful effects of the brain drain on East Europe might well be amplified by reduced foreign investment.

7.2.4 *Other Difficulties*

There are several additional difficulties that an Eastern enlargement might pose.

The Human Factor

To be part of the EU, member state governments, as well as public and private firms, must be staffed with highly capable and experienced personnel. It is not enough for the national parliament to adopt the right laws. The government must have trained and experienced personnel to interpret, apply and enforce these laws. To take just one example, membership means participation in the Single Market. Since this involves mutual recognition of industrial and health standards, member countries need to have the effective regulatory agencies. This is not a simple task. It is difficult to regulate a market economy. It is as easy to make the mistake of being too severe as it is of being too lenient. A hurried training course is probably not enough since the judgement of officials, even fairly low-level ones, is critical. It is easy to forget that West European agencies that perform these tasks have highly trained staffs, directed by officials with decades of experience. It could take a decade before the Central and Eastern European administrators gain sufficient experience. Even in the most advanced CEECs, government officials are inexperienced in the design and enforcement of health, safety and environment standards in a market economy. Moreover, Western businesses are run by people who have decades of experience in dealing with these agencies.

Private and public firms must also be able to operate in a transparent manner. For instance, it would be difficult to enforce competition and anti-subsidy policies until Western-style accounting are universally practised and strictly policed. This is not easy, since it takes years to train accountants and for them to get essential on-the-job training. A report by the Business Council for Sustainable Development (1993), which consists of many of Europe's largest corporations, notes that inexperienced personnel was a major problem in Central and Eastern Europe (BCSD, 1993). 'One of the biggest handicaps slowing down the region's transformation is the lack of experience of managing businesses in a modern market economy after 40 years of central planning and state control.'

The Balance between Deepeners and Wideners

The Maastricht Treaty promises extensive political integration. EU members will decide the extent and pace of this integration over the coming decades. An early Eastern enlargement means that Central and Eastern European government will vote on the shape of the EU. Since the CEECs are quite populous (64 million Visegraders alone), it is likely that their votes would have a significant impact on the pace of deepening as well as on the ultimate shape of the Union.

As with many of these issues, it is not possible to know which way the balance would tilt. One possibility is that an Eastern enlargement would delay the Council of Ministers, bringing EU decision making to a halt. This would hand victory to the wideners, who would like to avoid meeting many of the vague commitments made in the Maastricht Treaty. Moreover, a quick Eastern enlargement would significantly increase the economic diversity in the Union. An Eastern enlargement, even after the CEECs get much richer, would increase the political diversity of the Union. All this would favour the tendency towards a multi-tier or multi-speed European Union. It might prevent the monumental decisions that would be needed to move closer to the 'finalité politique'.

Another possibility is that the newly admitted CEECs would be avid promoters of deepening. In any case, they are likely to support stronger EU commitments to common foreign policies. A substantial Eastern enlargement might then hasten and deepen political integration.

Defence and Security issues

Defence and security issues are also likely to become more divisive. Once Poland and Slovakia are members, the EU will have a border with the Ukraine, Belarus and Russia (via Kaliningrad). Finland also brings with it a Russian border, but the position of Kaliningrad is quite special. This is likely to complicate significantly the foreign and security problems confronting the Union over the next two or three decades. The fact that one main reason the CEECs want to join the EU is the security guarantee they hope it will provide suggests that these problems could be important. An Eastern enlargement would transfer part of the CEECs' security problems to the EU.

As full members the CEECs could use their voting power to help to deepen the EU's commitment to common defence policies in an attempt to secure their own eastern borders. In a body such as the Council of Ministers even a small number of countries may be able to get their way on issues that they see as all-important. Increasing EU commitments to the defence of its members runs counter to the tendency of many EU incumbents. The EU's stance in the former Yugoslavia, and even in the Gulf War, suggests that many current EU members would be extremely reluctant to commit their military forces to security guarantees. After the current enlargement many EU incumbents will be formally neutral or will have strong pacifist traditions.

Notes

1. See El-Agraa (1990), Eurostat (1992) and Franklin (1992) for a more complete description of the EU budget. The EC Commission has recently produced an excellent study of spending and revenue entitled 'Stable money – sound finances' (Courchene et al., 1993).
2. Since 1988 each member's VAT base (for the purposes of EU contribution) was limited to no more than 55% of its GNP.
3. Agriculture shares were not available for all years for all countries. The figure plots all available data.

4. Recall that income levels in all CEECs fell substantially in 1992, and early data suggest that most fell in 1993, therefore attaining an average of 6% would require above-average growth in some years.
5. The issue is whether to change the number of votes needed to block a decision. Changing this rule could greatly alter the power of incumbents, especially the small countries.
6. This is not done directly under current EU practice. What is done is to change the Structural Funds rules in such as way so as to ensure that equal application of the new rules to all EU members will provide disproportionate benefits to certain countries. The creation of a fishing region objective is a good example of how Portugal won substantial benefits.
7. See Baldwin et al. (1992) Section 3.4.1 for more details. Also see Blanchard et al. (1992).

8

Early Enlargement on the Cheap

Chapter 7 argues that it would be at least two decades before the leading CEECs can be full members without threatening incumbents' special interests. The main difficulties concern EU agriculture and structural spending programmes, EU decision-making mechanisms, trade in sensitive products and migration. Let us take, as an example, an enlargement that granted full EU citizenship to the 64 million Visegrad citizens by 2000. The budgetary and institutional adjustments necessary to do this while 'maintaining the momentum of European integration' are very likely to harm incumbent farmers, poor regions and small countries.

A simple solution, one might think, would be to admit the CEECs early, but to exempt them from the full rights of membership for a long transition period. They could be excluded from structural spending until they are rich enough not to need it, and excluded from agriculture for however long incumbent EU farmers insist upon. Access to the EU labour market could be withheld until wages differences equalize. On many levels, this seems quite reasonable. The first Eastern enlargement, whenever it occurs, will include at least some aspects of this solution. Accessions always involve various derogations over various transition periods. Nevertheless, this 'solution' could be treacherous.

This chapter argues that this 'solution' could create considerable political complications in the European Union. The critical issue is the voting power of members that may come to feel they are being treated as second-class for ten years or more (once the ephemeral joys of 'marriage' fade). To put it colloquially, unpleasantness is unavoidable when second-class ticket holders have a say in what the first-class passengers are going to have for dinner. The potential for unpleasantness becomes more severe, the larger is the difference between the first- and second-class treatment and the longer is the train ride. If the enlargement-on-the-cheap excluded voting for the CEECs, membership would be mostly a matter of semantics. EFTAns participating in the European Economic Area would have more rights than the Central European 'members' of the Union.

8.1   Exclusions and Transition Periods

To prevent harming incumbent special-interest groups – farmers and workers in steel, coal, and textile industries in particular – an early Eastern enlargement may require long transition periods concerning free trade in sensitive goods. This section briefly discusses why these sectors are considered sensitive, why allowing the CEECs to have free access would harm these industries and how long the exclusion must last. Of course, Chapter 2 pointed out that EU consumers would gain more than the industries would lose. While true, this is moot since politics, not economics, is the driving force behind the junior-membership proposal.

8.1.1   *Trade in Food*

Food markets are a special case. This follows from two basic economic facts and one political economy fact. First, the demand for food is very insensitive to its price. If the price of bread doubles, people buy more or less the same amount. This means that if the supply of bread rises, prices must fall sharply to make people buy more of it. For this reason, prices for farm products are extremely sensitive to changes in supply. Second, farmers' incomes (and often their wealth as well) depend heavily on this potentially variable price. Very few other workers face this extreme season-to-season uncertainty. Third, farmers – who are usually concentrated geographically – are usually over-represented politically. The reason is that most representative democracies are based (at least partially) on geographical boundaries, instead of, say, economic ones.

For these reasons (and many more), agriculture is a highly political matter. Each government tends to favour its agricultural sectors. One tempting way to do this is to prohibit food imports and subsidize food exports. These tendencies operate throughout the world, so free trade in food is extremely rare. On this point the EU is an exception. However, a single EU market for food would not be politically feasible without the common agricultural policy.

The point of all these preliminaries is the following. If the CEECs are admitted to the EU, and this included free access to EU food markets, the cost of maintaining the Union's high food prices would rise very quickly.

Thus, it would not be enough to exclude the CEECs from CAP subsidies. They would have to be excluded from free trade in food.

Indefinite Transition or CAP Reform?

The number of years that trade in agriculture would have to be excluded is indeterminate. The Visegrad nations, particularly Poland and Hungary, are blessed with fertile land. Rising affluence usually reduces the fraction of the workforce in farming, as well as the share of agriculture in the GDP. However, steeply rising yields usually accompany these changes. One can easily imagine that in 20 years, Polish farmers would be as productive as the Danish and French. This means that it might never be cheap to allow Visegrad farmers access to EU food markets, to say nothing of access to more direct CAP payments.

This line of thought suggests that trade in food and access to CAP payments would have to be postponed for a very long time. The alternative is a further reform of the CAP.

8.1.2   *Trade in Other Sensitive Products*

Several other products share similar sensitivities to trade, so the same logic applies. Steel is one, since its demand is also fairly sensitive to supply. Moreover, steel workers and firms are typically concentrated geographically. The same is true of the EU coal industry. Textiles and clothing are not particularly price-sensitive but the workers in these industries are often poor compared with national averages. This creates a sympathy for protection. In fact, this is the second most protected sector in the industrial world following agriculture.

Incumbent production of steel and coal are on a long-run downward trend. A very optimistic scenario for Eastern enlargement is admission in 2000 with a ten-year transition period. By the year 2010, the political influence of the incumbent coal and steel industry (and unions) is likely to be greatly diminished. A similar transition period for trade in labour-intensive goods would also probably be sufficient provided the CEECs actually caught up with Western income levels. The relative competitiveness of CEECs' labour-intensive industries is likely to fall as they become richer.

8.1.3   *Structural Spending*

The role of structural spending in the current EU is manifold. It was intended to ease the pain that the poor-four and various poor regions would experience when they adopted the rigour of Community law, especially the Single Market Act. It is also supposed to promote 'economic and social cohesion'. Presumably, this means mainly a convergence of per capita incomes. In this role it is similar to development aid. The junior membership option would presumably provide the CEECs with very limited access to these funds in order to insulate the incumbent poor regions. The discussion in Chapter 2 cited Courchene et al. (1993) as saying that EU structural spending in the Visegrad nations could amount to 400 ECU per citizen in 1999. The junior-membership option would presumably limit this to a much lower number. Since there are 64 million Visegraders, providing even a quarter of this figure would cost over 6 billion ECU a year.

The economic effect of limited structural spending in the CEECs is not clear. At first, one would think that without this sort of aid the CEECs would grow more slowly and therefore prolong the length of their second-class status. The reason that the effects are unclear is that we have examples of countries, especially in Asia, which have grown rapidly without much direct foreign aid. Furthermore, the certitude of eventual access to the Single Market would make the CEECs very attractive to investors inside and outside the Union.

8.1.4   *Migration*

One of the most controversial issues in Europe during the 1990s is migration. There are many explanations for this that we need not address here. Chapter 7 argued that East–West migration flows are likely to be no more than 5–10% of the CEECs' labour force. However, it is quite likely that most of them would settle in northern EU countries, especially those that border the Visegrad regions. This means Austria and Germany.

If junior membership also excluded structural spending, migration pressures would be increased. It may be argued that one reason the EU-rich are willing to fund large investment programmes in the EU-poor is the desire to moderate intra-EU migration. Recall from Chapter 2 that the decision to migrate depends upon the expectations of the workers regarding future wage differences, in addition to current wage differentials. Insofar as structural spending brightens the future prospects of the EU-poor nations, it could play an important role in reducing intra-EU migration.

Chapter 2 argued that limiting out-migration of skilled workers from the CEECs may be economically beneficial to them. Moreover, except a few small developing countries, it is rare for a nation to care much about the migration rights that its workers have in other countries. This suggests that limiting migration would not raise a large amount of resentment in the Visegrad governments, apart from a vague feeling of being treated as inferior in some way.

8.1.5 *Membership with Limited Obligations*

Many EU incumbents resist the obligations of membership and would wish to be temporarily excused from them. For instance, France and Italy would like to give more money to their uncompetitive industries. The United Kingdom would wish to keep passport checks. Virtually all would like to be excused from certain parts of the Single European Act. The attraction of this sort of exception, however, is likely to carry less weight with the CEECs. At the moment, the Visegrad countries seem anxious to adopt even the most difficult of membership obligations. Of course, much of this is undertaken to make themselves look like the best candidate for membership. Once membership is promised, a whole new attitude may emerge. However, the basic point stands. The idea that junior membership would entail a gradual phasing in of the obligations of membership would do little to make it more palatable for the Visegraders and (eventually) other CEECs.

What the CEECs require from EU membership is political anchorage, security guarantees and rapid affluence. Excusing them from certain membership obligations would do almost nothing to further any of these basic goals. However, things may change in the CEECs. As their economies mature, they are likely to see a set of economic special-interest groups influence politics. If this occurs, the CEEC politicians may appreciate the ability to deviate from Union standards.

8.1.6 *The Iberian Analogy*

The political and economic motives for the Southern enlargement of the EU are similar to those for the Eastern enlargement. Politics was the engine; economics was the brake. Of course, one can argue that the consequences of instability in Central and Eastern Europe are potentially much more dire than those that were posed by instability in Spain, Portugal and Greece. However, it is probably fair to say that there is less consensus now about the urgency of CEECs membership than there was about Spain. The problems of Poland look quite different from Lisbon and Berlin. Despite the greater consensus on the Iberian problem, Spain's and Portugal's applications in 1977 led to membership in only 1986.

Accession offered Greece, Spain and Portugal a means of securing the recent adoptions of democracy. For incumbent members, securing democracy was desired for altruistic reasons as well as to ensure stability along the Union's Southern border. The problems of the Iberian enlargement are also analogous. Initially, Greece opposed the Iberian accession, and incumbent farmers in Mediterranean areas felt threatened.

There is a major difference, however. Then, the poor-country incumbents were much weaker and they had less to lose since structural spending was much lower. When the Iberians joined, the poor incumbents, Greece and Ireland, accounted for only 5% of the EU-10's population, so the poor-country coalition was quite weak. Moreover, structural spending was much less important at the time. Indeed, structural spending, i.e. the European Regional Development Fund, was increased as part of the Iberian accession. This was the so-called integrated Mediterranean policy (see Winters, 1992, for details). Now, the poor-four account for about one-fifth of the EU population and 28% of votes in the Council of Ministers. Structural spending has tripled since the mid-1980s and is set to rise much further.

To assuage opposition from incumbent farmers and workers in sensitive sectors, the EC insisted on long transition periods. For example, quotas on Iberian iron and steel were in place for seven years, and Spanish fruit, vegetables and vegetable fats will not have free access to the EU market until 1996. Furthermore, opposition from incumbent poor-countries was avoided since structural spending was increased substantially. Migration rights for Iberians were restricted for five years.

The increased structural spending served an important second purpose. While the Iberians received second-class treatment in terms of market access and the labour market, they were offered better than first-class treatment on Structural Funds. This balanced the impression that Spain and Portugal were joining as second-class members.

8.2   Political Unpleasantness

The calculations in Chapter 7 make clear that any Eastern enlargement, even one that included only the Visegrad countries, would require much broader and much longer transitions than those of the Iberian accession. The chapter argued that it will take at least two decades until the Visegraders are rich enough not to put a strain on the structural budget. Since the calculations were based on 1991 data, the suggested date is about 2010. Thus, if the most optimistic timetable is realized and the first Eastern enlargement occurs in 2000, a ten-year transition period would be necessary for access to the Structural Funds. Given the fertility of Visegrad farmland and the types of food it could produce, the CAP is likely to be threatened whenever the CEECs gain full access to EU food markets. Fully insulating EU farmers might then require an indefinite transition period. Since this is unlikely, let us consider a transition of, say, ten years. Note that these two temporary derogations would exclude the CEECs from 80% of EU spending for a decade.

Migration pressure would fade as wages equalized, so five years might be a sufficient transition period. Let us take five years as the transition period for other sensitive goods, just as an example.

8.2.1 *Political Implications*

In general, the EU commits itself to spending plans only for five-year periods. A ten-year transition period means that the CEECs would have second-class access to structural spending for part of at least two budget cycles. Therefore, if the newly admitted CEECs had the right to vote, they would have an opportunity to do so on at least one five-year budget package. One issue on which they would vote (while they had second-class access to structural spending) is reform of structural spending.

One cannot help but ponder the position the Visegraders – individually or as a group – would take in the European Council when Spain and others asked for a continuation or augmentation of the current spending programmes. On the one hand, the CEEC politicians may keep in mind the objective (stated in the Treaty on European Union) of 'strengthening economic and social cohesion'. In this case they would surely support the claims of the poor-four. On the other hand, they may decide that massive transfers to poor countries were not really as necessary for European integration as was once thought. Yet a third option would be that the new poor-four would support demands from the old poor-four in exchange for shorter-than-foreseen derogations on structural spending or agricultural trade. Another line of thought suggests that the CEEC politicians would rise above such petty reasoning. They would simply vote for whatever they decided was best for both the first- and second-class members of the Union. There is no end to such conjectures.

Many observers note that a further reform of the CAP is inevitable due to political pressures inside and outside the EU. Such a reform, if it does occur, is likely to be some time between 1999 and 2010. During this period, the CEECs will have second-class status as far as the CAP is concerned. How would Visegrad politicians vote on reform of the CAP? Supporting a quick phasing out of the CAP would make it easier to shorten the transition to first-class status. Alternatively, the Visegraders – individually or separately – might decide to 'sell' their votes on CAP reform to EU agricultural interests in exchange for, say, creation of a new fund (it might be called the Solidarity Fund) that financed infrastructure in regions east of Germany.

Another item that the Council of Ministers decides upon is external trade policy. This includes the imposition of anti-dumping duties and quantitative restrictions on sensitive products such as coal, iron, steel and clothing. Again, it is enlightening to speculate on what positions the CEECs would take given their second-class access to the EU markets for such goods. One line of thought suggests that the CEECs would informally offer to support easy contingent protection against third-country products in exchange for a faster-than-foreseen reduction of restrictions on their exports. Another suggests that opening EU markets for sensitive goods would force the closure of sensitive industries in the first-class member countries. This might lower the resistance to giving the CEECs full access to the markets of the first-class countries.

Restricted Voting Rights

One solution to the difficulties mentioned above would be to grant the CEECs restricted voting rights. For instance, they could vote on issues such as R&D programmes and foreign aid but they would be required to abstain on those related to CAP and structural spending, the common labour market, and the coal, iron, steel or textile industries. It is not clear that this would be feasible, but, in any case, it would not be enough to eliminate problems. Politics very often involves 'back-scratching'. That is, votes on totally unrelated issues are informally exchanged.

Alternatively, sufficiently radical institutional reforms could permit the Union to give the Visegraders full voting rights without the risk of them diverting EU largesse eastwards. Such reforms, however, are likely to be resisted by incumbent small nations. This would force small counties to choose: veto an early Eastern enlargement, or surrender even more of their power than would otherwise be necessary in the 1996 reforms.

8.2.2　*Some Conclusions*

The above examples illustrate a general point. The EU is a club, which has functioned better than most other international clubs. One reason is that members are more economically homogenous than those of other international clubs. Another is that members are treated as equals. This equality means that the Union only works well when members act in good faith. The same equality, however, encourages members to do so. Spain agreed to forgo access to the EU market for fruits and vegetables for ten years, but in its accession talks it won concessions from the incumbents on structural spending. Thus, on balance, it was not treated as a second-class member. The derogations and transitions necessary to make an Eastern enlargement palatable to incumbent special interests must be broad and long, if accession occurs before the CEECs are much richer and much less agricultural. In particular, they would have to be largely excluded from the benefits of 80% of EU expenditures. It appears that the CEECs would feel like second-class members because of this.

Despite this, the CEECs might eagerly accept junior membership for ten years. One of their primary goals in the short term is to secure political anchorage, win security guarantees and rapidly attain affluence. Yet once junior membership was a *fait accompli*, would they be satisfied? Would their voters, say five years after membership, be happy with governments that continued to support the CAP and Structural Funds while their own farmers and industries were denied equal access to EU markets? There is a very natural tendency for assertiveness to increase once the wedding ring is on the finger.

8.2.3   A Note of Caution

The point of all this is to sound a note of caution. Whether the first Eastern enlargement occurs in 6, 16 or 26 years, various derogations and transition periods will be involved. Crafting a membership package for the CEECs that insulated incumbent special interests is always difficult. The task becomes much more so if the transitions must very broad and very long. There is no clear demarcation between a long transition and junior membership. The critical issue is the voting power of members that may come to feel that they are being treated as second-class. A very uneven treatment of the CEECs and very long transition periods are a recipe for political complications in the European Union.

On the matter of voting over ten-year periods, no one can predict what will happen. As the years passed, political pressure would mount to shorten the transition periods. The carefully calculated transition periods intended to insulate incumbent farmers and poor regions from an Eastern enlargement could be cast aside. Additionally, the CEECs *sans* CAP and structural spending would undermine these programmes' *raison d'être*. The adjustment by the CEECs without transfers might foster the belief that structural spending was not as important for European integration as was once thought. After all, if the Easterners can live with membership without massive transfers, why should the EU-rich pay hundreds of ECU a year to the much richer Irish, Portuguese, Greeks and Spaniards? The only way for the poor-four to avoid raising such doubts would be to veto the creation of a prolonged second-class membership.

A final point is that the longer and broader are the derogations, the more difficult will be the accession talks. Spain's took six years. Although the CEECs, especially the leaders, are very keen to join, this does not mean that they would be docile in their accession talks. After accession talks began, both the EU and the CEECs would try to avoid failure. The CEECs may take heart from the very tough stance that served the Iberians well. Some of the sweetest courtships are followed by really unpleasant haggling over wedding arrangements.

9

A Proposal

The long-run design of pan-European integration was decided in 1993 in Copenhagen. All associated nations can join the European Union, eventually. The Europe Agreements and the tangle of CEEC–CEEC deals tell us where pan-European integration is now. Europe Agreements also contain vague indications of how integration will be deepened. What is missing is a well-marked path that gets Europe from here to there.

The required path must accomplish many things. It must correct the current pan-European trade system's shortcomings in order to avoid political difficulties and to seize the economic opportunity presented by the opening of Central and Eastern Europe. It should be a multispeed path to account for the great diversity among the Central and East Europeans. Most importantly, it must be politically viable. Three major constraints are posed by Eastern politics. First, the CEEC governments are very resistant to anything that resembles the old Council for Mutual Economic Assistance (CMEA). This rules out one natural route – creation of an Eastern free trade area. The second constraint is related. Many CEECs wish to join the EU as fast as possible. Thus, the path must make the journey to membership easier, not harder. Finally, there is no leader among the CEECs, so the initiative must come from the European Union. Equally important constraints are posed by Western politics. The path to full EU membership for the CEECs must avoid four 'political land mines' in West Europe, i.e. agricultural trade, competition for structural spending, migration and voting in the Council of Ministers. Lastly, Chapter 7 argued that an Eastern enlargement is unlikely for at least two decades (absent earth-shaking political events). This means that a makeshift road will not do. Whatever the path to membership is, it will govern pan-European integration for a very long time.

There is no way to be certain about what the best path should look like. Key elements depend upon opinions concerning events that are 10 to 20 years in the future. Obviously, reasonable people can differ over such things. This chapter puts forward one proposal for improving the pan-European integration process.

The proposal envisions two phases. The first would be a rather modest step. It would redress the current hub-and-spoke bilateralism by embedding the existing Europe Agreements into what could be called an Association of Association Agreements (AAA). The AAA would consist of an agreement and a new institutional framework. This would (1) immediately increase the EU's political and economic engagement in the integration of the CEECs and (2) bring the advanced CEECs into Western Europe's duty-free zone for industrial goods. The next phase is to create an intermediate step – resembling the EEA Agreement without migration – for the CEECs that need it. If the most optimistic timetable for EU enlargement holds, some CEECs – certainly not all – may have already passed this step by the time the necessary institutional framework could be in place. This intermediate step would turn the European trade arrangement into three concentric circles. Membership in all three circles should evolve.

9.1 A Stage One

The fundamental aim of the proposed first stage is to make the continuing bilateral association process more coherent. It serves two economic goals and one political goal. Economically, it is aimed at rationalizing and coordinating efforts to fulfil the liberalization promises made in the Europe Agreements and in Copenhagen. It is also aimed at redressing hub-and-spoke bilateralism by rationalizing the market-opening component of the Europe Agreements. Politically, it would complement the long-term Copenhagen decision with immediate action: creating a more coherent institutional framework and increasing the EU's engagement in the short- and medium-run economic integration of Europe. This stage concerns only the CEECs that already have Europe Agreements with the EU.

The Copenhagen decision reflects the EU's interest in opening trade and investment opportunities throughout Europe, not just bilaterally with the CEECs. To quote the Conclusions of the Presidency: 'The European Council, recognizing the crucial importance of trade in the transition to a market economy, agreed to accelerate the Community's efforts to open its markets. It expected this step forward to go hand in hand with further development of trade between those countries themselves and between them and their traditional trading partners.'

Much can be read into this quote, especially the part about further development of intra-CEEC trade. On the economic side, it might be interpreted as reflecting the EU's concern for CEECs' development. Chapter 3 showed that at current income levels, intra-CEEC trade would account for between 10% and 20% of total CEEC trade, if all of Europe was as integrated as Western Europe was in the 1980s. This figure rises to 20–30% if CEEC incomes increase to Western levels. The conclusion is that removing EU–CEEC barriers is by far the most important task, but failing to remove CEEC–CEEC trade barriers could inhibit a substantial amount of trade. East–East trade is tainted by its association with the old regime. However, the numbers in Chapter 3 indicate that even new private firms in the CEECs will want to sell their goods in the markets of surrounding nations. The quotation could also reflect more self-interested economic concerns. East–West and East–East trade liberalization would benefit West European multinational firms that have, or are considering, investing in the CEECs.

On the political side, there is a danger that the quotation could be viewed by the CEECs as a diversionary tactic. The problem is that the Europe Agreements lump together all aspects of pan-European integration in a very vague way. Consequently, any suggestion that one aspect of pan-European integration (i.e. liberalization of CEEC–CEEC trade) is important may be viewed as a suggestion that other aspects (i.e. an Eastern enlargement) are less so. The proposed first stage is aimed at providing a separate forum – and one in which the EU would be materially and politically engaged – for more technical market-access issues.

A practical solution to hub-and-spoke bilateralism is to embed the existing bilateral agreements – the Association Agreements – in a framework that transforms the current arrangement into a system of two concentric circles. This should involve a new portmanteau agreement and a new institution. It is useful to think of this as an Association of Association Agreements (AAA).[1] The member states of the AAA would consist of all EU members and all CEECs that have signed Europe Agreements.

9.1.1   A New Agreement

The aim of the new agreement is to regionalize the trade and investment liberalization components of the Europe Agreements (EAs). This would eliminate many marginalizing effects discussed in Chapter 5. It would do this by ensuring that enterprises located in any Central and Eastern Europe (CEE) member state has access to other CEE markets that is no worse than that accorded to EU-based firms. In other words, the new agreement would require the CEECs to open their markets equally to imports (only those covered in the Europe Agreements) from all AAA members. The principle of asymmetric East–West liberalization would remain, so the EU would still open its markets to the CEECs faster than the CEECs opened theirs to EU and CEE exports. Operationally, the CEE members would phase out tariffs and quantitative restrictions on imported manufactured goods from other CEE members of the AAA in tandem with their liberalization of imports from the EU. The Europe Agreements also contain provisions on national treatment of establishments, trade in services, the openness of competition for government contracts, and the liberalization of payments and financial transfers. The AAA would regionalize these liberalizations by requiring the CEE member states to offer non-discriminatory treatment to all AAA-based firms. Again, the principle of asymmetric liberalization by the EU would be maintained.

The liberalization of EU–CEEC trade and investment would continue to be governed by the Europe Agreements. This should not be viewed as a restriction. The EAs promise more EU–CEEC liberalization than has been accomplished to date. The AAA framework is a way to carry out those promises while fostering further development of trade between the CEEC members.

A moment's reflection reveals that the AAA would bring the advanced CEECs into Western Europe's duty-free zone for industrial goods. In other words, an industrial firm located in one AAA member state would have (eventually) duty-free access to any other AAA market. Figure 9.1 makes this point graphically. Recall that the current West European duty-free zone for industrial goods is created (indirectly) by three sets of accords: the Treaty of Rome (duty-free industrial trade within the EU), the Stockholm Convention (duty-free industrial trade within EFTA) and the bilateral EU–EFTA free trade agreements. Industrial firms based in the CEE members of the proposed AAA already have duty-free access to EFTA markets. The AAA agreement would complete the circle by locking in duty-free access to other CEE member states.

The envisaged system of agreements is really quite simple. After the continuing EFTA enlargement of the EU, the great majority of European trade will be among AAA members. Intra-EFTA trade will be negligible (Iceland, Norway and the Swiss–Liechtenstein customs union trade very little) and EFTA–CEEC trade will not be much larger. Thus, for practical purposes, the prospective duty-free zone would be created by the confluence of the Treaty of Rome and the proposed AAA agreement.

Does the AAA Postpone Enlargement?

The most important question for many CEECs is when they will get into the EU. This is a bilateral matter. EU accessions always have been. It is true

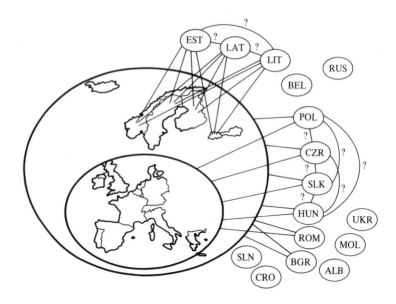

An Association of Association Agreements would bring the advanced
CEECs into the West European circle of free trade in industrial goods

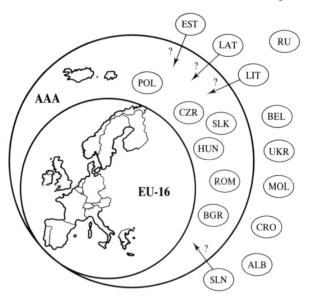

Figure 9.1 AAA versus current hub-and-spoke bilateralism

that the EU usually enlarges in waves, but the decision of who is included in the first wave must necessarily be bilateral. High-level politics inside the EU will determine the extent and timing of the first Eastern enlargement. The AAA is not intended to touch on such questions: it addresses much more modest problems.

This point is important to keep in mind. As László Csaba points out, the CEECs 'fear that their joint treatment serves as a pretext for the eternal postponement of their accession'. The AAA is a form of joint treatment, but only insofar as it regionalizes the liberalization generated by the Europe Agreements and rationalizes the efforts of the EU to assist with this. The progress of individual CEE members of the AAA will continue to be governed primarily by their internal political processes. For example, progress by the Czech Republic in, say, removing tariffs on EU imports or adopting the *Acquis communautaire* would in no way be tied to progress by slower CEE nations. The AAA agreement would merely require that the benefits of the resulting liberalization be extended to all AAA members.

The AAA might marginally hasten the first enlargement by increasing income levels and providing the CEECs with a record on multilateral cooperation in an EU-dominated organization dealing with complicated economic issues.

9.1.2   *A New Institutional Framework*

The patchy institutional arrangements that now govern the economic integration of the new Europe did not result from coherent reflection. They evolved helter-skelter. It would seem evident that they can be improved and this is one major goal of the AAA. There is no hard logic dictating the exact nature of these arrangements and the specifics of the AAA proposal depend upon issues on which reasonable people can differ. It seems reasonable, for instance, that the AAA would completely supplant the existing trade deals among its CEE members. Yet its reasonableness depends mostly on the fact that it would reduce the number of meetings and streamline legal arrangements. A reasonable counter-argument would be that keeping the CEEC–CEEC deals, but making them supplementary to the AAA, would allow sub-sets of AAA members to become even more integrated.

The proposed framework is referred to as the AAA Authority, and this would deal with EU–CEEC and CEEC–CEEC relations on the economic issues that are covered in the Europe Agreements: trade in goods and services, rights of establishment, the liberalization of payments and financial transfers, competition rules, state aids, government procurement and the approximation of laws. In each of these areas the AAA Authority would have four roles: surveillance, enforcement, coordination and assistance. The AAA Authority would:

1. Play a surveillance and enforcement role to ensure that promised liberalization actually occurred and was not offset (nullified and impaired) by subtle changes in domestic laws or regulations.
2. Have a coordinating role (where necessary) to smooth problems with the multitude of transition periods and derogations in the various Europe Agreements.
3. Assist in the coordination of technical and financial assistance to the associated countries.
4. Help directly with the human capital formation and national institution building that is necessary to operationalize the approximation of laws foreseen in the EAs.

Given legal, political and economic realities, the new institution must be dominated by the EU. In the EEA negotiations, the EU showed itself to be adamantly opposed to any institutional construction in which the Union entered as a component and therefore subordinate part. No Communauté bis, was the EU slogan. The European Court of Justice rejected the first draft of the EEA agreement for this type of reason. Clearly, the EU's judicial system would have to be supreme in all disputes involving trade with the EU. To reinforce the idea that the AAA was a step on the path to full EU membership, the AAA Authority should avoid creating a junior EC Commission. It should respect the distribution of tasks within the EC Commission. There should not, for example, be an AAA administrator making judgements on the acceptability of a merger between two CEEC firms without reference to the Merger Task Force. The room for direct participation by CEEC governments, and independent responsibility for the AAA Authority, would be much greater on issues involving only CEEC–CEEC trade.

As far as the CEECs who want to join the Union are concerned, a dominant role for the EU (e.g. the EC Commission and EU judicial system) should be a plus instead of a minus. The AAA Authority would materially and politically engage the EU in the task of integrating the CEECs into the Union. Take, for instance, the quotation from Copenhagen cited above: 'It expected this step forward [more open EU markets] to go hand in hand with further development of trade between those countries themselves and between them and their traditional trading partners.' The AAA would move the EU beyond simply demanding that the CEECs sign more trade deals among themselves. It would engage the EU directly in the task of encouraging further development of trade among the CEE members of the AAA. The development of East–East trade liberalization might look less like a diversionary tactic if it were part of a broad effort to liberalize pan-European trade and the EU participated in the organization promoting this effort.

The AAA would not only assist the CEE members with the adoption of EU standards, it would help the EU to learn more about the CEE economies. Every economy has its own peculiarities and the EC Commission tends to develop approaches, and sometimes policies, which are suited to them. Accession talks are often slowed by the fact that these peculiarities must be discovered and discussed by the EU and the prospective entrant. By increasing the involvement of the Commission Services in the CEE nations immediately, the AAA may shorten the length of accession talks whenever they occur.

As far as the EU is concerned, the AAA Authority could be a burden. Paying for the financial and administrative costs should be viewed as a contribution to pan-European integration. Nonetheless, the proposed AAA Authority is intended to streamline the current patchy institutional arrangements governing economic integration between the EU and the CEECs and among the CEECs. The idea is to reduce the number of meetings, not to add a new set. The AAA should be able to realize some efficiencies in this respect.

9.1.3 *Benefits of the AAA*

Although it would entail no immediate increase in East–West liberalization (the Association Agreements would continue to govern this), the new framework would promote the development of trade and investment on a pan-European basis. It would do this in two ways. By increasing the credibility, consistency and predictability of trade policy throughout the AAA region, the institution would be good for European business. International commerce is promoted by reductions in the uncertainty over future trade and investment policies as well as by increases in the transparency of current policies. Furthermore, by establishing credible free-trade links among the CEECs, it would eliminate the marginalizing effects of hub-and-spoke bilateralism. This would help firms to do business in the central and eastern parts of the continent. Accordingly, it should encourage investment in the CEECs, both foreign and domestic. This would spur Eastern growth.

The AAA Authority would help the CEECs in two more ways. The CEECs are short on experienced bureaucrats, so the attendant scale economies in administration should be welcome. The solid participation of the EU Commission staff in this institution would help. Additionally, a strong bureaucracy would help to smooth over difficulties created by the unevenness in the CEECs' administrations and transformations as well as the unevenness of policy caused by the many transition periods in the various Association Agreements.

If the AAA succeed in its first task – regionalizing the current bilateral trade liberalization – additional tasks might be added. The AAA could provide a forum for rational discussion of safeguard measures. All trade agreements have safeguard clauses and most countries use them. However, the EU's use of contingent protection against CEEC exports has hitherto been driven by political expediency, not coherent thought. Even without altering the letter or spirit of the safeguard clauses in the EAs, a forum for multilateral discussion of sector-specific problems may lead to more satisfactory outcomes for all parties.

One of the absurd aspects of the current hub-and-spoke bilateralism concerns the 'rules of origin' (see Chapter 2). It is possible that a product assembled from parts made in, say, three countries may not be granted duty-free status – even if each of the three has duty-free access to the EU market. Under current bilateral rules, the good may not count as originating in any one of the three. Some thinking is under way about how to redress this. The AAA may be used as a good vehicle for the adoption of sensible cumulation in rules of origin. Rules of origin in the AAA could be eliminated entirely if the non-EU members of the AAA eventually adopted the EU's Common External Tariff (CET) structure. The benefits of easier intra-European trade could be offset if adoption of the CET meant much higher barriers against non-AAA goods.[2] Since the EU's tariffs on industrial products are quite low on average, the CET would probably not involve a substantial increase in Eastern tariffs. However, elimination of rules of origin would also commit all AAA members to mimic the EU's anti-dumping and countervailing duties. Since the Union is an avid user of this sort of contingent protection, the economic implications of a customs union are likely to be mixed.

The AAA would also provide its CEE members with a track record on European integration. For many reasons, governments do not always get along. This is equally true in Western, Central and Eastern Europe (there must be times when France wishes it had never let the UK and Denmark into the Union). A favourable experience, even for 5 or 6 years, with an organization that included the EU and the associated countries may assuage some fears that an Eastern enlargement would bring decision making in the Council of Ministers to a halt. Since the CEECs would be independent members of the AAA, each CEEC could establish it own track record.

As noted above, the current association process combines most aspects of political and economic integration in a very vague way. There is no well-defined institutional framework that allows a separation of large and small economic issues. As a result, one finds a confusion of issues. In particular, encouragement of trade among the CEECs is seen as a diversionary tactic. By providing a separate forum (in which the EU was materially engaged) for more technical market-access issues, the AAA may help to boost the clarity of the various signals that the EU and the CEECs send to each other.

Chapter 3 showed that exporters based in the EU will be major winners if the economies in Central and Eastern Europe manage to grow rapidly. EU leaders should find substantial support in the business community for this rationalization of the existing pan-European trade system.[3]

Expanding Membership

Membership in the AAA should expand as more CEECs negotiate Association Agreements. The evolutionary nature of the AAA should be recognized from the start.

9.2   Stage Two: Creating an Intermediate Step

European integration could be stalled for a long time at the Association Agreements stage. Chapter 7 argues that it will be at least two decades before an Eastern enlargement is possible. Stage two of the proposal would create an intermediate step between free trade in industrial goods and full membership in order to avoid political difficulties and seize the economic opportunity presented by the opening of Central and Eastern Europe. The importance of creating an intermediate step does not require that the 'two decades before membership' premise apply to all CEECs. The most optimistic scenario envisages accession for Hungary, Poland, the Czech Republic and perhaps Slovenia in 2000 with a decade-long transition period excluding them from most structural spending and the CAP. Even if this does occur, many CEECs will not be in the first wave. For many of them, the wait may be much longer than two decades.

9.2.1   *At Least Two Decades to Wait*

Since the importance of creating an intermediate step depends upon how long the CEECs must wait, the arguments in Chapter 6 are summarized here.

Budget Burden

Because they are now so poor, so populous and so agricultural, an early Eastern enlargement would multiply EU expenditure. EU incumbents would have to pay more or receive less to cover the cost. Raising taxes or deficits to finance an Eastern enlargement would be unpopular with voters.

The only other alternative is to cut spending on two extremely powerful interest groups – EU farmers and poor regions. As a matter of self-defence, coalitions of farmers and poor regions are likely to veto an Eastern enlargement until the CEECs become much richer and much less agricultural. This problem is worse for earlier and greater enlargements.

Structural Funds

As the CEECs become richer, the cost of their membership would fall (under current Structural Funds rules). An important cut-off point occurs when a region's income reaches more than 75% of the EU average. If this average grows at 2% per annum, and the Visegrad group averaged three times that pace, it would take two decades before they passed the 75% cut-off. If the Visegraders managed to grow only twice as fast as the EU, it would take three decades. The periods would be longer for CEECs starting at lower income levels.

CAP Spending

The Visegrad countries are blessed with fertile farmland that is well-suited for the farm products most heavily protected by the CAP (e.g. dairy). Consequently, their accession is likely to bankrupt the post-McSharry CAP. One careful study puts the annual cost of extending the CAP to the Visegraders at US $47 billion in 2000. Rising incomes might never change this. Visegrad farmers could be as productive as French and Danish farmers in 20 years, so the most relevant fact is that a Visegrad enlargement would increase the EU landmass by more than a fifth.

Further CAP reform is inevitable, but an early Eastern enlargement would significantly alter the nature of the necessary reforms.

Voting Problems

Council of Ministers votes are currently allocated on population, with small countries receiving a disproportionate number of votes per citizen. Under current practices, the Visegrad group would receive more votes than the incumbent poor-four (Spain, Portugal, Ireland and Greece). This would drastically alter the EU decision-making process. Clearly, the problem increases, the further East the enlargement reaches.

A reform of EU voting is foreseen, but the nature of the necessary reforms will depend significantly on how soon, and how far, the Union enlarges to the East. The small incumbent member state may have to choose between accepting additional reductions in their own power and endorsing an early Eastern enlargement.

The Human Factor

Assuming that the obligations of EU membership require capable and experienced people, it is not enough to adopt EU law. Entrants' governments must have trained and experienced personnel to interpret, apply and enforce the laws. Take the example of health standards for products traded in the Single Market. A hurried training course for key staff might not enough. The judgement of even fairly low-level officials is critical. It is easy to forget that West European agencies that perform these tasks have highly trained staffs, directed by officials with decades of experience. It could take a decade before the Central and Eastern European administrators gain sufficient experience. Even in the most advanced CEECs, government officials are inexperienced in the design and enforcement of health, safety and environment standards in a market economy. Moreover, Western businesses are run by people who have decades of experience in dealing with these agencies.

Migration

Estimating East–West migration after an Eastern enlargement is very difficult. Much would depend upon how rich the CEECs were when they gained the EU citizen's right to 'move and reside freely within the territory of the Member States'. Chapter 7 suggests that no more than 3.2 to 6.4 million Visegraders would move West. If they spread themselves evenly about the Union, few problems would arise. If they all settle in Germany and Austria, there would be many problems.

Defence and Security Issues

If Poland joins, the Union would have a border with Belarus, the Ukraine and Russia (Kaliningrad). This would greatly enrich the range of foreign policy issue that might have to be resolved. It would also transfer some of the CEECs' security problems to the Union.

Deepeners versus Wideners

One schism in the EU involves members that wish to deepen EU integration and those that do not. Maastricht made bold, but vague, commitments to deeper social, economic and political integration. Voting by EU members over the coming decades will decide how the commitments are met. An Eastern enlargement would have important but unpredictable effects on the results of such voting.

9.2.2   *Early Membership on the Cheap*

One might think that an easy solution to the budget burden of an early enlargement would be to exclude CEEC entrants from CAP and cohesion cash. They could also be excluded from structural spending until they were rich enough not to need it, and from agriculture for however long incumbent EU farmers insist upon. Migration could be ruled out until wages equalize.

This 'solution' is a recipe for large political complications. There is no clear demarcation between second-class citizenship and a long and broad derogation. Once the joys of marriage wore off, this second-class status might be disruptive to the EU decision-making process. Furthermore, when it comes to decade-long transitions, 'pre-marital' promises are futile. There is a natural tendency for assertiveness to increase once the wedding ring is on the finger. During their long transition the CEECs would have a chance to vote on reform of structural spending and the CAP. One wonders what stance they would take towards programmes from which they were excluded.

All this suggests that an Eastern enlargement is likely to be vetoed by incumbents under pressure from farmers, poor regions and/or small countries.

9.2.3   *Moving from a Free Trade Zone to a Wider Single Market*

The EU grants much better access to EFTAn members of the EEA than to CEECs. Some CEECs should be ready for this deeper integration by, say, the end of the decade. Similarly, if CEECs grow rapidly, EU firms will want Single-Market access to CEECs. The proposed intermediate step – an 'Organization for European Integration' (OEI) – would guarantee CEEC and EU firms such access. A new agreement would be needed since not all CEECs would be ready simultaneously.

The proposed OEI would help to fulfil the Europe Agreement promise 'to make progress towards realizing between [the EU and each CEEC] the other economic freedoms on which the Community is based'. The Europe Agreements are specific about tariff and quota removal. They are asymmetrically vague about moving beyond this. It is clear what CEECs must do (approximation of laws, etc.) but not what the EU must do.

This will not be an easy task, as the EEA negotiations revealed. Access to the Single Market entails privileged treatment that goes far beyond zero-tariffs and no quotas, so the necessary controls surpass border formalities. The EEA, for example, suspended the right of all parties to impose anti-dumping and anti-subsidy duties. To prevent barriers created by spurious standards and regulations, it ensures that a product that has been approved in one EEA country can be sold freely in all. To prevent subtle collusion among local service providers, it ensures that a company that is registered in its home country can operate and establish branches in any EEA country without prior approval of the local authorities. Clearly, this sort of access requires that many rules be enforced credibly and uniformly. This, in turn, needs a strong institution. Within the EU, the EC Commission and judicial system play this role. A rather awkward two-pillar system performs this role in the EEA, so a new, more appropriate framework is needed.

No Immediate Action

The proposed stage two would not lead to immediate action, as would the proposed stage one. It will be a number of years before even the most advanced CEECs will be at a level where the EU could consider granting them Single Market access. It is therefore somewhat premature to discuss this stage in great detail. Nevertheless, as with road building, it is wise to have a good idea about the whole route before the first cement is laid.

9.2.4   *Shape of the New Agreement*

Eastern enlargement of the EU would step on at least four 'political land mines': agricultural trade, migration, competition for structural spending, and voting in the Council of Ministers. The solution, therefore, is to find an intermediate step that allows as much of economic integration as possible while avoiding these land mines. The EEA agreement is a good example, as far as access is concerned. This offered participation in the EU's Single Market without agriculture, without transfers and without voting.[4] Thus, something similar to the EEA could provide a good model of an intermediate step between Association Agreements and EU membership. The key modification, however, would be necessary. Migration would have to be excluded to make the closer integration politically acceptable in Western Europe. Thus, the proposed new agreement and accompanying institutions would allow the advanced CEECs to participate in the Single Market apart from trade in agricultural goods and migration. The CEECs would not have automatic access to structural spending, nor would they have the right to vote in the Council of Ministers.[5] Some supranational bodies would be necessary to deal with issues of competition policy, state aid and acceptability of national legislation concerning technical standards and regulation.

The exact shape of the OEI prescribes how soon the CEECs will be ready. For instance, if anti-dumping and anti-subsidy duties are prohibited, the CEECs must wait until they have attained a high level of transparency in all levels of government and in private and public firms. This would require Western-style accounting practices to be universally practised and strictly policed. This is not easy, since it takes years to train accountants and for them to get essential on-the-job training. If the OEI extends mutual recognition of industrial and health standards to the CEECs, these countries will need to have the right kind of laws and regulatory agencies to enforce them. Again this could take a decade, since even the most advanced CEECs are inexperienced in the design and enforcement of health, safety and environment standards in a market economy. A very strong surveillance authority, dominated by the EU Commission, would probably advance the date at which the new intermediate step could be created.

9.2.5   *New Institutions*

It was widely recognized that the EEA Agreement required new supranational bodies (see Chapter 1 for more detail on the EEA). Recall that the EEA institutions played two critical roles: surveillance and enforcement of the Agreement, and continual modification of the Agreement to match new EU laws concerning the Single Market. For similar reasons, the OEI would require the same sorts of institutions. The proposed institution, which might be called the 'OEI Administration Authority', would be particularly useful to West European businesses given the CEECs' general inexperience with the regulation of a market economy. For the same reason, it would be particularly helpful for the CEECs. Great skill is required in the design and enforcement of antitrust laws, the administration of health and safety standards, the certification of financial institutions, the regulation of capital markets, etc. In all West European nations, regulation and enforcement are performed by experienced staffs managed by senior officials who usually have decades of experience. Moreover, West European firms have learned to deal with this sort of regulation. The operation of the proposed administration authority could provide support for institution building in the CEECs.

This administration authority should probably be modelled on the parts of the EU Commission that deal with enforcement and surveillance. Of course, the proposed Administration Authority could not impinge on the mandates of existing EU institutions, so some sort of multi-tier arrangement would be necessary. The somewhat awkward two-pillar legal structure of the EEA Agreement is not a good model, but it is indicative. The EFTA Surveillance Authority polices the EFTA nations. The EC Commission polices EU nations. The EU has no direct involvement in the

EFTA Surveillance Authority. It is this last item that should be changed. As in the AAA Authority, the proposed OEI Administration Authority should be dominated by the EU. The CEECs very much want to join the EU, so they should welcome assistance in helping them to adopt Community standards on all Single Market issues. The EU should be interested in extending this assistance in order to promote pan-European integration that would increase trade, investment and growth throughout Europe.

9.2.6 *A Pan-European Trade System with Three Concentric Circles*

It is impossible to predict when the first CEECs will be prepared for this closer integration. Nonetheless, two facts are likely to be in evidence when the leading CEECs are ready. First, the leading CEECs will be ready before the EU is prepared to let them become full members (unless the optimistic scenario occurs). Second, not all the CEECs will be ready to move forward at the same time. This uneven readiness means that the creation of an intermediate step should not replace the Association of Association Agreements. The AAA would continue to exist for the slower CEECs.

The force of this observation is that the emergence of an intermediate step would turn Europe's trade arrangement into three concentric circles. The EU would make up the central circle with the smallest membership (at least until the Copenhagen vision is fully realized). The OEI would be the next largest comprising all the EU member states plus the leading CEECs. The outer circle, the AAA, would continue to delimit the boundary of a European duty-free zone for industrial products.

The basic idea is illustrated in Figure 9.2. The inner circle consists of EU members. The middle circle encompasses all countries that participate in the Single Market integrations excluding agriculture, transfers and migration. This would include all the EU members plus as many CEECs as are ready. The outer circle shows the limit of the European free trade zone. All countries in all circles would extend duty-free treatment to industrial products made anywhere inside the boundaries of the outer circle.

9.2.7 *How Much Integration Would the OEI Afford?*

The Single European Act was a radical increase in the degree of economic integration within the European Union itself. Agriculture, transfers and migration had little to do with the increased integration implied by the Single European Act. Consequently, by allowing the CEECs to participate in most aspects of the Single Market, the OEI would involve a quite profound degree of economic integration. More importantly, it should be

Structure: three concentric circles

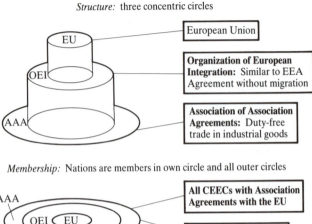

Membership: Nations are members in own circle and all outer circles

Figure 9.2   An integration 'wedding cake'

possible to obtain this integration without exploding the political land mines mentioned above.

Emerson (1988) writes that in the mid-1980s four types of barriers impeded intra-EU trade: (1) differences in technical regulations, (2) delays at frontiers and the related administrative burden for companies, (3) restrictions on competition for public purchases through excluding bids from other countries, and (4) restrictions on freedom to engage in certain service transactions, or to become established in certain service activities. The Single European Act strove to remove all these barriers. It did this by: (1) adopting an EU-wide strategy of mutual recognition of member states' standards with selective harmonization, (2) removing internal frontier checks (this has not yet been fully implemented), (3) opening public procurement, and (4) guaranteeing rights of establishment. Accompanying these moves was a partial harmonization of VAT rates in all Union nations. It seems that the EU and sufficiently advanced CEECs could eliminate all these barriers except the one dealing with border controls, which would be necessary to enforce restrictions on migration and agricultural trade. The Cecchini Report found that the direct cost of frontier delays was fairly small, so not removing this barrier would probably leave ample benefits.

Another very important increase in integration would involve a prohibition on the use of anti-dumping and countervailing duties among all members of the proposed OEI. Of course, the agreement would have to find another way of policing unfair competition. The most likely outcome – and the one that mirrors the solution in the EEA agreement – would be to institute supranational controls on competition policy and state aid in all OEI countries.

9.2.8   *Expanding the Circles*

Membership in the three circles in the proposed trade arrangement should evolve. In particular, the outer circle should be expanded as quickly as possible in order to include all European nations mentioned in the Copenhagen vision. At this point, integration of Belarus, the Ukraine, Moldova and Russia even into the AAA seems to be politically infeasible. If the political situation changes, there is no economic reason for excluding them from the AAA. On the contrary, there would be important economic benefits in doing so.

9.3   Conclusions

In a speech in Jauary 1994, Jacque Delors said 'Europe needs to know where it is going'. Given the decisions made in Copenhagen, a more appropriate comment might have been: 'Europe needs to know how to get where it has decided to go.' This book argues that an Eastern enlargement of the EU is at least two decades away, barring any drastic political or military event. Thus, an even more appropriate comment might have been: 'Europe needs to know how to get where it's going and what to do in the meantime.'

There can be no single best response to such questions. The way forward depends upon many unknowables. Perhaps the most one can hope for is to ask the right questions. It is my hope that this book meets this criterion.

Notes

1. Agreements cannot join an Association, so it would be more grammatical, but more awkward, to call it the Association of Nations Participating in Association Agreements. Indisputably, the new framework would require a more muscular name than AAA to reflect its importance.
2. See Chapter 2 for a more detailed analysis of geographically discriminatory tariffs.

3. Perhaps Germany's EU Presidency, which begins in the summer of 1994, could provide a rallying point for EU exporters interested in freeing up East–East trade in addition to further opening up East–West trade.
4. The EEA agreement did involve a small amount of transfers from the EFTAns to the EU.
5. Perhaps they might have some sort of observer status on the Council.

References

Aghion, P. and Howitt, P. (1990), 'A model of growth through creative destruction', NBER Working Paper 3223.

Anderson, K. and Blackhurst, R. (eds) (1993), *Regional Integration and the Global Trading System*, Harvester Wheatsheaf, Hemel Hempstead.

Anderson, K. and Tyers, R. (1993), 'Implications of EC expansion for European agricultural policies, trade and welfare', CEPR Discussion Paper No. 829.

Attali, J. (1992), 'A global European initiative', speech delivered to European Policy Forum, December, London.

Azariadis, C. and Drazen, A. (1990), 'Threshold externalities in economic development', *Quarterly Journal of Economics*.

Baldwin R. (1989), 'Growth effects of 1992', *Economic Policy*, **9**, 247–82.

Baldwin, R. (1992a), 'The economic logic of EFTA countries joining the EEA and the EC', EFTA Occasional Paper No. 41, Geneva.

Baldwin R. (1992b), 'Measurable dynamic gains from trade', *Journal of Political Economy*, **100**, No. 1, 162–74.

Baldwin, R. (1992c), 'On the growth effects of import competiton', NBER Working Paper No. 4045.

Baldwin, R. (1992d), 'A domino theory of regionalism', NBER Working Paper No. 4465.

Baldwin, R. (1992e), 'An Eastern enlargement of EFTA: Why the East should join and the EFTAns should want them', CEPR Occasional Paper No. 10.

Baldwin, R. (1992f), 'Asymmetric lobbying effects: Why governments pick losers', GIIS manuscript.

Baldwin, R. (1993), 'The potential for trade between the countries of EFTA and Central and Eastern Europe', EFTA Occasional Paper No. 44, Geneva.

Baldwin R. and Venables, A. (1994), 'International migration, capital mobility and transitional dynamics', GIIS and LSE mimeo.

Baldwin, R. et al. (1992), *Is Bigger Better? The Economics of EC Enlargement*, Monitoring European Integration 3, CEPR, London.

Barro, R. (1991), 'Economic growth in a cross-section of countries', *Quarterly Journal of Economics*, **106**, 407–44.

Barro, R. and Sala-i-Martin, X. (1990), 'Economic growth and convergence across the United States', NBER Working Paper 3419.

BCSD (1993), 'Accelerating sustainable development in Central and Eastern Europe', November.

Bergstrand, J. (1988), 'A Hecksher–Ohlin approach to the gravity model', *American Economic Review*.

Bergstrand, J. (1989), 'The generalized gravity equation, monopolistic competition and the factor-proportions theory in international trade', *The Review of Economics and Statistics*, **71**, 143–53.

Biessen, G. (1991), 'Is the impact of central planning on the level of foreign trade really negative?' *Journal of Comparative Economics*, **15**, 22–44.

Blanchard, O. et al. (1992), *Reform in Eastern Europe*, MIT Press, Cambridge, MA.

Brenton, P. and Gros, D. (1993), 'The budgetary implications of EC enlargement', CEPS Working Document No. 78.

Brown, D. (1992), 'The impact of a NAFTA: applied general equilibrium models', *Brookings Papers on Economic Activity*.

Caballero, R. and Lyons, R. (1989), 'Increasing returns and imperfect competition in European industry', *European Economic Review*.

CEPR (1992), 'Making the Association process work', Occasional Paper No. 11, London.

Cohen, D. (1992), 'Tests of the "convergence hypothesis": a critical note', CEPR DP 691.

Collins, S. and Rodrik D. (1991), *Eastern European and the Soviet Union in the World Economy*, Institute for International Economics, Washington, DC.

Commission of the European Communities (1988), 'The economics of 1992', *European Economy*, No. 35. Known as the Cecchini Report.

Courchene, T. et al. (1993), 'Stable money – sound finances', *European Economy*, No. 53.

De la Torre, A. and Kelly, M. R. (1992), 'Regional trade arrangements', Occasional Paper 93, IMF, Washington, DC, March.

El-Agraa, A. (1990), *Economics of the European Communities*, Philip Allan, Deddington.

Emerson, M. (1988), *The Economics of 1992*, Oxford University Press, Oxford.

EFTA (1987), *The European Free Trade Association*, EFTA Secretariat, Geneva.

EFTA Secretariat (1992), 'The EEA Agreement', EFTA Secretariat publication, Geneva.

EFTA Secretariat (1993), 'Institutional solutions ensuring a dynamic and homogeneous EEA', EFTA Secretariat publication, Geneva.

Eurostat (1992), *L'Europe en chiffres*, Eurostat, Luxembourg.

Fagerberg, J. and Lundberg L. (eds) (1993), *European Economic Integration: A Nordic perspective*, Avebury, Stockholm.

Flam, H. (1992), 'Product markets and 1992: full integration, large gains?' *Journal of Economic Perspectives*, **6**, 4, 7–30.

Franklin, M. (1992), 'The EC budget: Realism, redistribution and radical reform', Royal Institute of International Affairs, Discussion Paper No. 42, London.

Gasiorek, M., Smith, A. and Venables, T. (1992), 'Completing the internal market in the EC: factor demands and comparative advantage', in A. Venables and L. A. Winters (eds), *European Integration: trade and industry*, Cambridge University Press, Cambridge.

Grossman, G. and Helpman, E. (1991), *Innovation and Growth in the World Economy*, MIT Press, Cambridge, MA.

Haaland, J. and Norman V. (1992), 'Global production effects of European integration', in A. Venables and L. A. Winters (eds), *European Integration: trade and industry*, Cambridge University Press, Cambridge.

Hall, B. H. et al. (1986), 'Patents and R&D: is there a lag?' *International Economic Review*, **27**, 265–302.

Hall, R. (1989), 'Increasing returns: theory and measurement with industry data', Stanford University mimeo.

Hamilton, C. and Winters, L. A. (1992), 'Opening up international trade with Eastern Europe', *Economic Policy*, **14**, 77–116.

Helpman, E. and Grossman, G. (1991), *Innovation and Growth in the Global Economy*, MIT Press, Cambridge, MA.

Helpman, E. and Krugman, P. (1985), *Market Structure and Foreign Trade*, MIT Press, Cambridge, MA.

Helpman, E. and Krugman, P. (1989), *Trade Policy and Market Structure*, MIT Press, Cambridge, MA.

Herin, J. (1986), 'Rules of origin and differences between tariff levels in EFTA and the EC', EFTA Occasional Paper No. 13.

Hillman, A. (1989), *The Political Economy of Protection*, Harwood, New York.

Huang, S. (1993), *Explaining East–West Trade Flows*, Thesis, GIIS, Geneva.

IMF (1992), *Direction of Trade Statistics Yearbook 1985–1991*, Washington, DC.

Jaffe, A. (1986), 'Technology opportunity and spillovers of R&D: evidence from firms' patents, profits and market value', *American Economic Review*, **76**, 986–1001.

Krugman, P. (1988), 'Endogenous innovation, international trade and growth', Mimeo, published in P. Krugman (ed.), *Rethinking International Trade*, MIT Press, Cambridge, MA, 1990.

Krugman, P. (1990), *Rethinking International Trade*, MIT Press, Cambridge, MA.

Krugman, P. (1991), *Geography and Trade*, MIT Press, Cambridge, MA.

Krugman, P. and Venables, A. (1990), 'Integration and competitiveness of peripheral industry', in C. Bliss and J. Braga de Macedo (eds), *Unity with Diversity in the European Community*, Cambridge University Press, Cambridge.

League of Nations (1942), *The Network of World Trade*, Geneva.

Lipsey, R. (1960), 'The theory of customs unions: a general survey', *The Economic Journal*, **70**, 496–513.

Lucas, R. (1988), 'On the mechanics of economic development', *Journal of Monetary Economics*, **22**, 3–42.

Maddison, A. (1987), 'Growth and slowdown in advanced capitalist economies: techniques of quantitative assessment', *Journal of Economic Literature*, **25**, 649–98.

Mankiw, G., Romer, D. and Weil, P. (1992), 'A contribution to the empirics of economic growth', *Quarterly Journal of Economics*, May, 407–37.

Molle, W. (1990), *The Economics of European Integration*, Dartmouth, Aldershot.

Nerb, G. (1988), 'The completion of the internal market: a survey of Europe's industry perception of the likely effects', *Research on the Costs of Non-Europe*, Basic Findings, Vol. 3, Commission of the European Community.

OECD (1992), *Agricultural Policies, Markets and Trade*, OECD, Paris.

Owen, R. and Dynes, M. (1989), *The Times Guide to 1992*, Times Books, London.

Pelkman, J., Wallace, H. and Winters, A. (1988), *The European Domestic Market*, Chatham House, London.

Rodrik, D. (1992), 'Foreign trade in Eastern Europe's transition: early results', NBER Working Paper 4064.

Rollo, J. M. (1992), 'Association Agreements between the EC and the CSFR, Hungary and Poland: a half empty glass?' Mimeo, Royal Institute of International Affairs, London.

Rollo, J. M. and Smith, M. A. M. (1993), 'The political economy of Central

European trade with the European Community: why so sensitive?' *Economic Policy*, **16**.

Romer, P. (1983), *Dynamic competitive equilibria with externalities, increasing returns and unbounded growth*, PhD thesis, University of Chicago.

Romer, P. (1986), 'Increasing returns and long run growth', *Journal of Political Economy*, **94**, 1002–37.

Romer, P. (1987), 'Crazy explanations for the productivity slowdown', *NBER Macroeconomic Annual*, 163–210.

Romer, P. (1990), 'Endogenous technological change', *Journal of Political Economy*, **98**.

Rosati, D. (1992), 'Problems of Post-CMEA trade and payments', CEPR Discussion Paper 650.

Rosenstein-Rodan, P. (1943), 'Problems of industrialization of Eastern and Southeastern Europe', *Economic Journal*, **LIII**, 202–11.

Sapir, A. (1992), 'Regional integration in Europe', *Economic Journal*, Policy Forum.

Schumpeter, J. (1942), *Capitalism, Socialism and Democracy*, Harper, New York.

Shleifer, A. (1986), 'Implementation cycles', *Journal of Political Economy*, **94**, 1163–91.

Smith, M. A. M., Venables, T. and Gasiorek, M. (1992), '1992: Trade and welfare – a general equilibrium model', in L. A. Winters, (ed.), *Trade Flows and Trade Policies After '1992'*, Cambridge University Press, Cambridge.

Solow, R. (1956), 'A contribution to the theory of economic growth', *Quarterly Journal of Economics*, **70**, 65–94.

Summers, R. and Heston, A. (1988), 'A new set of international comparisons of real product and price levels: Estimates for 130 countries', *Review of Income and Wealth*, **34**, 1–25.

Tyers, R. (1993), *Economic Reform in Greater Europe and the Former Soviet Union: Implications for International Food Markets*, IFPRI Research Report, Washington, DC.

Van Bergeijk, P. and Oldersma, H. (1990), 'Detente, market-oriented reform and German unification: potential consequences for world trade system', *Kyklos*, **43**, 4, 566–609.

Venables, A. and Smith, M. A. M. (1988), 'Completing the internal market in the European Community: some industry simulations', *European Economic Review*, **32**, 1501–25.

Wang, Z. and Winters, L. A. (1991), 'The trading potential of Eastern Europe', CEPR Discussion Paper 610.

Widgren, M. (1991), 'A Nordic coalition's influence on the EC Council of Ministers', in J. Fagerberg and L. Luneberg (eds), *European Economic Integration: A Nordic perspective*, Avebury, Stockholm.

Widgren, M. (1993), 'Voting power and decision making control in the Council of Ministers before and after the enlargement of the EC', ETLA Discussion Paper No. 457, Helsinki.

Wijkman, P. M. (1993), 'A role for EFTA in the wider Europe?' Manuscript, EFTA Secretariat.

Winters, L. A. (1992), *Trade Flows and Trade Policies after '1992'*, Cambridge University Press, Cambridge.

Winters, L. A. (1993), 'Expanding EC membership and Association accords', in K. Anderson and R. Blackhurst (eds), *Regional Integration and the Global Trading System*, Harvester Wheatsheaf, Hemel Hempstead.

World Bank (1992), *Statistical Handbook: States of the former USSR*, Washington, DC.

World Bank (1993), 'World Development Report', Washington, DC.

Index